Rethinking Faith

Rethinking Faith

Heidegger between Nietzsche and Wittgenstein

Edited by
Antonio Cimino and Gert-Jan van der Heiden

Bloomsbury Academic
An imprint of Bloomsbury Publishing Inc

BLOOMSBURY
NEW YORK • LONDON • OXFORD • NEW DELHI • SYDNEY

Bloomsbury Academic
An imprint of Bloomsbury Publishing Inc

1385 Broadway
New York
NY 10018
USA

50 Bedford Square
London
WC1B 3DP
UK

www.bloomsbury.com

BLOOMSBURY and the Diana logo are trademarks of Bloomsbury Publishing Plc

First published 2017

Library of Congress Cataloging-in-Publication Data
Names: Cimino, Antonio, 1979– editor. | Heiden, Gerrit Jan van der, 1976– editor.
Title: Rethinking faith : Heidegger between Nietzsche and Wittgenstein / edited by Antonio Cimino and Gert-Jan van der Heiden.
Description: New York : Bloomsbury Academic, an imprint of Bloomsbury Publishing, Inc, [2016] | Includes bibliographical references and index.
Identifiers: LCCN 2016014915 (print) | LCCN 2016034163 (ebook) | ISBN 9781501321221 (hardcover : alk. paper) | ISBN 9781501321238 (ePub) | ISBN 9781501321245 (ePDF)
Subjects: LCSH: Heidegger, Martin, 1889–1976. | Nietzsche, Friedrich Wilhelm, 1844-1900. | Wittgenstein, Ludwig, 1889–1951. | Faith. | Religion. | Metaphysics.
Classification: LCC B3279.H49 R455 2016 (print) | LCC B3279.H49 (ebook) | DDC 121/.7—dc23
LC record available at https://lccn.loc.gov/2016014915

ISBN: HB: 978-1-5013-2122-1
ePub: 978-1-5013-2123-8
ePDF: 978-1-5013-2124-5

Typeset by RefineCatch Limited, Bungay, Suffolk
Printed and bound in the United States of America

Contents

Acknowledgments

The present volume is partially the outcome of the international conference *Radical Experiences: Faith and Reason in Nietzsche, Heidegger and Wittgenstein*, organized by Antonio Cimino and Gert-Jan van der Heiden at Radboud University in November 2013. The conference and the volume are linked to the research project *Overcoming the Faith-Reason Opposition: Pauline* Pistis *in Contemporary Philosophy*, carried out at Radboud University and at the University of Groningen. The project was generously financed by the Netherlands Organisation for Scientific Research (NWO; project no. 360-25-120).

Jussi Backman's participation in the conference was made possible by a travel grant from the Academy of Finland (research project: *The Intellectual Heritage of Radical Cultural Conservatism*).

Claudio Tarditi's essay results from the research project *A Phenomenological and Hermeneutical Development of Saint Paul*, financed by the Netherlands Organisation for Scientific Research (NWO; project no. 040-11-390) and carried out at the Center for Contemporary European Philosophy, Radboud University.

Parts of Vincent Blok's essay have already been published as "Heidegger and Derrida on the Nature of Questioning: Towards the Rehabilitation of Questioning in Contemporary Philosophy," *The Journal of the British Society for Phenomenology* 46, no. 4 (2015): 307–23.

List of Contributors

Editors

Antonio Cimino is a postdoctoral researcher at Radboud University in Nijmegen, the Netherlands. He holds a PhD in philosophy from the University of Pisa. He conducted research in Pisa, Tübingen, Freiburg im Breisgau, Fribourg and Wuppertal. His main fields of research are metaphysics, contemporary European philosophy, practical philosophy and philosophy of religion. His books include *Phänomenologie und Vollzug: Heideggers performative Philosophie des faktischen Lebens* (in German; Phenomenology and Enactment: Heidegger's Performative Philosophy of Factical Life, Frankfurt am Main, 2013).

Gert-Jan van der Heiden is full professor of metaphysics at Radboud University in Nijmegen, the Netherlands. He holds a PhD in mathematics from the University of Groningen and a PhD in philosophy from Radboud University. His main fields of research are metaphysics, hermeneutics and contemporary French thought. His books include *The Truth (and Untruth) of Language* (Pittsburgh, 2010) and *Ontology after Ontotheology* (Pittsburgh, 2014).

Contributors

Jussi Backman is a university lecturer in philosophy at the University of Jyväskylä, Finland. His main fields of research are contemporary continental philosophy and ancient philosophy. He is the author of *Complicated Presence: Heidegger and the Postmetaphysical Unity of Being* (Albany, NY, 2015) and *Omaisuus ja elämä: Heidegger ja Aristoteles kreikkalaisen ontologian rajalla* (in Finnish; Property and Life: Heidegger and Aristotle at the Limits of Greek Ontology, Tampere, 2005) as well as numerous articles on ancient philosophy, Martin Heidegger, Hannah Arendt, Jacques Derrida, Alain Badiou and Quentin Meillassoux. He has also translated Heidegger's *Einführung in die Metaphysik* into Finnish (2010).

Chantal Bax is an NWO VENI researcher at Radboud University in Nijmegen, the Netherlands. Having written her dissertation on Wittgenstein and subjectivity, she is currently working on a project about community and intersubjectivity in Levinas and Nancy. Her publications include *Subjectivity after Wittgenstein: Wittgenstein's post-Cartesian Subject and the "Death of Man"* (London, 2011) and "Reading *On Certainty* through the lens of Cavell: Scepticism, dogmatism and the 'groundlessness of our believing'" (published in *International Journal of Philosophical Studies*, 2013).

Vincent Blok is associate professor in Philosophy of Technology and Environmental Philosophy at the Philosophy Group, and in Business Ethics and Responsible Innovation at the Management Studies Group, Wageningen University, the Netherlands. His main research interests are continental philosophy, philosophy of technology and innovation, and environmental philosophy. Blok's work appeared among others in *Journal of the British Society for Phenomenology, Studia Phaenomenologica, Heidegger Studies* and *Environmental Philosophy.*

Ezra Delahaye is a PhD candidate in metaphysics and philosophy of religion at the Faculty of Philosophy, Theology and Religious Studies of Radboud University in Nijmegen, the Netherlands. He holds a degree in philosophy from Radboud University and a degree in theology from Tilburg University. In his PhD project, he is developing a new theory of subjectivity based on the contemporary philosophical readings of the apostle Paul.

Tobias Keiling pursued his graduate studies at the University of Freiburg, Germany, and Boston College, Boston, USA. In 2013, he received a PhD from Boston College and completed his doctoral studies in Freiburg. His main research interests are in phenomenology and hermeneutics, in classical German philosophy and Nietzsche, with a view on both art and literature and current debates in the analytic tradition. His publications include *Seinsgeschichte und phänomenologischer Realismus: Eine Interpretation und Kritik der Spätphilosophie Heideggers* (in German; The History of Being and Phenomenological Realism: An Interpretation and Critique of Later Heidegger, Tübingen, 2015). Currently, he is a postdoctoral researcher at the University of Freiburg.

Carlotta Santini is a postdoctoral associate fellow at the Seeger Center for Hellenic Studies of Princeton University, Princeton, USA. Her main fields of research include nineteenth-century German philosophy and culture, aesthetics, history of religion and Nietzsche's philosophy. Her most recent publications include (with Christian Benne) "Nietzsche und die klassische Philologie" (in *Nietzsche und die Wissenschaften*, edited by H. Heit and L. Heller, Berlin/New York, 2014) and "L'enfance des Grecs et l'épos homérique" (in *Herder und die Künste*, edited by E. Décultot and G. Raulet, Heidelberg, 2013).

Claudio Tarditi is a postdoctoral fellow at the University of Turin, Italy. His publications include *Con e oltre la fenomenologia* (in Italian; With and beyond Phenomenology, Genoa, 2008) and *Abitare la soglia: Percorsi di fenomenologia francese* (in Italian; Inhabiting the Threshold: Paths of French Phenomenology, Milan, 2013).

Ben Vedder studied theology in Utrecht and philosophy in Leuven. He wrote his dissertation on Heidegger and Scheler. He was university teacher in Amsterdam and had a special chair for philosophy at Wageningen University. He was full professor for systematic philosophy at Tilburg University, and professor of metaphysics and philosophy of religion at Radboud University in Nijmegen, the Netherlands. From June 2013 on, he is emeritus professor. His publications include *Was ist Hermeneutik? Ein Weg von der Textdeutung zur Interpretation der Wirklichkeit* (Stuttgart, 2000), *De voorlopigheid van het denken: Over Heideggers hermeneutisering van de filosofie* (Leuven, 2004) and *Heidegger's Philosophy of Religion: From God to the Gods* (Pittsburgh, 2007). At present, he is working together with other colleagues on Paul in contemporary philosophy, and preparing a book on hermeneutics and religion.

Introduction

Antonio Cimino and Gert-Jan van der Heiden

Heidegger has often been considered as the proponent of the end of metaphysics in post-Hegelian philosophy due to his persistent attempts to overcome the onto-theological framework of traditional metaphysics. Yet, Heidegger's dismissal of metaphysical, theological and religious motives is deeply ambiguous because new forms of metaphysical and religious experience eventually re-emerge in his writings. Heidegger shares this complex relation to faith and religion with authors such as Nietzsche and Wittgenstein, whose works are also marked by a critique of metaphysics and by a characteristic rethinking of the role of faith and religion.

In this volume, we have collected essays that explore how the phenomena of religion and faith are present in the works of Heidegger, Nietzsche and Wittgenstein, and how these phenomena are brought into play in their discussion of the classical metaphysical motives they criticize. The volume especially discusses how the phenomena of faith and religion are rethought in their work and placed in a new relation to reason and rationality. Clearly, these three philosophers offer different accounts of this relation and the goal of the present volume is not only to clarify this relation between faith and reason, but also to show what this newly understood relation implies for the role of faith and religion in philosophy.

To this end, the volume is divided into three parts. The first part explores how the phenomenon of religion determines the agenda of contemporary philosophy. It is especially Heidegger's works that set this agenda for both a hermeneutics of religion and reflections on the fideistic core of contemporary philosophy. The second part offers analyses of the concepts of faith and reason in the works of these important critical accounts of metaphysics, theology and religion. These essays discuss Nietzsche's, Heidegger's and Wittgenstein's conceptions of faith in relation to more classical metaphysical themes such as truth, reason and questioning. Finally, the third part explores how the important contemporary turn to Paul, as a new theological turn in present-day philosophy, changes and sets the standard for the contemporary reflections on faith and religion. In particular, as the essays in this part argue, Paul's letters are at the basis of both the critique and reappraisal of faith. This allows the authors of these essays to disclose Pauline resonances in the contemporary philosophical explorations of faith and religion.

The first part, devoted to "The Phenomenon of Religion," opens with the essay "Understanding Religious Faith: A Hermeneutical Approach," in which Ben Vedder discusses the phenomenon of faith and religious behavior. Vedder provides useful conceptual and methodological clarifications with a view to outlining a hermeneutical approach to religious experience. The assumption underlying Vedder's analysis of the phenomenon of faith is that the question of the meaning of religious behavior is something different from religious behavior itself. Thus, if one tries to analyze someone else's behavior (or if one wants to clarify someone else's actions), a distance is needed insomuch as the reflecting act is a different activity than the act the reflecting act of thinking refers to. Against this background, Vedder poses the question of how religious behavior can be understood from a hermeneutical point of view. In this vein, in the first part of his essay, he explains why onto-theological rationality is not in a position to understand religious behavior. The second part focuses on the question of whether a religious person can be understood through hermeneutical reason.

In his essay, "Is Ontology the Last Form of Idolatry? A Dialogue between Heidegger and Marion," Claudio Tarditi discusses the problem of idolatry in Heidegger's and Marion's approaches to the question of God. First, Tarditi analyzes both the ambiguities and the fruitfulness of the way Heidegger articulates the relationship between "the last God" and Being. In this context, Tarditi focuses on the thesis according to which "the last God" cannot be reduced to Being, although it can only become manifest within an ontological horizon. Second, Tarditi examines Marion's notion of "double idolatry" and shows that Marion views Heidegger's thought of Being as a form of idolatry because it does not succeed in thinking of God as pure absoluteness. Even though Marion shares a number of Heideggerian insights into Western metaphysics as onto-theology, he tries to dismiss Heidegger's ontological idolatry by using the notions of "excessiveness" and "saturation." However, as Tarditi shows, an ontological commitment can be noticed in Marion's approach as well. In the last part of his contribution, Tarditi contends that a hermeneutical approach can overcome the contradiction between ontology and saturation.

Jussi Backman's essay, "A Religious End of Metaphysics? Heidegger, Meillassoux and the Question of Fideism," analyzes Quentin Meillassoux's conception of the fideistic approach to religious faith intrinsic to the "strong correlationism" that he considers pervasive in contemporary thought. Backman presents the basic elements of Meillassoux's "speculative materialism," and especially, the thesis according to which strong correlationism involves a "fideistic" approach to religiosity. In doing so, Backman critically examines Meillassoux's notions of postmetaphysical faith, religious absolutes and contemporary fanaticism, especially against the background of Heidegger's philosophy. According to Backman, Meillassoux's logical and conceptual critique of strong correlationism is innovative, and it may remain legitimate if its presuppositions are accepted. And yet, Backman argues that Meillassoux's allegations of fideism seem to rely on the questionable application of Enlightenment conceptions to the contemporary situation.

The second part of the volume is devoted to "Faith and Reason" in Nietzsche, Heidegger and Wittgenstein. In her contribution, "'How we, too, are still pious': The Status of Truth and the Irreducibility of Faith in the Work of Nietzsche," Carlotta Santini contextualizes the question of faith, or belief, in Nietzsche with particular reference to the notion of truth. Santini offers an in-depth analysis of the complex aspects that characterize Nietzsche's dealing with the question of truth and takes the concept of "instinct toward the truth" (*Trieb der Wahrheit*) as guiding theme. According to Santini, in conjunction with the paradox of the world of lies and the intriguing re-evaluation of the believer (i.e., who "believes in truth"), Nietzsche introduces a "weak" (i.e., procedural and nondogmatic) notion of truth, that is, "truthfulness" (*Wahrhaftigkeit*). In the last part of the essay, Santini examines Nietzsche's account of the will to truth (*Wille zur Wahrheit*), which is closely linked to the well-known notion of the will to power.

The point of departure of Tobias Keiling's essay, "Dionysius, Apollo and Other *Göttliche*: Denial and Excess of Meaning in Nietzsche, Heidegger and Wittgenstein," is the distinction between two ways of understanding the radicality of an experience, that is, as an excess and as a denial of meaning. Keiling uses and tests this differentiation in terms of a heuristic and interpretive framework. In so doing, he analyzes Nietzsche's, Heidegger's and Wittgenstein's accounts of radical experience. With regard to *The Birth of the Tragedy*, Keiling contends that Nietzsche conceives of radicality as a double excess of the Apollonian and the Dionysian, but not in terms of a denial of meaning. Thus, in a radical experience, everything can be reintegrated in that dual interpretive pattern. According to Keiling, Heidegger adopts a different approach in that he does not reduce the divine to representations of opposed metaphysical principles and contends that the experience of poetry, understood as the beckoning of the divine, is the paradigmatic radical experience. Keiling shows that Heidegger describes radical experiences in terms of an exposure to a meaning that is extraordinary and withdrawn at the same time. In this context, Keiling analyzes some difficulties of this conception. The last part of Keiling's essay concentrates on Wittgenstein and shows that the *Tractatus* gets entangled in a paradoxical attribution of excessive as well as denied meaning. Instead, the later Wittgenstein focuses on the disputes that result from the difficulty of catching the meaning of radical experience.

In her essay, "'A way of living, or a way of assessing life': Wittgenstein on Faith, Reason and Philosophy," Chantal Bax shows that Wittgenstein had an enduring interest in religious themes throughout his life, and that his well-known antimetaphysical attitude does not imply any dismissal of theology and religion. By analyzing texts of the early as well as the later Wittgenstein, Bax argues that he always defended a strict distinction between faith and reason. As Bax points out, this also holds true for Wittgenstein's very last collection of remarks, *On Certainty*, which may seem to contend that reason completely relies on something like faith. On closer inspection, however, Wittgenstein need not be said to see everything in (quasi-)religious terms in *On Certainty*. Even so, as Bax underlines, in her concluding remarks, Wittgenstein's texts on religious belief lead us to qualify the customary picture of him as a radical antiphilosopher. In his reflections on religion, Wittgenstein does not confine himself to dismissing erroneous views on religion. He also uses these analyses to give a more appropriate account of faith, that is, as a "way of living, or a way of assessing life."

Vincent Blok's contribution, "A Question of Faith: Heidegger's Destructed Concept of Faith as the Origin of Questioning in Philosophy," analyzes the relationship between Heidegger's method of philosophical questioning and his ambiguous attitude toward faith and religion. Blok scrutinizes Heidegger's thesis according to which religion is excluded from the questionability specific to philosophical thought. After analyzing Heidegger's characterization of philosophy as questioning and discussing three essential aspects of this conception, Blok raises the question whether the concept of faith can be separated from Heidegger's method of philosophical questioning. In this context, Blok shows that, in the 1930s, Heidegger developed a formal analysis of thought in terms of faith (or belief), where belief is understood as a "holding-to-be-true." According to Blok, Heidegger's notion of faith as a holding-to-be-true is a necessary aspect for the "original stance of inquiry" essential to philosophy since the "truth of Being" can only resonate in a philosophical questioning characterized by faith as a holding-to-be-true.

The third and last part of the volume, "Pauline Resonances," addresses the reception of Paul in contemporary thought, especially in Heidegger and Nietzsche. In his contribution, "Heidegger on Religious Faith: The Development of Heidegger's Thinking about Faith between 1920 and 1928," Ezra Delahaye analyzes Heidegger's notion of faith in two texts of the 1920s, *Introduction to the Phenomenology of Religion* and *Phenomenology and Theology*, in which he develops two different accounts of faith. In the first part of his essay, Delahaye examines the lecture course held by Heidegger during the winter semester 1920–21 and devoted to crucial methodological questions as well as to a groundbreaking phenomenological reading of Paul. Delahaye focuses on how Heidegger interprets the relation between Pauline faith and *parousia* in the context of factical life. The second part of the essay concentrates on *Phenomenology and Theology*, and explains the extent to which Heidegger's discussion of faith is reshaped on the basis of his analysis of Dasein. In this context, faith implies a radical transformation of Dasein. In the last part of the essay, Delahaye analyzes both similarities and relevant differences between the two notions of faith developed by Heidegger.

Gert-Jan van der Heiden's contribution develops "The Experience of Contingency and the Attitude to Life: Nietzsche and Heidegger on Paul." In the first letter to the Corinthians, Paul offers a radical experience of the world in his account of the *schēma tou kosmou toutou* when he writes: "the form of this world is passing away" (1 Cor. 7:31). Although the world has a particular present form, Paul announces this form as one that is passing away. This means, as Van der Heiden argues, that Paul lets the world appear in its contingency. Moreover, Van der Heiden argues that the present-day philosophical interest in Paul's letters concerns exactly this experience of the contingency of the world. In addition, this experience goes hand in hand with a new comportment to the world and a new attitude to life, as Paul explicates. Van der Heiden shows how philosophers interpret this complex of experience of the world and comportment to the world. He does so against the background of Nietzsche's account of this complex because the important contemporary readings of Paul agree in their rejection of this Nietzschean reading. In particular, Van der Heiden shows how some of the basic insights of the contemporary readings concerning the afore-mentioned complex of experience and attitude to life already take shape in Heidegger's reading in which the experience of contingency leads to an attitude to life that neither affirms this world nor rejects this world in resentment and nihilism, but rather leads to a third attitude in accordance with the contingency of this world.

Antonio Cimino's contribution, "Paul as a Challenge for Contemporary Philosophers: Nietzsche, Heidegger and Agamben," explores the multilayered reception of Paul in Nietzsche, Agamben, and especially, Heidegger. Cimino shows that Paul is a challenging interlocutor for those thinkers because he leads them to very different ways of understanding the complex relationship between philosophical rationality and religious experience. It should not go unnoticed that Agamben's and Heidegger's comments on Paul's letters are a reversal of the theses developed by Nietzsche in *The Anti-Christ*. Nietzsche sees Paul within the horizon of the Western theological-philosophical tradition and describes him as a dogmatic priest who wants to suffocate the primordial tendencies of life. By contrast, Heidegger uses Paul's letters as a source of inspiration for his own phenomenological hermeneutics of facticity. Thus, Paul helps Heidegger to overcome the traditional way of conceptualizing human existence and outline a new philosophical approach. Likewise, Agamben overcomes Nietzsche's reading, and sees Paul as the proponent of a messianic apostleship that acts against any institutionalization or dogmatization of religious experience.

Along these three lines of investigations, in which the phenomenon of religion, the relation between faith and reason, and the resonances of Paul's letters in contemporary philosophy are examined, this volume offers new insights in the present-day debate on faith in philosophy. By combining interpretive readings and more systematic analyses, the volume maps the complex and fascinating relations among Nietzsche, Heidegger and Wittgenstein, who have powerfully influenced the way twentieth-century philosophy reflected on the themes of religion and faith. At the same time, the essays collected here show the extent to which these three thinkers remain pivotal sources of inspiration for discussions in philosophy of religion and metaphysics at the beginning of the twenty-first century. The volume eventually documents that Nietzsche, Heidegger and Wittgenstein still lead us to rethink the relation between faith and rationality, regardless of whether we accept their theses on the phenomenon of religion or not.

Part One

The Phenomenon of Religion

1

Understanding Religious Faith:

A Hermeneutical Approach[1]

Ben Vedder

In today's philosophy, and not only there, but also in parts of the public debate, there is an intense discussion about the question of the meaning of religion; this is done in the form of the question into the existence of God. The public opinion seems to be that God does not exist, and that therefore religion and religious behavior are meaningless. In addition, philosophers who think that God's existence is unprovable regard religion, and religious behavior such as rites, to be meaningless, and therefore, superfluous. But wouldn't this mean that a large part of human behavior is meaningless? And would this conclusion be right, given that a large portion of humanity today understands itself as religious?

1. The impotence of onto-theological reason

The rejection of the meaningfulness of religion would, in my view, be justified if the God of the philosophical construction, as is the case in onto-theology, were identical with the God to whom people pray in rites and prayers. The God of the philosophical paradigm or the philosophical conceptuality is seen as identical with the God to whom one prays in rites, readings and sacraments (see Heidegger 1957, 64). In this case, the philosophical God is not distinguished from the God of faith and prayer. The rejection of the onto-theological paradigm, together with the effort to get an intellectual entrance to religion, raises the question of what the meaning of such a "superfluous" behavior that understands itself as religious could be.

1 The present essay is part of the project *Overcoming the Faith–Reason Opposition: Pauline* Pistis *in Contemporary Philosophy*, financed by the Netherlands Organisation for Scientific Research (NWO; project nr. 360-25-120), carried out at Radboud University and the University of Groningen.

From the point of view of a hermeneutical approach to religious behavior, we try to understand what someone is doing if he or she behaves religiously. The hermeneutical task is to ask for the meaning of something, especially if we don't see the meaning of that phenomenon, or if we don't see it yet. We then try to make something understandable for ourselves or for someone else. In other words, the question of the meaning of religion or religious behavior brings us into an explication of religion as a hermeneutics of religion.

What could that be—a hermeneutics of religion? In my book on hermeneutics, I differentiate among (1) *hermeneuse*, (2) hermeneutics, (3) philosophical hermeneutics and (4) hermeneutic philosophy (Vedder 2000, 9–23). It would go too far to explain here again these differentiations. This is not necessary because there it concerns a philosophical discussion about the status of philosophy. Therefore, I will confine myself to the first three. A *hermeneuse* is the concrete interpretation of a text, for instance, the Bible; the interpretation of the parable of the lost son is an example. It can be an interpretation of a piece of literature; this can be a text by Hegel or another author. In hermeneutics, by contrast, we are stricter: We ask for the rules according to which—and possibly, without even being aware of it—someone interprets a text. But in the question of religious behavior that concerns us at present, philosophical hermeneutics is the most important. In philosophical hermeneutics, we not only interpret a text, we not only ask for the rules that are used or are to be used, but we also ask especially for the philosophical presuppositions that are present in a text, or in this case, in someone's religious behavior.

Philosophical hermeneutics means also that something has to become understandable by reason. The understandability of religion is obtained and received by asking for the philosophical presuppositions. These presuppositions are to be expressed in an understandable way. The understandability is obtained through a common reason. In onto-theological reason, one of the most important presuppositions seems to be that someone prays or behaves religiously with regard to a God who exists and who must be seen as a highest and almighty being. The onto-theological paradigm then supports the understanding of religion. This is the dominant presupposition if we must believe today's approach. If this presupposition, which means this first position or stand, is not given, the whole building collapses.

To return now to the task of philosophical hermeneutics, we intend to make something understandable, or make it better understandable, by giving an explication of the proposition or by understanding the propositions from the perspective of its presuppositions, which are its conditions of possibility. In this way, the task of hermeneutics is making someone or something understandable for another or for oneself. I explicate a behavior or a text to someone who doesn't understand what is meant in that situation or context. So a broader context, the context of presuppositions, is needed in order to understand the meaning of a certain behavior.

But whether something is understandable depends on, to a great extent, the historical situation in which what is said or meant takes place. For instance, in a family in which one is used to reading the Bible after dinner and in which everyone is familiar with the Bible, it is not necessary to explain what Dad is doing when he reads the Bible. But more explanation is needed if someone who wants to understand is completely unfamiliar with or alienated from reading the Bible, and is not familiar with the meaning of a biblical text or a certain behavior.

The explication is necessary if there is a situation of distance or alienation. The need for a hermeneutics of religion is the result of the alienation of religion. We see this also in the fact that hermeneutics appears on the scene in the modern age, when the obviousness of religious texts disappears, and therefore, must be called back by an explication that is supported by a common reason.

The Christian religious tradition has also become as unfamiliar as if it were a foreign religion. The Christian Holy days must be explained in the same way as the Ramadan of Islam. In today's culture, it is necessary to explicate what Christmas, Easter and Pentecost are. The immediate familiarity with these religious days has been lost.

Heidegger points out that where the experience of the Holy fades out in a culture, there also dancing and praying for a God are marginalized. This means that the understandability of an explication of praying has to lean on a context in which common experiences of the Holy can be thematized. Only within such a context of common understanding and experience is it possible for an explication to be understandable. Therefore, Heidegger can say that the experience of the Holy is a preliminary condition for the appearance of the gods, not the other way around. The experience of the Holy comes before the possible appearance of the gods (Vedder 2005a).

If it is said that the gods are gone and that we wait for new ones, as Heidegger does, then it means that the familiarity with the religious and the Holy is gone. The old gods are gone, and possible new ones have not come yet because the experience of the Holy is gone. Therefore, a hermeneutics of religion is also a symptom of a disappeared obviousness or understandability. Asking for the meaning of religion indicates that its meaning has been lost. And we do not know whether its obviousness will come back again. We stand between a past that we lost and a future that has not yet arrived. Today, religious behavior has become so unfamiliar and so foreign to many people that it needs a lot of explication in order to make this behavior understandable. This is the task for a hermeneutics of religion.

But if one wants to make religious behavior understandable, then this has to be done, in my view, with respect for the religious intention. The religious intention has to be left intact. This means that this intention should not be reduced to an element in which it does not recognize itself. The aim of the explanation is then to remove the strangeness of religious behavior for the one who wants to understand what the meaning of this behavior is. It seems as if we no longer understand what religion is and that therefore we need someone to explicate it for us. As I said, this means also that a hermeneutics of religion presupposes that religion is no longer obvious. The philosophical explication or interpretation has to justify its interpretation for a public that wants to understand it in order to be able to accept it. The question, however, is when and under which conditions something is understood and justified as understandable.

Generally, something is accepted as understandable and as meaningful if it answers to the standard of reason, since reason (*logos*) is the instance as such that wants to recognize the sense and the meaning of things. This is not because of reason itself, but because of the (pre)judice that if something is justified for and by reason, then it is accepted and understandable for everyone. This was Spinoza's motivation to estimate reason, thinking, as higher than religious faith because the former concerns a universal domain, and faith is just the domain of imagination and of individual contingency in which only historic variety dominates. This (pre)judice of the Enlightenment seems to be accepted up until today, motivated by the idea that one attains a broader and more universal understanding. So, if one has made something reasonably understandable, one has reached a greater acceptance of the phenomenon, in this case, the phenomenon of religion. To achieve a more common degree of meaning and sense, and thereby to be accepted, religious behavior has to be reasonable. This is almost literally how Kant formulates it. Religion is only meaningful within the limits of reason.

Nevertheless, it seems to me that in an era of hermeneutic reason, in which human reason is seen as historically determined, it must be seen that the rejection of a philosophical God (which means the onto-theological God) is historically embedded. The rise and fall of the onto-theological paradigm is a process that happens in a certain time and within a certain culture: namely, Western culture. The historicizing of reason brings onto the scene the realization that the onto-theological structure of Western metaphysics itself is a historic project that is crumbling. The onto-theological structure of Western thinking no longer has a basis.

This leads to the insight that the idea of rejecting the existence of an onto-theological God from a rational position, in order to reject religion as a cultural phenomenon and as meaningless, is at the same time a misunderstanding of the multiplicity and the historic multiculturality of religion. For one presupposes that together with the rational rejection of an onto-theological God, one rejects also a current religion, other religions and religion as such. The question must be posed whether this onto-theological conclusion does not imply an ethnocentrism.

The onto-theological paradigm, with the help of which religion is understood, is a product of Western thinking that has its highest point in Hegel's philosophy. If one misunderstands the historic and culturally determined context, then it is a way of thinking that has strong marks of ethnocentrism. The onto-theological character of understanding in Western thinking, whereby one rejects or confirms the highest being, is not something that also counts for other cultures and religions. If this is presupposed, then one remains in an ethnocentrism that pretends universal claims. For one's own historically determined reason is centralized as an a-historical paradigm that is not aware of its own historicity in attempting to understand something.

2. Toward a hermeneutic understanding

But now the question becomes more urgent: What is rational? Isn't there a threat of historical relativism here in which different traditions clash? And is it possible to understand religion rationally? If we go back to a philosophical understanding of religion, then we see that especially in philosophy there are a lot of reductionist approaches with regard to religion. Reason brings religion back to something in which it doesn't recognize itself. Kant reduces religion to ethics. Hegel neutralizes religion to philosophical conceptuality. According to the masters of suspicion (Marx, Nietzsche and Freud), religion is a derivative of unconscious impulses. Here, my first objection is not the reductionism. Rather, it is a question of whether these approaches are enough for a hermeneutic approach to the phenomenon of religion.

Not one religious person would recognize him- or herself in this reductionist approach. But the question is whether and to what extent this is necessary. At the beginning of this essay, I said that the question of the meaning of religion is something different from acting religiously. A hermeneutics of religion is not a religious act. If I return to my concept of hermeneutics and emphasize that something has to be made understandable that is not from itself understandable, then I cannot simply repeat what was said. Religion will not become understandable by praying, just as mathematics does not become understandable by writing mathematical formulas on the blackboard. Nevertheless, it is necessary that what I explicate and what I say with regard to the phenomenon to be interpreted must be recognizable *as* that phenomenon. The phenomenon has to recognize itself, as it were, in my wording of it. In addition, the result of my explication has to be understandable for others and has to be recognizable as the phenomenon that I want to interpret. Reductionism is there where the phenomenon is no longer recognizable. A hermeneutics does not want to be reductionist because in that case the phenomenon is no longer recognizable. Religion is not completely reducible to ethics. On the other hand, the religious phenomenon has to be interpreted with the help of words that are not a mere repetition of that phenomenon; it has to be different in order to make it understandable since the immediate understandability is lost.

The strange and unfamiliar phenomenon has to be explicated and brought back to a familiar and historic level of understanding out of which a living community lives and understands itself. That which is understandable for a person or a group is grounded in that with which they are familiar. What cannot be brought back to such a familiarity will remain strange for the interpreter who wants to understand.

It seems that the rationality of the current human community, especially in Northwest Europe, has become alienated from the gods and the godhead that it once worshipped. The gods are alienated from reason. There is no longer a reasonable entrance to religion since the death of God. This thinking or reasonable entrance had (as I already mentioned) its glorious height in Hegel's philosophy, in which the religiously highest is also thought as the philosophically highest. The God of faith reaches its completion in the God of thinking. This construction for thinking religion does not appear out of the blue, but rather is prepared for in Western thinking as onto-theology.

Christianity and other religions are usually understood within an onto-theological paradigm in which religion is grafted onto a highest being. The rational entrance that one has to religion is an entrance to something that appears as the highest being. Here, the rational understandability of religion is grafted onto a concept of the absolute. An initially external ontological concept becomes an entrance to religion and is then used as an internal moment of religion in which this highest and absolute being is worshipped as a religious God. Concepts such as "transcendence" and "absolute transcendence" are the bases on which the entrance and the rationality of religion are grounded. In another article, I interpret this with the help of the concept "transcendentology" (Vedder 2003a).

With this concept of "transcendentology," I mean to indicate that the conceptual framework with which one understands something dominates the phenomenon that has to be interpreted. We see a parallel of this in the question of "meaning as such" as an explicit recapitulation of the concern with meaning as regards content. Human beings are normally not concerned with meaning as such, but they listen to music, read books, take their children to school and so on. From the perspective of meaning as such, one understands oneself in a formal way, instead of from the contents with which one is concerned. The question of meaning, and the duty to do meaningful things and to behave meaningfully that is connected with this, keeps rather away from an immediate concern with reality (Marquard 1986). So it is important to see that meaning as such is just a formal concept that has to be completed with contents. In the same way, the concept of transcendence is a formal concept with which initially concrete contents are meant. Transcendence can only be made clear with the help of concrete concern with respect to content. It is this concrete concern that it is about; it is not about the transcendence. In this way, a praying person is concerned with God and with the object of his or her prayer, not with transcendence. Generally, these formal notions of transcendence and meaning are recapitulated in an onto-theological paradigm. But there is a gap between concepts like transcendence and meaning and the concrete behavior that is directed toward a content.

My question therefore is whether religious behavior can be understood with the help of this onto-theological paradigm. In that case, religion is understood from the perspective of an ontology that posits a highest being as the cause of reality. Such an onto-theology is the target of criticism now, which I find appropriate. But this criticism is not so much appropriate from the perspective of a religion or faith, but rather from the perspective of a philosophy that wants to take seriously Nietzsche, the death of God, phenomenology and the development of hermeneutics in philosophy (Vedder 2003b).

In the end, the problem of the onto-theological paradigm is not that something is rejected which may or may not exist. The paradigmatic structure of onto-theology remains also in a-theism, as that which is needed in order to be rejected. The question is whether such a paradigm is able to make a religious behavior understandable.

This question counts in two ways: Is the onto-theistic approach capable of making the religious phenomenon understandable, either in its confirmation or its denial? And does the ontological or logical proof of the existence of a highest entity do justice to the understandability of religious behavior? In my view, it does not. Certainly not as long as such a proof and the rationality that belongs to it remain external to the religious praxis. Second, from the perspective of the religious person, one can also ask whether religious behavior wants to be grafted onto reason in order to become understandable. There are strong indications—at least in the Christian religion—that reason cannot be seen as the basis of religion. One does not want religious faith to be overtaken by reason.

Generally speaking, we may say that the classic discrepancy between faith and reason is also present in the background of the current discussion. The question here is whether we have to understand credibility from the perspective of thinkability as the basis on which credibility is grounded. We have already seen the problem of the tension between credibility and thinkability in Anselm. Anselm's ontological proof is formulated within the context of a prayer. The reasoning with which he confirms God as the highest being is as it were an excursus. When he resumes praying he begins with a question: "Are thou this Lord whom I found in my reasoning?" In other words, he situates his reasoning under the authority of his religious faith in God. In this case, thinking has to be credible, not vice versa. Faith is not based in the ground of reason since it would then be superfluous as religious faith, as Spinoza teaches us in chapters 14 and 15 of his *Tractatus Theologico-Politicus*.

Religious faith does not want to be thinkable, but rather credible. Therefore, next to the question of the historicity of reason, the question also arises whether religious behavior and faith can be understood by rational thinking. If I want to make religion, which has become unintelligible, more understandable, then I have to interpret it on the basis of a common, which means reasonable, understandability. The claim that a philosophical hermeneutic presents with regard to its object, in this case religion, is that religious faith does not have to be credible, but rather understandable—that is, reasonable. Is it meaningful to bring faith back to reason? Is this not what we always do if we ask for the meaning of something?

But which reason are we left with? With regard to onto-theological reason, I have just said that it (1) does no justice to the phenomenon of religion, and (2) itself has become historical. This leads to the fact that I have to understand religion with the help of a historic hermeneutic reason.

Don't we have here a repetition of the same tension between faith and reason? The hermeneutic approach, which nears the phenomenon of religion as an object, reflects the relation between philosophy and religion as religious faith (Vedder 2002). According to Jean-Luc Marion, this is an impossible relation: "The field of religion could simply be defined as what philosophy excludes or, in the best case, subjugates" (Marion 1996, 103). From this point of view, the task of a hermeneutics of religion would be to objectify, and with this, it would lose its object as a religious object. Is it possible to describe religious phenomena objectively or separate these phenomena from their specific religious identity in a phenomenological description?[2] Therefore, the question arises: Does a philosophically hermeneutic understanding of religious words entail that the words are no longer religious, but neutralized philosophical concepts?

Indeed, the philosophical concepts are neutral with regard to the question of whether or not the philosopher agrees with the presented religious content. A hermeneutics that asks for the presuppositions of religion is not capable of taking such a confirming position. The question of presupposition is neutral and external with regard to confirmation. It is capable of indicating such a confirming position, but precisely because it wants to interpret in an understandable way, and wants to make something understandable at the level of presuppositions, it is unable to give a subjective confirmation. Philosophical hermeneutics does not situate its thinking under the authority of faith, for in that case, it would lose its thinkability. Hermeneutics remains formal and neutral with regard to what it wants to make understandable.

Because understanding, which means also hermeneutical understanding, is determined as general and doesn't touch the individual in the end, an interpreting hermeneutics also remains general and formal. The general character of a formal hermeneutics offers room for an individual completion. Therefore, the philosophical interpreter can say in the end, I understand you (generally and formally). This, however, is different from agreeing with a concrete religious content.

[2] "Either it would be a question of phenomena that are objectively definable but lose their religious specificity, or it would be a question of phenomena that are specifically religious but cannot be described objectively" (Marion 1996, 103).

In the Hegelian absolute concept, the individual is lost in the end. There, a paradigm is used in which everything is determined beforehand; this is the opposite of a hermeneutic paradigm that remains formal and gives room for an individual interpretation.

This means that religion has to be understood with the help of an empty and provisional form that can be interpreted individually. This formal paradigm remains provisional with regard to the religious phenomenon since it can turn out that the phenomenon appears differently (phenomenological motive). But with regard to the religious phenomenon, the paradigm is also provisional because of the religious content; the Godhead can reveal something different from what the initial anticipation expected (theological motive). Therefore, the provisionality of philosophical hermeneutics is determined here by the nature of the phenomenal as well as by the specific religious content of this phenomenon. For hermeneutics, it is important that parallel to the sociological and cultural priority of the God-talk (the religious phenomenon), God is also prior in the theological and faithful speaking of God (the content of the religious phenomenon). In hermeneutics, it is difficult to make clear whether God is prior as a theme of culture or as the God to whom a pious believer subjects himself in religious faith.[3]

But what is at stake in a hermeneutic understanding of religion? Hermeneutical understanding doesn't bring us back to an understanding of a highest being from where the total reality is understood, but it brings us to a hermeneutics that is by its nature provisional since its understanding is directed, at least where it concerns religion, to a whole that we do not have in our possession. Understanding and interpretation is understanding and interpreting within a whole. But this whole is not the totality that makes reality understandable from the point of view of a highest being. Hermeneutical understanding is always surrounded by a whole that we have neither in our possession nor at our disposal. It is a wholeness that comes down and over to us as a future we do not yet know. With this, the historicality of hermeneutical reason is also determined.

We see the structures of this hermeneutical understanding as well in a hermeneutics or reading as is developed by Heidegger and (in a different way) by Ricoeur. According to Heidegger's understanding of hermeneutics, we always read toward a future horizon that we ever again do not yet know. This determines the provisionality of our thinking and reading. In our anticipating and running

[3] See Vedder 2004. In this article, I point out the ambiguous meaning of the word *giving*.

ahead, a horizon comes to us that makes our reading provisional (Vedder 1996 and 2005b).

Against the same background, Ricoeur says that we can read the text like a revelation, as something that is a message to us and which lets itself be known to us. With this, Ricoeur means that biblical hermeneutics is not a specific case of hermeneutics, but that biblical hermeneutics has a model that counts for every formal hermeneutics of reading. We read what is coming down to us (formal); it is also possible that this comes down to someone as revelation (religious completion).

Hermeneutical understanding means an interpretation and anticipation of what can happen to us in our contingency. What can happen to me is not determined and controlled by me, but is, so to speak, in the lap of the gods, or as a religious person might say, it is received as a gift of grace. To what extent it is possible to understand what happens to us as a gift of grace? That is the domain of subjective confirmation and completion.

In philosophical hermeneutics, religion is understood with the aim of unfolding its presuppositions. It is understood as an explication of the longing for wholeness, the salvation that comes down to human being. This salvation, this wholeness, is understood in such a way that human beings cannot control this wholeness as a possession. I expressly say here "a longing for salvation," and not a striving or a wanting, because from a religious perspective wholeness does not belong to the domain of control, just as the Holy does not belong to the domain of human control (Vedder 2005a). Tuning to it is rather a matter of chance. This means that it is a tuning into what can happen to us in its pure contingency. But a culture that has found its wholeness in all kinds of manageable pleasures has this salvation and wholeness already under control and treats it as a possession. It denies that this wholeness is something that comes down to humans and structurally cannot be controlled from the temporality and finiteness of human existence. Religion is the explication of a longing for salvation about which the religious person implicitly says that it is not under his or her control or in his or her possession. Religion is based on a vision of human beings as a presupposition that explicates that they cannot effect or realize their own wholeness, just as they do not have their own historicality and temporality under control.

Now what would be a hermeneutics of religious behavior? In a hermeneutics of religious behavior, this acting is interpreted and explicated as an explication or an expression of the relation of knowing and receiving: of nature, will and anticipating, on the one hand, and receiving a gift, on the other. If I understand religious acting as an expression of this relation, then it is at the same time also the explication of this relation. With this, I bring back religious acting to something that is explicated or unfolded in it, namely: a manner, a way of dealing with the contingency of salvation or wholeness. With this explication, religion is something that can be understood, at a broader level, by someone who is initially foreign to the phenomenon of religion.

By this I do not understand religion and religious acting as a control of contingency, or *Kontingenzbewältigung*, as Hermann Lübbe has called it (Lübbe 1986, 127–218). Since contingency is not mastered in religion, it remains open. According to religious faith, the initiative to solve the contingency in granting salvation does not lie in the hands and the control of man, but it is parted with or relinquished, in which case contingency itself is kept. Contingency is characterized by the fact that we cannot master it; it comes down to us or happens to us. We can prepare in a certain way for what comes down to us, we can attune to it and make ourselves ready for it, but we cannot master it. Religion is not a mastering of contingency, but it is rather a manner in which contingency is left open. This manner exists like an attuning. The concrete completion of this manner is based in someone's most personal and most intimate experiences that have been more or less lucked into. Or it is determined from the tradition that is founded in the experience of a group to which someone belongs. From this background, a person will more or less react to what happens to him or her. In my view, sacraments and rites must also be understood as manners for handling the contingency of life and with which salvation can happen to man. So religion is a manner of dealing with the contingency of life, yet it does this in such a way that it does not resolve the contingency; the contingency remains because the gift of salvation is not mastered by man. In a certain sense, the gift of salvation is also contingent. Besides religion as a manner of dealing with the contingency of wholeness, metaphysics as onto-theology is an effort to avoid and escape from contingency. Metaphysics as onto-theology wants to escape from contingency by understanding reality within an overseeable totality that is knowable as a whole in the end.

With these only sketchily worked out ideas, I have tried to develop a formal understanding of religion, in which it concerns an attuning to what happens and comes down to me in my contingency. This is a attuning that exists in part as an anticipatory longing and hoping, but which is at the same time determined by an unmasterable, overcoming given. Within this formal framework we can understand the Christian religion, because the most important truths of the Christian religions concern nature and grace as the domain in which this relation of contingency and salvation receive their shape in a religious way and with religious words. To what extent other religions are also about this relation and can be understood from this framework, I am not sure. Within this formal framework, however, everyone can interpret and complete his or her religiosity, for instance, as a life that completely depends on God's mercy. I can say to that person, I understand you, but I don't agree with you. Or on the other hand, if someone says that he or she will provide for his or her own wholeness, which means salvation, once again, I can say that I understand, but I do not agree. For I understand that visions about how salvation is received are in between these extremes.

If I present the idea that religion is an expression of a manner for dealing with the contingency of life, then the avoiding of contingency and/or the mastering of it mean a misunderstanding of religion. Philosophy as onto-theology, insofar it wants to avoid contingency, will misunderstand religion from the very beginning. Pelagianism has the idea that humans can realize their own salvation. It understands human freedom as a complete autonomous self-determination and denies in this way the necessity of Grace. This is a vision in which religion as such is pushed aside. This is why the Church had to condemn it because it tends to neutralize religion as such. If there is less understanding of religion in our age and region of the world, then it might have to do with the fact that we live in a very pelagianistic time. One can understand such a Pelagianism, but it is not necessary to agree with it. To what extent is it necessary for a thinking religious person to recognize him- or herself in this proposal? The thinking believer may recognize him- or herself in it because he or she wants to make his or her faith understandable. This means to explicate it to someone who does not belong to that faith or religion. He or she may also accept this common understandability from the perspective of his or her own faith, as long as his or her individual faith is not hampered by it. Does he or she come to a better understanding by understanding the presuppositions and the implicit vision of humans that is expressed in his or her faith and religion? Is a religious person interested in this? In my view he or she is; since a believer can make his or her faith understandable on a level that is general and formal without prescribing his or her subjective completion of it. The individual and personal expression and manner is an explication of something that is generally understandable. It can be understood by a hermeneutic reason. For this hermeneutic reason, religious behavior and acting appears as meaningful. Christian faith unfolds as a way of handling the contingency of life. A religious person confirms this contingency with his or her religious behavior, without avoiding or rejecting it.

As a hermeneutic philosopher, I have tried to understand the meaning of religious behavior and to interpret it. As a philosopher, I understand the religious person in a formal way; I understand him or her as a religious person, and try to do justice to that person. Nevertheless I can agree or disagree with that person, especially from the perspective of my own subjectivity, but that is not under discussion here. I want to present a philosophical hermeneutics of religious acting. This means presenting religious behavior on a common reasonable and understandable level, for a time that has lost the meaning of that phenomenon, and therefore, has to ask for its meaning and sense.

References

Heidegger, Martin. 1957. *Identität und Differenz*. Pfullingen: Neske.

Lübbe, Hermann. 1986. *Religion nach der Aufklärung*. Darmstadt: Wissenschaftliche Buchgesellschaft.

Marion, Jean-Luc. 1992. *Phénoménologie et théologie*, Paris: Criterion.

Marion, Jean-Luc. 1996. "The Saturated Phenomenon." Translated by Thomas A. Carlson. *Philosophy Today* 40: 103–24.

Marquard, Odo. 1986. *Apologie des Zufälligen. Philosophische Studien*, Stuttgart: Reclam.

Vedder, Ben. 1996. "Die Faktizität der Hermeneutik: Ein Vorschlag." *Heidegger Studies* 12: 95–107.

Vedder, Ben. 2000. *Was ist Hermeneutik? Ein Weg von der Textdeutung zur Interpretation der Wirklichkeit*. Stuttgart: Kohlhammer.

Vedder, Ben. 2002. "Religion and Hermeneutic Philosophy." *International Journal for the Philosophy of Religion* 51: 39–54.

Vedder, Ben. 2003a. "The Question into Meaning and the Question of God. A Hermeneutic Approach." In *Transcendence in Philosophy and Religion*, edited by James E. Faulconer, 35–52. Bloomington: Indiana University Press.

Vedder, Ben. 2003b. "The Disappearance of Philosophical Theology in Hermeneutic Philosophy: Historicizing and Hermeneuticizing the Philosophical Idea of God." In *Religious Experience and the End of Metaphysics*, edited by Jeffrey Bloechl, 14–30. Bloomington: Indiana University Press.

Vedder, Ben. 2004. "Godsdiensfilosofie tussen ontologie en theologie." *Tijdschrift voor Filosofie* 66: 99–118.

Vedder, Ben. 2005a. "A Philosophical Understanding of Heidegger's Notion of the Holy." *Epoché. A Journal for the History of Philosophy* 10 (1): 141–54.

Vedder, Ben. 2005b. "The Provisionality of Thinking in Heidegger." *Southern Journal of Philosophy* 43 (4): 643–60.

2

Is Ontology the Last Form of Idolatry?

A Dialogue between Heidegger and Marion

Claudio Tarditi

1. A basic ambivalence

As is well known, there is no Christian cross on Martin Heidegger's grave at Messkirch's cemetery.[1] Rather, there is a little star that seems to remind us of a famous note on his text *Gelassenheit* (Releasement): "To follow one star, only this. To think is to concentrate on one thought, motionless like a star fixed in the heavens above the world" (Heidegger 1966, 7). Nevertheless, one cannot gather either that Heidegger is an atheist philosopher or that his philosophical perspective is completely indifferent to religion. Indeed, there is evidence he accorded great importance to religious experience throughout his entire philosophical career, even when faith and religion were not his explicit subject of inquiry. The absence of any cross on his grave probably means that, during the last years of his life, he had no faith. Or rather, that he had lost his faith many years before while developing his fundamental ontology. Nonetheless, his attention both for religion in general and the problem of the divine has never decreased throughout all his life, from his early education in theology until his latest reflections about the "last god" (Heidegger 2012, 16). In my interpretive hypothesis, although he lost his faith in the Christian God, he never quit his reflections about the experience of the divine. More precisely, Heidegger's critique of onto-theology does not lead him to a radical atheism, but rather to pose anew the question of the divine. As is well known, in his later texts,

1 The present essay results from my research project *A Phenomenological and Hermeneutical Development of Saint Paul*, financed by the Netherlands Organisation for Scientific Research (NWO, project nr. 040-11-390) and carried out at the Nijmegen Center for Contemporary European Philosophy (Radboud University).

Heidegger develops such a new inquiry on the divine through the image of the "escaped gods" (Hölderlin 1994, 318) in line with Hölderlin's verse: "But, friends, we have come too late for the gods!" (ibid.). This notion of an "escaped god" is doubtless to be understood with reference to Heidegger's concept of the "overcoming" (Heidegger 2003, 84) of Western metaphysics as well as the "common understanding of time" (Heidegger 1996, 15). Indeed, "being late for the gods" (Hölderlin 1994, 318) does not mean that they are not *anymore*, but rather that they have *never* been. Therefore, in Heidegger's view, the escape of the gods does not exclude a different variety of experience of the divine, provided that the end of the onto-theology allows for the disclosure of a new manifestation of god (or gods?) throughout the history of Being.[2] In other words, the escape of the gods erases our metaphysical conception of the divine in order to prepare the revelation of "what is thinkable by a thinking which is itself ungrounded" (Heidegger 2012, 88), namely, an unknown god to come. Moreover, as Heidegger affirms, this "passing by of the last god" (Heidegger 2012, 23) will *save* us. Accordingly, since the last god breaks with the onto-theological idea of god, his action of salvation is to be understood in a different way from the traditional one. More closely, in Heidegger's view, the "passing by of the last god" (Heidegger 2012, 23) will save us from the "danger" (Heidegger 2012, 375) of perpetuating the oblivion of the ontological difference. This means that the task of this last god will be to safeguard Being from the danger of being metaphysically interpreted as a being. Thus, this new divine epiphany is not grounded on Being; rather, the last god protects Being from the tendency of beings to cover and falsify it. First and foremost, in this essay, I intend to provide an in-depth analysis of how Heidegger develops his account of the last god as the most radical attempt to overcome onto-theology. Second, I pose the question whether such an overcoming of metaphysics leads to the overcoming of any variety of ontology. With regard to this second point, I discuss Jean-Luc Marion's core argument in *Dieu sans l'être* (God without Being), according to which ontology derives from idolatry.

During his seminar in Zürich in 1951 (Heidegger 2001), Heidegger is reported to have said to a group of scholars: "I will never attempt to think God's disclosedness through Being.... I think that one cannot conceive of Being as ground and disclosedness of God. Nevertheless, since the experience of God and

[2] As usual, in the secondary literature on Heidegger, I employ *Being* to indicate *Sein* and *being* to indicate *Seiendes*.

his manifestation happen to man, they accomplish themselves within the dimension of Being" (Fedier 1980, 38; my translation). This passage reveals both the ambivalence and the fruitfulness of Heidegger's account of religious experience. Indeed, what is at stake for Heidegger in religious experience is a new manifestation of the divine completely independent from Being, and at the same time, originally intertwined with the history of Being. In other words, in order to develop Heidegger's perspective on religion, one should be able to conceive of a god *with* and *without* Being at the same time. Accordingly, in this essay, my aim is to demonstrate that such an ostensible contradiction could be overcome through an appropriate hermeneutical approach.

It is worth emphasizing the ambivalence of Heidegger's account of religious experience in two other passages. The former is drawn from a series of conversations reported by Jean Beaufret: "Some of you maybe know that I had a theological education, that theology was my first love. If I would like to write a theology, as I wished so many times, therefore the word *Being* would not have any role. *Faith does not need the thought of Being*" (Heidegger 1976, 22). By contrast, in the *Brief über den Humanismus* (Letter on Humanism), Heidegger argues: "Only in the light of the essence of divinity can it be thought or said what the word 'God' is to signify: Being" (Heidegger 1998, 267). These two passages demonstrate the inner tension between ontology and religious experience in Heidegger's approach. Whereas, in the second passage, he explicitly connects god and Being, in the former, he flatly distinguishes philosophy from theology, reaffirming the core thesis of *Phänomenologie und Theologie* (Phenomenology and Theology): "Theology is a positive science and as such is absolutely different from philosophy" (Heidegger 1998, 41). From this viewpoint, thought and faith have nothing in common. Nevertheless, the passage from the *Letter on Humanism* suggests that, in Heidegger's view, there is a fundamental interaction between Being and the divine, which reveals itself through the "language of divinity" (Vedder 2006, 2), namely, a poetic language totally different from onto-theology. According to Heidegger, such a poetic language of the divine represents the highest manifestation of what he calls "remembrance thought" (Heidegger 2000, 108), whose peculiar feature is to take into account the ontological difference between Being and beings. This means that the remembrance thought requires a poetic language insofar as it rejects the principles of metaphysics. Under this premise, one can conclude that the overcoming of onto-theology makes room for a poetic experience of the divine. As a consequence, from Heidegger's perspective, the "other beginning" (Heidegger 2012, 139) of philosophy after the end of metaphysics inaugurates a new way of conceiving of god, or at least, opens this possibility.

In order to recapitulate Heidegger's perspective, one could argue that, although the last god exceeds the ontological horizon, he reveals himself through the "screen of Being" (Marion 1991, 37). "Faith does not need the thought of Being" and "God is to signify: Being": Can this ostensible contradiction be resolved? One can approach this problem by posing two further questions:

1. Does Being offer the most original horizon of God's manifestation?
2. Does the experience of faith require an ontological clarification in order to reveal its own meaning?

As demonstrated above, in certain texts, Heidegger seems to separate ontology from faith, whereas in other texts he explicitly puts them in connection. At first glance, one could conclude that Heidegger's perspective suffers from inconsistency; rather, I intend to show how this inner tension can be overcome by a hermeneutical investigation.

In this framework, one should remember that the notion of faith has several meanings. Indeed, on the one hand, faith means belonging to a religious tradition[3] whereas, on the other hand, being open to the experience of the divine. With respect to the meaning of faith in Heidegger, it is worth distinguishing between faith as a theological subject, "mortal enemy" (Heidegger 1998, 53) of philosophy, and faith as openness and trust in the event of the "passing by of the last god" (Heidegger 2012, 23). From Heidegger's viewpoint, both meanings of faith have a deep connection with the *Destruktion* of metaphysics and the "construction" (Heidegger 1982, 22) of a new ontology as remembrance thought. More precisely, this means that even the radical experience of faith (as trust) in the last god complies with Being's evental structure. On this basis, the core problem I approach is the following: Does god's manifestation depend on ontology or is a more original horizon needed?

2. God: With or without Being?

In dealing with the problem of faith in Heidegger, one must take into account a particular moment within Heidegger's French reception when the relationship

3 For instance, see article 144 of the *Catechism of the Catholic Church* (1994, 36): "To obey (from the Latin *ob-audire*, to hear or listen to) in faith is to submit freely to the word that has been heard, because its truth is guaranteed by God, who is Truth itself."

between religion and ontology has been strongly discussed. As a matter of fact, a curious event takes place throughout the 1980s. In 1982, Jean-Luc Marion publishes his *God without Being*, destined to give rise to a remarkable debate in France and abroad, and a few years later, in 1986, the Dominican theologian Dominique Dubarle publishes his *Dieu avec l'être* (God with Being). This coincidence is interesting inasmuch as the second book is not a sort of polemical response to the former; rather, it provides us with very useful insight about the relation between faith and ontology. As is well known, in *God without Being*, Marion approaches the question of how theology develops after Heidegger's assessments of onto-theology in order to overcome the traditional equivalence between God and Being. Marion's core argument is that the absolute transcendence of God, well expressed by the tradition of negative theology, has been covered throughout the history of metaphysics by an idolatric concept of God.[4] This means that every attempt to define God definitively consists of a mystification, namely, a reduction of God's absoluteness to a conceptual idol created by man. Although God is defined as the highest and most perfect being possible, according to Anselm's idea of God as "something than which nothing greater can be thought" (Anselm 1995, 7), he is considered as a being, and accordingly, destroyed in his profound otherness and radical unthinkability. As a consequence, in Marion's view, although Heidegger strongly emphasizes the difference between Being and beings, the notion of the last god suffers from a certain kind of "double idolatry" (Marion 1991, 25) inasmuch as he definitively reveals himself through Being.

Instead, in *Dieu avec l'être*, Dubarle reaffirms the original homogeneity between God and Being that characterizes the history of Western thought. In Dubarle's perspective, the God of Exodus 15 is substantially equivalent to Parmenides's concept of Being, and their similarity prefigures Thomas Aquinas's definition of God as "*ipsum esse subsistens*" (*Summa Theologiae*, I 2, 1). Nevertheless, Dubarle's analysis of the history of metaphysics (Parmenides, Plato, Aristotle, Augustine and Thomas Aquinas) does not aim at the reintroduction of onto-theology. Rather, Dubarle discerns two acts of naming God: the "naming of mercy" and the "naming of substance" (Dubarle 1986, 230; my translation). This distinction is based on the difference between the *ontic* understanding of God

4 As is well known, throughout the 1970s and 1980s, a sort of *Negative Theology Renaissance* took place in France, whose main exponents are Jean Délumeau, Jean Daniélou and Jean-Marie Lustiger. Although one can find some traces of negative theology in J. Derrida's works, it is through Marion's early thought, deeply influenced by Lustiger and Daniélou, that the discussion on negative theology developed within contemporary French philosophy (see also Marion 2012).

(his infinity, perfection, absoluteness, etc.) and the *ontological* one, namely, the possibility for man to grasp the "ontological intention of the divine essence as such" (Dubarle 1986, 306; my translation). When considering God's reality, the human mind conceives of God as a *suppositum*, that is, something existing as a substance, in order to translate this notion of substance into the concept of God. In other words, such an intellectual operation consists in turning the notion of "something having essence" into "what is the essence as such" (Dubarle 1986, 306). It is worth noting that Dubarle concedes that these definitions are never fully suitable for expressing the divine essence since this latter always exceeds any human conceptual understanding. Nevertheless, in Dubarle's view, certain aspects of our knowledge—for instance, the scientific truths—aim at expressing the divine essence as such, and accordingly, consolidate our faith by opening the possibility of naming God. Ultimately, Dubarle struggles to synthesize the admission of the impossibility to give an adequate definition of God with the attempt to save the traditional equivalence between God and the concept of substance. For this reason, since he was never really committed to the post-Heideggerian debate on religion, the relevance of his work is limited to his attempt to develop the Thomistic ontology after the crisis of metaphysics. As a result, he cannot play a relevant role in this discussion.

The philosophical framework of *God without Being* is completely different. When Marion claims, in the preface to the English translation, that his work "does not remain 'postmodern' all the way through" (Marion 1991, xxi), it is because of the delegitimization both of metaphysics and of "Being, thought as such, without its metaphysical figure" (ibid.). Here, Marion seeks to push the Heideggerian conception of Being beyond its limits, or rather, to deconstruct it. Nonetheless, as Marion repeated many times, this deconstructive practice is directed at the destruction of neither the notion of Being nor God's existence. Accordingly, Marion argues:

> Was it [*God without Being*] insinuating that the God "without Being" is not, or does not exist? Let me repeat now the answer I gave then: no, definitely not. God is, exists, and that is the least of things. At issue here is not the possibility of God's attaining Being but, quite the opposite, the possibility of Being's attaining to God. . . . Does Being define the first and the highest of the divine names?
>
> Marion 1991, xix–xx

Nevertheless, the structure of *God without Being* reveals a certain tension in Marion's treatment of Heidegger. Indeed, although his explicit purpose is to develop a new notion of God after the crisis of metaphysics, his book is completely focused on the analysis of how the problem of God has been approached throughout the history of metaphysics. More closely, Marion shares Heidegger's critique of the metaphysical notion of God, but he does not follow his account of ontology.

It is worth clarifying this point. There is no doubt that Marion develops his core thesis about the radical inadequacy of ontology to deal with the question of God after Heidegger's critique of Western metaphysics. Most notably, Marion argues that turning the notion of God into a rational concept means to reduce it to an *idol*. As a consequence, in Marion's view, throughout modernity, the ideas of God as *causa sui* (Spinoza) or source of morality (Kant) have largely given up any authentic attempt to conceive of God's absoluteness. Marion ultimately inherits Heidegger's view on Western culture as the progressive forgetting of the ontological difference and follows his critique of onto-theology, whose essential tendency is to confuse Being with beings, and accordingly, to define God as a supremely perfect being. Thus, in Marion's view, the appearance of the concept of God in Western thought depends much more on metaphysics than on God himself. From this perspective, Heidegger glimpses the necessity of separating the questions of Being and God, but at the same time, he admits their bind: "The truth of Being is . . . preparedness for the passing by of the last god" (Heidegger 2012, 23).

For the sake of clarity, for both Heidegger and Marion, Being is not the same as God. Nevertheless, although Heidegger's critique of metaphysics is decisive for Marion's notion of idolatry, in *God without Being* Marion argues that also Heidegger's ontology suffers from the same tendency to fall into idolatry. Indeed, Heidegger insists that the divine manifests itself only after Being has been experienced in its "unconcealment" (Heidegger 1998, 144). Instead, in Marion's view, Being is of no help in order to conceive of the absoluteness of God. Thus, Marion concludes that Heidegger's notion of the last god reveals its structural idolatry by virtue of its secondariness with respect to the question of God (Marion 1991, 41).

According to Marion, Heidegger's idolatry is strongly connected with Dasein's ontic and ontological priority over the other beings in posing the question of Being. There is no doubt that, in Heidegger's view, the coming of the last god does not depend on Dasein, and accordingly, cannot be idolized. Nevertheless, Marion locates this very tendency to reduce the divine to the human in what Heidegger calls the "ontic-ontological priority" (Heidegger 1996, 12) of Dasein in the formulation of the question of Being: "Phenomenologically, the anteriority of Being can be developed and justified only by the anteriority of the analytic of Dasein" (Marion 1991, 42). This means that ontology derives from the analytic of Dasein. Furthermore, since any investigation of God is based on the ontological clarification of the difference between Being and beings, one can conclude that, in Heidegger's perspective, any discourse about God is based on the analytic of Dasein. From a theological point of view, Heidegger's account of the problem of God "implies an instance anterior to 'God,' hence that point from which idolatry could dawn" (Marion 1991, 43). Therefore, Marion reprimands Heidegger for conceiving of God as a being, and in doing so, taking him for an idol. To closer inspection, for Marion the question is whether God is to be conceived of uniquely within the confines of Being: "Undoubtedly, if 'God' is, he is a being; but does God have to be?" (Marion 1991, 44). In brief, in Marion's view, Heidegger's mistake consists in the fact that, for him, a new manifestation of the divine after the crisis of metaphysics ultimately depends on Dasein. Following Heidegger, since the last god is supposed to safeguard the ontological difference between Being and beings, he should be conceived of within an ontological framework. In other words, according to Marion, thinking of God after onto-theology does not simply mean overcoming the metaphysical concept of the divine; rather, it requires to overcome the ontological difference as well. In line with this view, in *God without Being* (from the third chapter onward), Marion writes the word *God* "under erasure" or "crossed out" (Marion 1991, 70).

Also, due to the strong influence of negative theology on his education, in *God without Being*, Marion's goal is to emancipate the notion of God from the limits of ontology. Nevertheless, one can pose the question whether rationality is still possible beyond the ontological difference. Both in Heidegger's and Marion's views, religious experience has no need of ontology. The problem comes to light when faith is described and understood as an experience of thinking. In this case, how could one avoid any use of the ontological language without being condemned to silence at all? According to Marion, Heidegger does not posit Being in a realm beyond beings; rather, he conceives of Being as "what brings something up into view" (Heidegger 1998, 187). This means that Being is to be conceived of as the light illuminating phenomena and bringing them to manifestation, as suggested by Heidegger's account of truth as *alētheia*. Accordingly, thinking of Being as disclosedness instead of ground requires a complete deconstruction of the metaphysical principle of sufficient reason. Following Marion, conceiving of God independently of ontological difference means to prevent any relapse into a metaphysical framework. As already demonstrated, Marion's claim is not to prove that God does not exist: "God *is*, exists, and that is the least of things" (Marion 1991, xix–xx). Rather, in Marion's view, Heidegger's idolatry is connected to his account of God *only within* the horizon of Being. Nevertheless, Marion's approach to the problem of God reveals a certain tension as well, inasmuch as he apparently conceives of God at the same time *within* ontology and *outside* ontological difference. At first glance, such a contradiction is unavoidable. In an important passage, Marion declares:

> *To think outside of ontological difference eventually condemns one to be no longer able to think at all.* But precisely, *to be no longer able to think, when it is a question of God, indicates neither absurdity nor impropriety,* as soon as God himself, *in order to be thought*, must be thought as ... that which surpasses, detours, and distracts all thought, even non-representational. By definition and decision, God, *if he must be thought*, can meet no theoretical space to his measure, because his measure exerts itself in our eyes as an excessiveness. Ontological difference itself, and hence also Being, become too limited to pretend to offer the dimension, still less the "divine abode" where God would become thinkable.
>
> Marion 1991, 45

In this passage, Marion argues that, although ontological difference is probably insurmountable for human rationality, this theoretical impossibility is perfectly compatible with a nonmetaphysical account of God. The passage just quoted, largely influenced by Levinas's idea of "otherwise than Being" (Levinas 1991), reveals the necessity of reconsidering "excessiveness" (Marion 2008, 34) in a nonmetaphysical way, as testified by Marion's works on the *saturated phenomenon*.[5] It is worth emphasizing that Marion argues in *The Idol and Distance* that the idea of distance overcomes Heidegger's account of ontological difference as well as Derrida's notion of *différance* (Derrida 1982, 1–28). In the same chapter of *God Without Being*, Marion claims:

> Liberation from Being does not at all mean abstracting from it, precisely because abstraction strictly renders possible one of the metaphysical modes of the Being of beings.... Nor does liberation from Being signify undoing oneself and stealing away from it, since this very evasion opens onto nonbeing, hence remains within the dominion of the Being of beings. Finally, liberation from Being does not mean that one claims to criticize it or revoke it—for that discourse

5 See, in particular, Marion 2002a, 2002b, 2006, 2008.

> still supposes a logos and a site from which to set it into operation, hence prerogatives of Being.
>
> Marion 1991, 83

In this passage, Marion explains that any attempt to overcome the metaphysical approach to the problem of God does not entail a reintroduction of the concept of a transcendent Being. Rather, in line with Levinas and Derrida, Marion observes that the *impossible* does not correspond to the *unthinkable*. Thus, the core task of phenomenology is to provide a new approach to the question of God without reducing it to a being, although the being of beings. In other words, according to Marion, what is at stake in contemporary phenomenology is the deconstruction of metaphysics in order to develop a new philosophical framework based on the notion of excessiveness. Indeed, in Marion's view, excessiveness is what overcomes the order of beings without destroying them. Furthermore, if such a notion of excessiveness is especially fruitful for the question of God's revelation, Marion applies it to phenomenality in general. In this perspective, excessiveness is acknowledged as the paradigm of givenness (Marion 2002a, 227). As a consequence, in Marion's view, God is not graspable by a concept, for in this case, it would be reduced to an idol. This means that, after Marion's assessment of Heidegger's double (ontological) idolatry, there is evidence that any conceptual understanding of God definitively remains inappropriate for grasping God's excessiveness. In other terms, God infinitely resists to the human attempt to designate him through a concept, namely, to an ontological framework. Rather, Marion argues that God can be conceived of uniquely as absolute excessiveness. Such an attempt to overcome idolatry requires a progressive deconstruction of Western metaphysics as well as a serious search for a new paradigm of rationality.

3. A hermeneutical attempt

On this basis, one can conclude that Marion develops a phenomenology of excessiveness following two main strategies. On the one hand, from a strictly phenomenological point of view, the paradigm of excessiveness—or saturation—has an intelligible structure, but inconceivable content: something Derrida would have called "the coming of the impossible" (Derrida 2002, 360). Thus, excessiveness overcomes the traditional idea of objectivity as well as ontological difference since it deposes any ontological framework. Hence, excessiveness marks the limits of all thoughts. On the other hand, from a theological perspective, all thoughts are definitively vain with respect to the excessiveness of Revelation. Accordingly, every concept requires to be demystified and loses its importance on behalf of the nonmetaphysical rationality of excessiveness.

Both of these strategies leave unsolved the following question: Provided that revelation's goal is to upset human rationality, how can revelation be given to thought? In Marion's defense, it could be argued that in more recent works he is much more careful about the philosophical problem of faith.[6] More precisely, in these texts, faith is no longer an affair of theological certainty, but rather a *hermeneutical risk-taking*, and there is an enormous difference in between. Indeed, as Marion emphasized during a number of recent interviews and lectures, excessiveness is not to be understood as a concept, but rather according to the structure of *appeal* and *response*.[7] In other words, excessiveness does not manifest itself as full visibility, but rather as an appeal waiting for a response. It is precisely in this sense that, in Marion's perspective, excessiveness perfectly describes the *radical experience* of the divine, inasmuch as it upsets our *ordinary experience* based on perceptions, objects and concepts. It is worth emphasizing that excessiveness cannot be reduced to a concept. Rather, it is given as an originary appeal. Although subjectivity can respond negatively, it cannot elude such a radical appeal. Thus, in Marion's view, the experience of the divine consists in the response to the appeal of excessiveness: This means that every theoretical elaboration of such an experience—included ontology—is to be understood as a response to the originary appeal of the divine.

As a result, humans cannot but conceive of God within the limits of rationality, namely, within the limits of ontology. As Marion emphasized, God *is*, *exists*, so one must take into account his or her relation with Being. Nevertheless, humans must be aware of the fact that God's revelation does not depend on Being, but rather is given as an originary and invisible appeal to subjectivity. In other words, God's manifestation is not reducible to an ontological framework precisely because it represents the very source of any ontological concept. In a certain sense, we can turn *to* God only on the basis of our originary dialogue *with* God.[8]

6 See, in particular, Marion 2008 and 2015.

7 I refer mainly to Marion's lectures *Le phénomène saturé et l'herméneutique* (The saturated Phenomena and Hermeneutics) at the seminar directed by Claude Romano, Ecole Normale Supérieure, Paris, December 3, 2011, and *Dieu, ou l'ambivalence de l'être* (God, or the Ambivalence of Being), University of Bucarest, October 8, 2013.

8 Heidegger himself emphasizes the common root of the German words *denken* (to think) and *danken* (to thank), where *danken* is to be understood as an explicit modality of response to the *Anspruch* (appeal) of Being.

In Marion's last works, there emerges the conviction that our involvement in the manifestation of the divine is a hermeneutical issue. Thus, provided that ontology demonstrates its inappropriateness to grasp the originary appeal of excessiveness, only interpretation can offer a rational paradigm able to overcome the limits of subjectivity and approach the (radical) experience of excessiveness. Conceiving of God's excessiveness *within the limit of our hermeneutical rationality* does not mean to reduce him to our finite rational structures; rather, it means to treasure our openness to his inexhaustible ways of manifestation. In other terms, only a hermeneutical approach can illuminate excessiveness as "inexhaustible source."[9] It follows that interpretation can overcome the objective inadequacy of our conceptual rationality in order to describe religious experience. From this viewpoint, the question whether a philosophical reflection on religious experience depends on ontology can be answered as follows: To avoid the danger of falling into idolatry, a philosophical reflection has to approach the problem of faith as an *ontological hermeneutics of religious experience*. More precisely, the ontological hermeneutics approaches the problem of God by developing a hermeneutics of excessiveness.

My last aim in this essay is to clarify such a notion of hermeneutics of excessiveness. In other words, it remains to explain how the notion of excessiveness can clarify the difficult relation between philosophy and faith. In more detail, a fruitful model of dialogue between hermeneutics and faith is now at stake. As I already mentioned, faith does not depend on ontology. This latter appears together with the philosophical reflection on the experience of faith. On the one hand, in line with Marion's perspective on the hermeneutics of the saturated phenomenon, one can define the radical experience of revelation as excessiveness. On the other hand, dealing with a philosophical approach to the experience of faith, ontology represents the ground zero, namely, the impassability of human finitude. It is up to hermeneutics to grasp the infinite source of excessiveness, not in a conceptual shape, but rather by the risk-taking of interpretation. On closer inspection, this risk consists in the constant possibility to objectify the truth expressed in interpretation, and accordingly, to turn the dialogue among different interpretations in a "conflict of interpretations" (Ricoeur 1974). Shortly, interpretation is always exposed to the danger of relativism. Rather, interpretation only safeguards its essential connection to truth by affirming truth's inexhaustibility and attesting it through the existential

[9] One can find this expression, referred to the concept of truth, in Pareyson 2013.

commitment of the interpreter. In this sense, as argued by Luigi Pareyson, "there is authentic interpretation only of truth, and truth is always given only by interpretation" (2013, 36).

The task hermeneutics of religious experience entrusts to us is to think *together* the different claims of thought and faith without any attempt to reduce them from one another, but rather safeguarding their own autonomy as well as their reciprocal dialogue. As is well known, philosophy and religion have often been characterized by a sort of *totalizing temptation* throughout the history of modern and contemporary Western culture: Whereas philosophy attempted to absorb theology, faith and the idea of God in its categories (as it happens, for instance, in Spinoza or in Hegel), theology tried to subordinate philosophy to the revealed faith (for instance, Thomas Aquinas and his doctrine of *philosophia ancilla theologiae*). On any account, this temptation of absorbing faith in philosophy is somehow present in Heidegger, whereas Marion (at least in *God without Being*) shows the opposite tendency to subordinate rationality to God's excessiveness. Indeed, according to Marion, conceiving of God within a conceptual framework always means to reduce him to an idol. In my view, this constant danger to fall into idolatry puts us in front of the urgent necessity to develop furthermore the hermeneutics of faith: Religious experience strongly involves the sphere of rational thought, it "gives to think," but at the same time, to measure the constitutive finitude of human *Logos*.

In conclusion, I do emphasize that this interpretive work can be done only by a hermeneutical approach able to deal with the radical and paradoxical experience of faith in a God which manifests himself as absolute excessiveness. Such a paradox raises from both the necessity and the impossibility to conceive of God within our rational limits: In line with Marion's account of the saturated phenomenon, one could conclude that a radical experience, to be as such, raises from paradox, upsetting, contradicting and overcoming the subjective conditions of our ordinary experience. So much work has to be done in this direction, but—as argued by Matthew—"the harvest is plentiful, but the workers are few" (Matt. 9, 37).

References

Catechism of the Catholic Church. 1994. Translated by Geoffrey Chapman. London: Burns & Oates.

Derrida, Jacques. 1982. *Margins of Philosophy*. Translated by Alan Bass. Chicago: University of Chicago Press.

Derrida, Jacques. 2002. *Negotiations: Interventions and Interviews, 1971–2001*. Edited by Elizabeth Rottenberg. Stanford. CA: Stanford University Press.

Dubarle, Dominique. 1986. *Dieu avec l'être*. Paris: Beauchesne.

Fedier, François. 1980. *Heidegger et Dieu*. In *Heidegger et la question de Dieu*, edited by Richard Kearney, 37–45. Paris: Grasset.

Heidegger, Martin. 1966. *Discourse on Thinking*. Translated by John Anderson. New York: Harper & Row.

Heidegger, Martin. 1976. *The Piety of Thinking: Essays*. Translated by James Hart and John Maraldo. Bloomington: Indiana University Press.

Heidegger, Martin. 1982. *The Basic Problems of Phenomenology*. Translated by Albert Hofstadter. Bloomington: Indiana University Press.

Heidegger, Martin. 1996. *Being and Time*. Translated by Joan Stambaugh. New York: SUNY Press.

Heidegger, Martin. 1998. *Pathmarks*. Translated by William McNeill. Cambridge: Cambridge University Press.

Heidegger, Martin. 2000. *Elucidations on Hölderlin's Poetry*. Translated by Keith Hoeller. New York: Humanity Books.

Heidegger, Martin. 2001. *Zollikon Seminars*. Translated by Franz Mayr. Evanston, IL: Northwestern University Press.

Heidegger, Martin. 2003. *The End of Philosophy*. Translated by Joan Stambaugh. New York: Harper & Row.

Heidegger, Martin. 2012. *Contributions to Philosophy (of the Event)*. Translated by Richard Rojcewicz. Bloomington: Indiana University Press.

Hölderlin, Friedrich. 1994. *Selected Poems and Fragments*. Translated by Micheal Hamburger. London: Anvil Press Poetry.

Levinas, Emmanuel. 1991. *Otherwise than Being, or Beyond Essence*. Translated by Alphonso Lingis. Dordrecht: Kluwer.

Marion, Jean-Luc. 1991. *God without Being*. Translated by Thomas Carlson. Chicago: University of Chicago Press.

Marion, Jean-Luc. 2002a. *Being Given: Toward a Phenomenology of Givenness*. Translated by Jeffrey L. Kosky. Stanford, CA: Stanford University Press.

Marion, Jean-Luc. 2002b. *In Excess: Studies of Saturated Phenomena*. Translated by Robyn Horner. New York: Fordham University Press.

Marion, Jean-Luc. 2006. *The Erotic Phenomenon*. Translated by Stephen E. Lewis. Chicago: University of Chicago Press.

Marion, Jean-Luc. 2008. *The Visible and the Revealed*. Translated by Christina M. Gschwandtner. New York: Fordham University Press.

Marion, Jean-Luc. 2012. *La rigueur des choses*. Paris: Flammarion.

Marion, Jean-Luc. 2015. *Negative Certainties*. Translated by Stephen Lewis. Chicago: University of Chicago Press.

Pareyson, Luigi. 2013. *Truth and Interpretation*. Translated by Robert Valgenti. New York: SUNY Press.

Ricoeur, Paul. 1974. *The Conflict of Interpretations*. Translated by Don Ihde. Evanston: Northwestern University Press.

St. Anselm. 1995. *Proslogion*. Translated by Thomas Williams. Indianapolis: Hackett.

The Holy Bible. New International Version. 1988. Lutterworth: The Gideons International.

Thomas Aquinas. 2006. *Summa Theologiae, Questions on God*. Translated by Brian Davies. Cambridge: Cambridge University Press.

Vedder, Ben. 2006. *Heidegger's Philosophy of Religion: From God to the Gods*. Pittsburgh: Duquesne University Press.

3

A Religious End of Metaphysics?

Heidegger, Meillassoux and the Question of Fideism

Jussi Backman

The publication of Quentin Meillassoux's *After Finitude: An Essay on the Necessity of Contingency* (*Après la finitude: Essai sur la nécessité de la contingence*, 2006, English translation, 2008) started a minor upheaval within French philosophy, one that rapidly spread into the Anglophone philosophical world. Marked by a rare intellectual audacity that is barely concealed by its modest and measured tone and its sober argumentative style, the book not only attempts a clear break with some of the most established points of departure of post-Heideggerian phenomenology, hermeneutics, (post)structuralism, post-Quinean naturalism and post-Wittgensteinian philosophy of language, but in fact, seeks to upset the foundations of most of post-Kantian thought. In his preface to the book, Meillassoux's mentor Alain Badiou (2006, 11; 2008, vii) maintains that *After Finitude* does nothing less than offer a new *speculative* alternative to the three main philosophical options outlined by Kant, that is, dogmatic (rationalist), skeptical (Humean) and critical (Kantian) philosophy, different versions of which still dominate the contemporary philosophical scene.[1]

What Meillassoux essentially claims is that the new period of modern philosophy introduced by Kant's "Copernican revolution" is fundamentally oriented by an approach that Meillassoux terms *correlationism*. The first part of this essay briefly introduces this notion, focusing on Meillassoux's distinction between Kant's "weak" correlationism and a contemporary "strong" version, most prominently represented by Heidegger and Wittgenstein, and on Meillassoux's intricate argument designed to reveal an inherent inconsistency in strong correlationism. However, our main focus is on one of the central *motives* cited by Meillassoux for his attack on strong correlationism: his diagnosis of the

[1] For Kant's distinction, see Kant 1998a, 33–34 (B XXXV–XXXVI); 1998b, 119.

fideism that he sees as inherent to this ultimate outcome of the Kantian heritage. The finitization of reason launched by Kant's critical project progressively deprived philosophy of any dogmatic or speculative claims to an *absolute* reference point. Nonetheless, Meillassoux claims, this deabsolutization of thinking cannot avoid surrendering the room vacated by the metaphysical absolutes to the realm of *faith*, which now becomes increasingly immunized against the claims of critical reason—provided that faith, in turn, makes no more claims on the finite domain of rational, discursive thought. By highlighting certain problematic aspects in Meillassoux's account of contemporary fideism, the present essay questions the cogency of this specific diagnosis. This permits us to pose some more general questions regarding the kind of modernity Meillassoux seeks to recover through his proposal of a speculative way out of the ravages of contemporary correlationism.

1. Strong correlationism and speculative materialism

Let us start by elucidating the key notions of "correlationism" and "speculative" thinking. *Correlationism* is defined by Meillassoux (2006a, 18; 2008a, 5) as a primarily epistemological principle according to which being and thinking—the latter understood in the widest possible sense of any activity related to the reception, articulation or constitution of meaning—cannot be conceived or accessed apart from each other, but only in terms of their reciprocal correlation, that is, in terms of the (meaningful) givenness of being to thinking and of the corresponding inherent orientation of thinking to being. *Speculative* is to be understood here in the sense of an approach professing access, by logical and conceptual means, to knowledge about the absolute reality of "things in themselves," a claim proscribed by Kant's critical philosophy, but later vindicated by the German Idealists in a dialectical form (Meillassoux 2006a, 47–48; 2008a, 34). The defining principle of what Meillassoux (2006a, 26–27, 42, 48–49; 2008a, 10–11, 30, 35) terms Kant's "weak" correlationism is that we have access to being only *insofar as* it is an objective phenomenal correlate of our experience, structured by the transcendental forms and categories of our sensory intuition and discursive understanding, while the absolute, correlation-transcendent *source* or *cause* of empirical experience remains epistemically inaccessible.[2] This

[2] For Kant's argument for the intelligibility and necessity of the notion of "things in themselves," suggesting that while the validity of this notion is theoretically unknowable, it could be justified on a practical basis, see Kant 1998a, 27–28 (B XXVI–XXVII); 1998b, 115–16.

was transformed by speculative idealism into an absolute metaphysical principle that denies the very coherence of the notion of noncorrelational things in themselves and absolutizes the correlation itself in the form of an absolute subjectivity. Meillassoux's *speculative materialism*, however, is based on another kind of absolutization. What Kant's "weak" correlationism was for Hegel, the "strong" correlationism of Heidegger and Wittgenstein is for Meillassoux.

In order to understand the premises of Meillassoux's own position, we therefore need to understand how he defines the strong version of correlationism. One of the key accomplishments of Meillassoux's book is undeniably its articulation of the fundamental presuppositions of this specific position, which cuts across many established lines of division in contemporary thought. While Meillassoux (2006a, 51–52, 71; 2008a, 37–38, 51–52) regards thinkers such as Schopenhauer, Bergson and Deleuze as, in fact, committed to forms of absolute idealism that hypostasize will or life into an ultimate principle, "strong correlationism" is a category that apparently binds together orientations as diverse as Heideggerian hermeneutics, Derridean deconstruction, Habermasian discourse ethics and Wittgensteinian linguistic philosophy (Meillassoux 2006a, 42, 48–67; 2008a, 30, 35–48). Like absolute or speculative idealism, strong correlationism denies the coherence of the notion of a completely correlation-transcendent reality. However, it further denies the conceptual intelligibility of *any* kind of absolute, including absolute subjectivity. Strong correlationism holds that the correlation itself, even though it is the condition of possibility for any intelligibility or conceivability, is not given as an absolute provided with necessitating reasons or grounds. The correlation is rather accepted as an unmotivated given or "gift," that is, as radically *factical*. For the strong correlationist, however, this does not imply any actual knowledge of the nonnecessity of the correlation or of its specific structures, but rather refers to the intrinsic *finitude* of thinking: While thinking is unable to grasp its own total absence as such, it is also incapable of giving any absolute and necessary grounds for the fact of its correlatedness with being.

Strong correlationists will disagree among themselves whether or not thinking is committed to any universal transcendental structures. While those inspired by Habermas and Apel will argue that the possibility of rational communication and argumentation depends on certain universally accepted criteria of validity and phenomenologists of the Merleau-Pontyan persuasion will point to the transcendental role of human embodied perception, Heideggerian hermeneutics will insist on the historically constituted and situated nature of all a priori conditions. However, they will all agree on the incapacity of thinking to attain any absolutely necessary point of reference, either beyond itself or within itself. In the end, thinking will have to accept an ultimate given—the simple fact of language, perception, experience or willing—that it is no longer able to rationally justify or derive from something more fundamental. Strong correlationism is a postmetaphysical approach, in the Heideggerian sense of renouncing aspirations to an absolute reference point. It is inherently committed to the historical thesis of a contemporary end of metaphysics (Meillassoux 2006a, 61–63; 2008a, 44–46).

Meillassoux's most original and striking move, elaborated in the third chapter of his book (2006a, 69–109; 2008a, 50–81), is to argue that the strong correlationist insistence on the facticity of the correlation, on the one hand, and on the inconceivability of its absence, on the other, harbors an implicit contradiction. This is illustrated by way of an intricate fictitious dialogue (2006a, 74–81; 2008a, 54–59) between several interlocutors, the most important of whom are the absolute idealist, the strong correlationist and the speculative materialist. The topic of their dispute is mortality and the fate of the thinking ego in death. The absolute idealist must maintain that death is an empirical event affecting only the empirical, finite and personal aspects of the ego; the transcendental core of egoity, the "I think" as the subject of thought and as an absolute point of reference for all conscious acts, necessarily remains unaffected by the death of a particular individual. The strong correlationist, however, accepts no such necessity, and therefore, has to choose agnosticism regarding the ego's mortality. Since we have no access to any necessitating grounds for the continued preservation of thinking and of the ego or the self as the focal point of thought, the strong correlationist reasons, thinking is equally conceivable as mortal, even though its death and absence *as such* remain inconceivable. This approach is particularly prominent in Heidegger (2001, 260–67, 316–23; 2010, 249–55, 302–9), for whom Dasein's mortality—its being-toward-death in the sense of an orientation to the constant possibility of the closure of its existential possibilities (the "possibility of impossibility" as an "ultimate" possibility)—is a constitutive structure that precisely limits and situates Dasein's existence, and thus, individuates and singularizes it.[3]

[3] However, see also the remarks in Wittgenstein's *Tractatus* on death as the "end of the (my) world," as a limit that is not an event, but rather like a horizon, as something that one cannot live through, and on the complete uncertainty of a preservation of the soul after death; Wittgenstein 1960, §§6.431, 6.4311, 6.4312.

But here, the speculative materialist spots an inconsistency. For Hegel (1985, 31, 47; 2010, 27, 41), Kant's delimitation of the realm of knowledge "from the inside" is incompatible with the latter's denial of any epistemic access to what remains beyond this limit, since establishing a limit in a way presupposes that one has already grasped both its sides, which implicitly makes Kant's "things in themselves" an intellectual abstraction, and thus, a correlate of thought. In an analogous manner, Meillassoux regards the Heideggerian affirmation of thinking's constitutive relationship to its own death as a *possibility* and the simultaneous denial of any access to the *actuality* of one's death as incompatible. To say that thinking can conceive itself as mortal, Meillassoux argues, can have no plausible meaning other than to say that it can conceive its own undoing and absence as such—that is, that it can conceive a reality beyond the correlation of thinking and being.

> [I]f I maintain that the possibility of my not-being only exists as a correlate of my act of thinking the possibility of my not-being, then *I can no longer conceive the possibility of my not-being,* which is precisely the thesis defended by the idealist. For I think myself as mortal only if I think that my death has no need of my thought of death in order to be actual.
>
> Meillassoux 2006a, 78; 2008a, 57

In other words, egoity is conceivable as mortal only if the death of the ego, *my* death, is itself conceivable in some way—but not, to be sure, from a first-personal perspective since what is at stake in one's own death is precisely the disappearance of the first person. Strong correlationism thus has two coherent options: It must either collapse back into absolute idealism, which denies the real possibility of "mortality" as anything more than a mood of an inherently absolute egoity, or convert to speculative materialism, which recognizes that the only consistent way to deny the absoluteness of any *instance* or *level* of reality is to absolutize the *facticity* of all things and to reinterpret this facticity in the sense of *contingency*. From accepting that all things, including givenness itself, are *given* without absolutely and necessitating grounds, the speculative materialist proceeds to attribute to them a *real* capacity for *not being* the way they currently happen to be. Such contingency is no longer seen as a phenomenological description of the givenness of things, but rather as a speculative thesis concerning the way in which all things *as well as givenness itself* are "in themselves," independently of their correlation with thinking. Any attempt to make contingency itself contingent would be self-defeating, since it would amount to a regressive suggestion that things in themselves could be merely *contingently* contingent—invoking, once more, a more fundamental contingency—as well as the absurd view that things could just as well, contingently, be noncontingent, that is, *necessarily* the way they are. The strong correlationist who refuses to become an absolute idealist is thus ultimately committed to an absolute contingency which is "an absolute that cannot be de-absolutized without being thought as absolute once more" (Meillassoux 2006a, 79; 2008a, 58).

If this reasoning holds, it follows that the only true option to absolute idealism is asserting the *absoluteness of contingency*. This is to maintain that everything there is, including the fact *that there is* a meaningful givenness of being to thinking, is not only *factical* in the sense of not being given as necessary, but simply *contingent* in the sense of being really *non*necessary, that is, inherently capable of *not* being there. As we saw, such a concept of contingency, which does not merely express an epistemological limitation ("*x* cannot be known to be necessary"), but an ontological thesis ("*x* is indeed nonnecessary"), can be applied to the correlation between being and thinking only if we presuppose the conceivability of a reality without this correlation. In order to grasp itself as contingent rather than simply factical, thinking must have access to its own possible absence and to a level of being that is independent of the correlation. However, the criteria for such conceivability clearly cannot be phenomenological, as the absence of the correlation is never "given." Perhaps unsurprisingly, Meillassoux asserts that they must be *mathematical*: The terms under which absolute contingency can be thought must be purely formal and structural, without any phenomenal content of meaningful presence. This is why he insists (Meillassoux 2006a, 13–16; 2008a, 1–3) that the Cartesian and Lockean distinction between secondary qualities (phenomenal and nonquantifiable qualities, such as color) and primary qualities (measurable and mathematizable quantities, such as extension) must be rehabilitated. Only the latter qualities, by virtue of being conceivable in mathematical terms, can claim to be absolute and noncorrelational features of things in themselves. Following Badiou, Meillassoux suggests that mathematics has an absolute ontological scope as the formal science of being *qua* being. However, in order to be true to the rational and deductive nature of his Cartesian-style system, Meillassoux cannot simply presuppose this status of mathematics, but faces the task of deriving it from his fundamental thesis of absolute contingency. In *After Finitude*, this task is postponed to later works (Meillassoux 2006a, 37, 152–53, 176–78; 2008a, 26, 110–11, 127–28).

Even though Meillassoux's argumentation is quite novel and compelling, many of its crucial individual steps remain underdeveloped and still require a detailed critical analysis. We should also note that it seems to rest on certain presuppositions that can arguably be contested from a Heideggerian perspective. Notably, the notion that the conceivability of death as a *possibility* logically entails the conceivability of death as an *actuality* would undoubtedly be unacceptable for Heidegger, who precisely seeks to overturn the Aristotelian hierarchy of act and potency and insists on the ontological primacy of possibility over actuality, that is, of the dimension of future over that of the present.[4] One's own death, for Heidegger (2001, 261–62; 2010, 250–51), is the ultimate and pure limit-possibility that *remains* a possibility. Phenomenologically, mortality is simply a futural reference without a referent that could be directly present in itself.

A critical examination of Meillassoux's premises along these lines would, however, require an extensive study of its own.[5] Here, we rather take a look at what seems to be one of Meillassoux's central grievances against strong correlationism in addition to its alleged incoherence, namely, the *fideism* that he perceives as an unacceptable consequence of the strong correlationist deabsolutization of thinking.

2. Fideism: The "other name" of strong correlationism

At the end of the second chapter of *After Finitude*, "Metaphysics, Fideism, Speculation," Meillassoux (2006a, 60–68; 2008a, 43–49) associates the contemporary predominance of strong correlationism with what he sees as the contemporary liberation of religious faith from the constraints of discursive rationality. An essential difference between the Kantian weak version and the Heideggerian and Wittgensteinian strong versions of correlationism is their respective understanding of the relationship between faith and reason. While Kant (1998c; 2003b), the philosopher of the Enlightenment, subjected religion to rational scrutiny "within the boundaries of mere reason"—even though he concludes that in depriving speculative philosophy of its pretension to absolute insights into the nature of God, freedom and immortality, he must "deny knowledge in order to make room for faith" regarding these topics in the practical and moral realm (Kant 1998a, 30 [B

4 This is emphasized by Heidegger in his 1925 lecture course: "[T]he relationship of being toward a possibility must be such that it lets the possibility stand as a possibility, and not such that the possibility becomes actuality [*Wirklichkeit*]" (Heidegger 1979, 439; 1985, 317; translation modified).

5 For a more extensive discussion of Meillassoux's account of correlationism and his "argument from mortality," see Backman 2014b.

XXX]; 1998b, 117)—philosophical late modernity has made a point of regarding such subjection as in itself illegitimate. The reason for this, Meillassoux thinks, is precisely the radical finitization of discursive thinking, the culmination of a process initiated by Kant himself.

> It ... becomes clear that this [strong correlationist] trajectory culminates in the disappearance of the pretension to *think* any absolutes, *but not in the disappearance of absolutes*.... Far from abolishing the value of the absolute, the process that continues to be referred to today as "the end of absolutes" grants the latter an unprecedented licence—philosophers seem to ask only one thing of these absolutes: that they be devoid of the slightest pretension to rationality. The end of metaphysics, understood as the "de-absolutization of thought," is thereby seen to consist in the rational legitimation of any and every variety of religious (or "poetico-religious") belief in the absolute, so long the latter invokes no authority beside itself. To put it in other words: *by forbidding reason any claim to the absolute, the end of metaphysics has taken the form of an exacerbated return of the religious.*
>
> Meillassoux 2006a, 61–62; 2008a, 44–45

Meillassoux recognizes, of course, that the strong correlationist project of deabsolutization was rooted in a broadly shared thesis of the end of metaphysics, understood by Heidegger as the historical closure of *onto-theology*, a term with which he designates the ontological and epistemological foundationalism dominating the Western metaphysical tradition.[6] According to Heidegger's grand historical narrative, Plato and Aristotle introduced the initial onto-theological models (Heidegger 1996, 235–36; 1998c, 180–81), which referred the totality of beings to a supreme, ideal and absolute—"divine" (*theion*)—instance of beingness, such as the Platonic Idea of the Good or the Aristotelian metaphysical divinity. Since Descartes, onto-theology was gradually reoriented toward a metaphysics of subjectivity that shifted the metaphysical Archimedean point into the realm of the self-consciousness of the thinking ego. In the Heideggerian account, this development attains its point of culmination and exhaustion in Hegel and Nietzsche (Heidegger 1991a, 200–10; 1996, 335–36; 1998a, 202–13; 1998c, 255–56; 2000b, 63; 2002d, 57). Nietzsche elaborates the ultimate "negative" onto-theological model in which the absolute metaphysical reference point—the will to power as the essence of life—becomes a dynamic principle of the endless, nonteleological

6 On onto-theology, see, for example, Heidegger 1991d, 207–11; 1996, 378–79; 1998b, 311–15; 1998c, 287–88; 2002a, 31–67; 2002b, 42–74.

and self-referential process of life's self-intensification (structurally characterized as the "eternal recurrence of the same") that ceaselessly generates and annihilates meanings or "values" as its temporary instruments. The fact that the Nietzschean model entails an "inversion" of basic Platonic hierarchies—a preference for the transient, the multiple and the sensuous over the intransient, the one and the ideal—reveals the model's fundamental conceptual dependency on precisely those hierarchies, and thus, discloses its basic nature as a final stage of onto-theological metaphysics and of its modern phase in particular.[7]

Meillassoux (2006a, 62–63; 2008a, 45–46) rightly adds, however, that this diagnosis of the contemporary exhaustion of onto-theology affected, in truth, only a very specific historical framing of religion. First and foremost, it involved the Christian and Islamic natural theologies, both strongly influenced by Aristotle, that assert the *rational* necessity of God as a supreme and absolute being. Far from being a contribution to intellectual secularization, the undermining of onto-theology has simply contributed to a final divorce between theology and philosophy—a tendency that had always existed within the Christian and Islamic theological traditions—and has resulted merely in the total *exemption* of divinity from the sphere of rational conceptual analysis and debate. According to Meillassoux, the fact that in the strong correlationist context, the divine can no longer plausibly claim the status of a rationally necessary supreme being whose existence can be deduced by strictly rational means, in no way prevents the divine from retaining its absolute status in the realm of *faith*. In terms of the relationship between philosophy and religion, the philosophical rejection of onto-theology is the victory of *fideism*, defined by Meillassoux as skepticism regarding the capacity of metaphysical reason to access the proper objects or sources of faith. Meillassoux (2006a, 63–64; 2008a, 46) concludes: "[I]t is our conviction that the contemporary end of metaphysics is nothing other than the victory of such a fideism.... *The contemporary end of metaphysics is an end which, being sceptical, could only be a religious end of metaphysics*."

Unlike the various fideisms of previous centuries, however, the fideism of strong correlationism is no longer primarily a Catholic or Protestant fideism, or even a Christian fideism in general. It is rather, in Meillassoux's view (2006a, 64; 2008a, 46), a "fideism of any belief whatsoever," a general postsecular apology of *religiosity as*

[7] On this reading of Nietzsche, see Heidegger 1968, 48–110; 1991a, 3–6; 1991b, 198–208, 222–30; 1991c, 3–9, 150–58, 159–83, 185–251; 1991d, 147–96; 1997b, 19–47, 62–78; 1998a, 1–4, 415–23, 425–32, 585–94; 1998b, 1–22, 177–229, 231–300; 2000a, 72, 77–86, 109–19; 2002c, 157–99; 2003a, 89, 93–102; 2003b, 209–67.

such. That Wittgenstein and Heidegger are seen as the masterminds of this new "religionizing" (*enreligement*) of thinking is evident from the very choice of the term *fideism*, commonly associated with Wittgensteinian philosophy of religion (although not used by Wittgenstein himself).[8] Meillassoux (2006a, 66; 2008a, 48) specifically alludes to Wittgenstein's references to the "mystical" fact that there is a (my) world, limited by the limits of (my) language (Wittgenstein 1960, §§5.6, 6.44, 6.45, 6.522). He also cites (Meillassoux 2006a, 66; 2008a, 48) Heidegger's rather cryptic mention, in his 1951 Zürich seminar, of a temptation to write a theology "without the word 'being'" (Heidegger 2002e, 291; 2005, 436–37), a suggestion extensively developed in Jean-Luc Marion's *God Without Being* (1982).[9] *Fideism*, in the end, is thus simply "the *other name* for strong correlationism" (Meillassoux 2006a, 67; 2008a, 48).

Why this fideism is not to be regarded as a mere intellectual curiosity experimented by a handful of academics in an increasingly secularized Western world is then stated in strikingly strong terms. In its incapacity to subject religiosity to rational analysis, Meillassoux (2006a, 65; 2008a, 47) claims, the strong correlationist framework effectively renounces the Enlightenment struggle against *fanaticism* by means of reason. Armed solely with moral arguments in the realm of religion, intellectually the contemporary correlationist philosopher must "capitulate to the man of faith" in the domain proper to the latter. Hence, Meillassoux's dramatic conclusion: As the completion of the Kantian critical quest against dogmatism and ideological foundationalism, strong correlationism inadvertently falls into the arms of skeptical fanaticism.

> It is thanks to the critical power of correlationism that dogmatism was effectively vanquished in philosophy, and it is because of correlationism that philosophy finds itself incapable of fundamentally distinguishing itself from fanaticism. The victorious critique of ideologies has been transformed into a renewed argument for blind faith.
>
> Meillassoux 2006a, 68; 2008a, 49

Meillassoux's notion of contemporary fideism clearly addresses a prominent intellectual trend manifested by Heidegger's important influence on late twentieth-century theology and philosophy of religion. This trend is visible particularly in the Levinasian "theological turn" of French phenomenology

8 In the context of Wittgenstein studies, the label of "fideism" was introduced by Kai Nielsen (Nielsen 1967; cf. Nielsen and Phillips 2005).

9 For a related reading of Heidegger and Wittgenstein as two key philosophers of facticity and finitude, see Braver 2012.

critically described by Dominique Janicaud (1991; 2000) and in the renewed interest in faith and religion in the work of post-Heideggerians such as Jacques Derrida (1996; 1998) and Gianni Vattimo (1999; cf. Rorty, Vattimo and Zabala 2005). Moreover, we know that the critique of fideism is related to the intended role of *After Finitude* as a prelude to Meillassoux's projected *magnum opus*, known by its working title *Divine Inexistence: An Essay on the Virtual God*, to which he defers a more elaborate discussion of the contemporary role of fideism (Meillassoux 2006a, 67n1; 2008a, 132n15). Even though this work still remains unpublished in its definitive form, we know its general line of argumentation, at least in its projected form, from Meillassoux's 1997 doctoral dissertation, from the manuscript excerpts published in Graham Harman's (2011, 175–238) introductory work on Meillassoux, and from an article published independently by Meillassoux (2006b; 2008b). This rather astounding project apparently aims to introduce an entirely novel and rational perspective on the divine, but one that diverges completely from rational theism in maintaining the present inexistence of God, and also from scientifically oriented atheism in vindicating, on the basis of the thesis of absolute contingency that entails the contingency and real capacity to be otherwise of even the most established regularities of nature,[10] the rationality of a hope for the completely unmotivated emergence of an omnipotent and benevolent (but nonetheless contingent and nonnecessary) "god to come" that would redeem the promise of ultimate justice attributed by Kant to God as a postulate of practical reason (Meillassoux 2006b; 2008b; Harman 2011, 189–93).[11] Such an entirely groundless and inexplicable emergence of a "world of justice" is compared by Meillassoux to the equally groundless emergence of the worlds of matter, life and sentience. In brief, Meillassoux's project seems to consist in a rectification of modernity's fateful excursion into correlationism and fideism with the help of a new concept of divinity that would allow us to replace traditional notions of religious faith as well as Kant's "moral faith" with a fully rational, posttranscendental moral *hope* of a world of divine justice to come. Significantly for our present topic, this project—to the extent

[10] Meillassoux (2006a, 111–53; 2008a, 82–111) devotes considerable energy to arguing that the true solution to Hume's problem regarding the validity of inductive generalizations and of general empirical laws is that (1) as Hume showed, there is nothing rationally necessary about the laws of nature; and that (2) post-Cantorian set theory allows a mathematical model in which the (finite or infinite) amount of all possible cases does not form a closed totality, which makes even probabilistic or statistical reasoning in favor of the stability of natural laws invalid.

[11] Cf. Kant's (1996, 239–46 [A 223–37; AA 124–32]; 2003a, 167–77) account of the existence of God as a postulate of practical reason. For a discussion of Meillassoux's "virtual god" in comparison to Heidegger's "ultimate god" and Badiou's "contemporary atheism," see Backman 2014a.

that it has been made public—effectively suggests that instead of a fideistic sanctioning of religious faith, or of a naturalistic antireligiosity based on the sanctioning of scientific inductive reasoning, philosophy must propagate a rationally legitimized *hope* and *demand* for a morally rational and just world, a world essentially different from the one presently familiar to us.

3. Faith, the absolute and contemporary fanaticism: Critical reflections

Challenging approaches to the divine focused on faith rather than reason is thus at the heart of Meillassoux's wider speculative enterprise. However, his diagnosis of the fideistic core of strong correlationism is among the most disputable claims of *After Finitude*. Let us look at three particularly problematic aspects of this account. Since post-Heideggerian philosophy of religion seems to be its primary frame of reference, it will be instructive to use Heidegger as a key reference point here.

3.1. Faith, belief, religion

First of all, Meillassoux's use of the term *fideism* is extremely general. The term is notoriously ambiguous and refers to several quite different historical traditions; Thomas Carroll (2008) has distinguished no less than six different connotations of the word.[12] Meillassoux (2006a, 63, 66; 2008a, 46, 48) explicitly refers to the early modern fideistic stances of sixteenth- and seventeenth-century thinkers such as Michel de Montaigne, Pierre Gassendi and Pierre Bayle, who used the arguments of Pyrrhonist skepticism against the rational establishment of beliefs in order to make room for faith. Somewhat surprisingly, Meillassoux describes fideism as an invention of the Catholic Counter-Reformation; however, this Catholic fideism was, above all, a reaction to Protestant theology and one that never found particular favor within official Church theology. It was most recently condemned by Pope John Paul II (1998, no. 55; 1999, 49), who, in his 1998

[12] Carroll distinguishes three historical usages and three more or less pejorative usages of the term *fideism*. Historically, it refers to (1) the early modern "conformist" skeptical fideism of Erasmus of Rotterdam, Michel de Montaigne and Pierre Bayle; (2) the "evangelical" skeptical fideism of Blaise Pascal and Søren Kierkegaard; and (3) the late-nineteenth-century "symbolo-fideism" of the French Protestant theologians Eugène Ménégoz and Louis Auguste Sabatier. The pejorative senses of *fideism* are (4) Catholic traditionalism; (5) fundamentalist Biblicism; and (6) the "antimetaphysical" philosophical and theological trends of the twentieth century.

encyclical *Fides et Ratio*, voices his concern over an apparent "resurgence of *fideism*, which fails to recognize the importance of rational knowledge and philosophical discourse for the understanding of faith."[13]

The term *fideism* itself was coined in the late nineteenth century by the French Protestant theologians Eugène Ménégoz and Louis Auguste Sabatier, founders of the "symbolo-fideistic" movement, which emphasized the relativity of dogmatic religious doctrines as different historical expressions of faith. The emphasis on faith and the undermining of rational access to its content has been most prominent in the Lutheran theological tradition, where it is sometimes referred to as "solifidianism" in reference to the doctrine of justification *sola fide*, "by faith alone" (Vainio 2010, 9–10). Luther himself was perhaps the first early modern critic of the onto-theological "metaphysics of presence." Thomas Sheehan (1979, 322) and John van Buren (1994a, 161, 167–68; 1994b, 157–68, 198) have shown that Luther's distinction, in his 1515–16 *Lectures on Romans* (Luther 1938, 371; 2006, 235), between the future-oriented thinking of the Apostle Paul and the present-oriented thought of "philosophers and metaphysicians," was decisively important for the young Heidegger, as was Luther's (1883, 350–74; 2012, 14–25) attack on the rational and natural "theology of glory" in his 1518 Heidelberg disputation. In addition to a fideistic epistemology of religion, the Lutheran emphasis on the primacy of the existential message of the Gospel also tended toward an existential, rather than cognitive, notion of faith. This tendency is most evident in the thought of Kierkegaard and visible also in Rudolf Bultmann's "demythologization" of the New Testament; under the strong influence of Heidegger's *Being and Time*, Bultmann (1960, 29; 1961, 19)[14] defines *faith* as an act of "opening ourselves freely to the future" and argues that "[a] blind acceptance of the New Testament mythology would be arbitrary, and to press for its acceptance as an article of faith would be to reduce faith to works" (1960, 17; 1961, 3–4). The same heritage is also visible in Paul Tillich's (1999, 101) notion of faith as "a state of being grasped by an ultimate concern."

Meillassoux's notion of a pluralistic "fideism of any *belief* [*croyance*] whatsoever" thus becomes doubly problematic. On the one hand, we see that

[13] As an example of contemporary fideism, the Pope mentions (Protestant) "Biblicism" and also makes a rather indeterminate reference to the "latent fideism" apparent in "the scant consideration accorded to speculative theology, and in disdain for the classical philosophy from which the terms of both the understanding of faith and the actual formulation of dogma have been drawn."

[14] Bultmann (1960, 33; 1961, 24) also notes that "Heidegger's existential analysis of Dasein would seem to be no more than a profane, philosophical exposition of the New Testament view of human existence." (Translation modified.)

fideism per se is inherently linked to Christianity and to the Protestant tradition (or the Catholic reaction to it), in particular, and that the Christian notion of faith cannot be transposed as such onto Islamic or Jewish, let alone nonmonotheistic, contexts. Nonetheless, Meillassoux seems to presuppose that "faith" is a universal and defining feature of "religiosity" as such. On the other hand, while Meillassoux seems to think that "faith" invariably involves "beliefs," post-Kierkegaardian existential-fideistic approaches, such as those of Bultmann and Tillich, have precisely tended to distinguish sharply between *faith* as an existential attitude and *beliefs* as epistemic attitudes with propositional content.

It should be noted that while Heidegger was indisputably influenced by Lutheran fideism in the early part of his career and consistently argued that faith, properly understood, has no need of philosophy or of rational articulation, these remarks are limited to the specific context of Christian faith; they do not apply to a "religiosity as such." In his 1927 lecture on "Phenomenology and Theology," he argues: "[F]aith [*Glaube*] does not need philosophy.... Accordingly there is no such thing as a Christian philosophy; that is simply an oxymoron [*hölzernes Eisen*]" (Heidegger 1996, 61, 66; 1998c, 50, 53; translation modified). In a 1953 discussion at the Evangelical Academy at Hofgeismar, he notes: "Within thinking nothing can be achieved which would be a preparation for, or have a determining influence on, that which occurs in faith and in grace. Were I addressed by faith in such a way, I would close up my shop" (Heidegger and Noack 1954, 33; Heidegger 1976, 64; translation modified). A notion of a fideism of any religious belief whatsoever would have remained void for Heidegger, who questioned the validity of the very concept of "religion," rooted in the Roman state cult, as a generic term for all ways of relating to the dimensions of the divine or the holy. The ancient Greeks, Heidegger (1994, 13–14) maintains, had divinities but no "religion." Moreover, his mention of a theology without the word *being*, cited by Meillassoux as an instance of Heideggerian fideism, as well as the notions of the divine developed in his later work, are sharply distinguished from metaphysical as well as Christian theological notions and are not framed in terms of faith. The enigmatic figure of the "ultimate god" (*der letzte Gott*) outlined in Heidegger's *Contributions to Philosophy* (*Beiträge zur Philosophie*, 1936–38) is emphatically said to be "entirely other than the ones that have been and especially other than the Christian one" (Heidegger 1989, 403; 2012, 319; translation modified), and in his subsequent monograph *Mindfulness* (*Besinnung*, 1938–39), Heidegger explicitly detaches his figures of divinity and divinities from all senses of "religion" and "devoutness" (*Gläubigkeit*; Heidegger 1997a, 243, 249; 2006, 214–15, 220).

3.2. The absolute

The second problematic aspect in Meillassoux's account of fideism is related to his suggestion that strong correlationism's deabsolutization of rational thought and its abandonment of metaphysical absolutes would nonetheless allow the retention or reintroduction of an "absolute" in a nonrational religious context. This claim is even more perplexing. On a very general level, one can ask to what extent, and in what sense, a strong correlationist approach to faith could concede the legitimacy of *any* notion of an "absolute."

It is true that Kierkegaard, in *Fear and Trembling* (1843), defines *faith* as the pure paradox in which the singular individual stands in an "absolute relation to the absolute" (God), unmediated by any universal form. This relation assumes "absurd," that is, intersubjectively inaccessible and ethically nonuniversalizable manifestations, such as God's terrible command to Abraham to slay his son Isaac (Kierkegaard 1985, 84–85). This clearly comes very close to what Meillassoux seems to mean by a purely religious relationship to the absolute. Here, the "absoluteness" of God no longer consists in ontological perfection or rational necessity, but simply in the power of faith as the "absolute relation" to elevate the singular individual beyond discursive rationality and ethical concerns. However, the fact that the "absolute" is thus manifested only in faith as a singular *relation* already in a sense dissolves the classical, literal concept of absoluteness, analyzed by Heidegger as a pure self-identity completely "absolved" from all relations to anything other than itself.[15]

It is important to see that the Heideggerian overcoming of the absolute entails not only a renunciation of onto-theological absolutes such as the Aristotelian God of metaphysics or absolute subjectivity, but also a formulation of a radically nonabsolute notion of divinity. In his 1934–35 Hölderlin lectures, reading the eighth stanza of Hölderlin's hymn "The Rhine" which introduces a notion of divinities that "need" or "require" mortals since they are unable "feel" by themselves, in other words, since they are radically *non*-self-sufficient and *non*absolute, Heidegger exalts the poetic formulation of such a notion as a true upheaval in the Western tradition of thinking the relationship between the

[15] Cf. Heidegger 2002c, 102; 2003b, 136: "The absoluteness of the absolute is characterized by the unity of absolvence [*Absolvenz*] (disengagement from relation), absolving (completeness of disengagement), and absolution (acquittal on the basis of that completeness)." (Translation modified.)

divine and the human.[16] Accordingly, the notion of gods or "divinities" (*die Göttlichen*) employed by the later Heidegger in *Contributions* and in his figure of the fourfold (*Geviert*) is utterly relational. The Heideggerian divinities are dependent on the relational dimension of the "between" (*Zwischen*), suspended between two poles—the historical, communal and linguistic pole of the humans or mortals, and the superhuman pole of divinities as the purposes, aims or supreme possibilities of a specific human community—and have no real subsistence apart from this relation.[17] These divinities are not objects of religious faith. Indeed, we must note that "faith" (*Glaube*) and "piety" (*Frömmigkeit*) are specifically associated by the later Heidegger with the "questioning" attitude, that is, with the openness of thinking to the nonobjectifiable and nonepistemic dimension of truth (*Wahrheit*) in Heidegger's idiosyncratic sense of the contextual and referential structure that first grants meaningful presence to beings, and thus, allows truth in the sense of the "unconcealment" (*alētheia, Unverborgenheit*) or the intelligible accessibility of meaningful things.[18] In *Contributions*, Heidegger (1989, 368–70; 2012, 291–92) collapses the traditional opposition between knowing (*Wissen*) and believing or having faith (*Glauben*) by making them both expressions for exposing oneself to truth in the sense of

16 In the eighth stanza of "The Rhine" ("Der Rhein"), Hölderlin (1951, 145; 2002, 223) declares: "But the gods have enough / Immortality of their own, and if there be / One thing the celestials need [*bedürfen*] / It is heroes and men / And mortals generally. For since / The serenest beings [*Seligsten*] feel nothing at all, / There must come, if to speak / Thus is permitted, another who feels / On their behalf, him / They use and need [*brauchen*]." ("Es haben aber an eigner / Unsterblichkeit die Götter genug und bedürfen / Die Himmlischen eines Dings, / So sinds Heroën und Menschen / Und Sterbliche sonst. Denn weil / Die Seeligsten nichts fühlen von selbst, / Muß wohl, wenn solches zu sagen / Erlaubt ist, in der Götter Nahmen / Theilnehmend fühlen ein Andrer, / Den brauchen sie.") Heidegger (1980, 269; 2014, 244) comments: "With the eighth stanza the poet's thinking scales one of the most towering and solitary peaks of Western thinking, and that is to say, at the same time: of beyng [*Seyns*]. . . . On the peak that is now attained, Hölderlin dwells in proximity to the thinkers of the inception [*Anfang*] of our Western history, not because Hölderlin is dependent on them, but because he is an inceptor [*Anfänger*] in an inceptual manner." (Translation modified.)

17 In *Contributions to Philosophy*, Heidegger (1989, 470–71; 2012, 370–71) wards off the "mistaken view" that the situatedness of the event (*Ereignis*) in the intermediate space "between" the gods and the human being would imply that the event is a mere relation between pre-established relata. Rather, gods and human beings are poles or dimensions of the event itself; in their inextricable reciprocity, gods and humans are dependent on the intermediate space of meaning suspended between the two.

18 Heidegger (1977, 35; 2000a, 40) famously concludes his 1953 lecture on "The Question Concerning Technology" by characterizing questioning (*Fragen*) as the "piety" (*Frömmigkeit*) of thinking. On the Heideggerian sense of the "truth of being" (*Wahrheit des Seins*) as the contextual background-foreground structure of meaningfulness, as the "clearing harboring" (*lichtendes Bergen*) that refers back to the ecstatic temporal contextuality thematized in *Being and Time* as the "sense" (*Sinn*) of being, see the note appended to the end of the 1930 lecture "On the Essence of Truth" (Heidegger 1996, 201–2; 1998c, 153–54).

the contextualization of meaning. Rather than implying *certainty*, both knowing and having faith here indicate a mode of *questioning* (*Fragen*), that is, of active openness to nonobjectifiable meaning-dimensions. Those who question in this way are those who "have faith" (*die Glaubenden*) in the proper sense as the ones "who in a radical way take seriously *truth* itself [in the Heideggerian sense], not only what is true" (Heidegger 1989, 369; 2012, 292).

Rather than any extrarational sense of "absolute" that religious faith could relate to, the Heideggerian postmetaphysical notion of divinity thus designates a purely relational and nonabsolute dimension of contextual meaningfulness. Rather than a religious relationship to a nondiscursive absolute, postmetaphysical and postreligious "faith" indicates, in the later Heidegger, an openness to the inherent contextuality and singularity of all meaning. At least in the context of Heideggerian "strong correlationism," Meillassoux's notion of an intellectual legitimation of "religious absolutes" thus seems unwarranted.

3.3. Fanaticism

The third—and perhaps the most—problematic feature of Meillassoux's account is his notion of a contemporary *fanaticism* against which skeptical fideism is not only defenseless, but which can even be seen as an *effect* of the culmination of Western critical reason in strong correlationism and of philosophy's subsequent inability to combat "blind faith." "Contemporary fanaticism" is seemingly not perceived by Meillassoux as a mere risk or possibility but as an existing reality; however, what precise phenomenon he has in mind remains rather puzzling. Who are the contemporary fanatics exactly? It is even more unclear what kind of intellectual support or shelter any presumably fundamentalist type of religious fanaticism could plausibly gain from existential and phenomenological approaches such as those of Bultmann or Marion. Alberto Toscano (2010) has disclosed the highly politicized nature of the concept of "fanaticism," arguing that ever since Luther's attack against the peasant revolts triggered by the Reformation, the term has been predominantly applied to socially marginalized groups opposing elites.[19] Meillassoux (2006a, 65; 2008a, 47) emphasizes that his notion of fanaticism is that of the Enlightenment. In his 1756 contribution to Diderot's great encyclopedia, Alexandre Deleyre (1756, 393; 1967, 104) describes

[19] For Toscano's critical notes on Meillassoux's account of fanaticism, see Toscano 2011.

fanaticism as "superstition put into practice," and Voltaire (1764, 190–93; 2011, 137–38) echoes this definition in his philosophical dictionary: *fanaticism* is obscurantism and blind faith for the sake of faith combined with the will to violently enact one's conviction. However, even the Enlightenment thinkers seem to be equally hard put to come up with unequivocal contemporary examples of fanaticism. They are apparently thinking first and foremost of the violent religious conflicts of the sixteenth and seventeenth centuries; a main point of reference for them was the 1572 St. Bartholomew's Day massacre of French Protestants (Voltaire 1764, 191; 2011, 137).

It should also be noted that the Meillassouxian notion of fideistic fanaticism seems to be opposed to Kant's (1996, 208–9 [A 84–86; AA 150–54]; 2003a, 114–17; cf. Toscano 2011, 86; Zuckert 2010) general definition, in *Critique of Practical Reason*, of fanaticism or "enthusiasm" (*Schwärmerei*) as precisely a *dogmatic* tendency to transcend the limits of reason, for example, by claiming some form of direct cognitive or emotional access to the supersensible divinity—a tendency that can have particularly pathological consequences in the form of *moral* fanaticism, involving claims that one's moral acts are motivated not by rational duty, but by a "holy will" without immoral inclinations and with immediate affective access to a divine or sublime source of morality. Understood as an heir of Kant's critical philosophy, Heideggerian strong correlationism can hardly be accused of being defenseless against *this* form of dogmatic fanaticism. Meillassoux's claim concerning contemporary fanaticism thus remains conspicuously vague and indeterminate.

4. Conclusion: Meillassoux's problematic modernity

Taking these problematic aspects of Meillassoux's notion of fideism into consideration, we may thus conclude that while his argument regarding the internal contradictions of strong correlationism may remain compelling if one accepts its presuppositions, his understanding of strong correlationism as the herald of a "religious end of metaphysics" remains, in its present form, unconvincing. While it is clear that strong correlationism, at least its Heideggerian version, allows the formulation of post-onto-theological notions of divinity and faith that are not susceptible to the same type of rational critique as the speculative and natural theologies criticized by Kant, the "theological turn" in post-Heideggerian thought has mostly been limited to certain reinterpretations of the Christian tradition and has not resulted in a "fideism of any religious belief whatsoever," particularly not in the rehabilitation of a religious "absolute" in any traditional sense of this term. Moreover, it is extremely difficult to see what kind of "fanaticism" could be justified in terms of, say, Marion's account of saturated phenomena or of Vattimo's notion of "weak faith."

In its present form, Meillassoux's critique of fideism employs a very traditional Enlightenment vocabulary and rhetoric against modes of thinking that are fundamentally different from those battled by the historical Enlightenment, for which "fanaticism" was one of the names for essentially *pre*modern modes of thought. The contemporary fideism of "any religious belief whatsoever" diagnosed by Meillassoux is not a pre- or antimodern orientation, nor is it even a properly "postmodern" phenomenon. Meillassoux himself emphasizes that it is first and foremost a late modern guise assumed by the Kantian project of modernity itself.

> Contrary to the familiar view according to which Occidental modernity consists in a vast enterprise of the secularization of thought, we consider the most striking feature of modernity to be the following: *the modern man is he who has been religionized* [*enreligé*] *precisely to the extent that he has been de-Christianized.* The modern man is he who, even as he stripped Christianity of the ideological (metaphysical) pretension that its cult was superior to all others, has delivered himself body and soul to the idea that all cults are equally legitimate in matters of veracity.
>
> Meillassoux 2006a, 65–66; 2008a, 47–48; translation modified

Meillassoux's core aim is thus not really a recovery of a modernity "lost" by postmodernism, but rather the rational *development* of modern thought toward what he sees as its logical conclusion: The realization that the downfall of metaphysical absolutes is not consummated in a philosophy of facticity and finitude, but in the discovery of a new postmetaphysical absolute, namely, contingency. This insight is, for Meillassoux, a key step on modernity's way to its true calling, speculative materialism. While we have not attempted to deny the basic legitimacy or potential intellectual fruitfulness of such an innovative project, we have cast some doubts on the way it is framed through allegations concerning the complex relationship between strong correlationism and "religiosity." However, as we have seen, Meillassoux's thinking remains "philosophy in the making." We have reason to hope that his future work will complement his account of fideism in important ways and disclose, in detail, the definitive role of his approach to faith and religion in his overall project.

References

Backman, Jussi. 2014a. "From the Ultimate God to the Virtual God: Post-Ontotheological Perspectives on the Divine in Heidegger, Badiou and Meillassoux." *META: Research in Hermeneutics, Phenomenology, and Practical Philosophy*, Special Issue: *New Realism and Phenomenology*, edited by Diego D'Angelo and Nikola Mirković, 113–42. Accessed January 11, 2016. http://www.metajournal.org/download.php?id=189&type=articles.

Backman, Jussi. 2014b. "Transcendental Idealism and Strong Correlationism: Meillassoux and the End of Heideggerian Finitude." In *Phenomenology and the Transcendental*, edited by Sara Heinämaa, Mirja Hartimo and Timo Miettinen, 276–94. New York: Routledge.

Badiou, Alain. 2006. Preface to *Après la finitude: essai sur la nécessité de la contingence*, by Quentin Meillassoux, 9–11. Paris: Seuil.

Badiou, Alain. 2008. Preface to *After Finitude: An Essay on the Necessity of Contingency*, by Quentin Meillassoux, vi–viii. Translated by Ray Brassier. London: Continuum.

Braver, Lee. 2012. *Groundless Grounds: A Study of Wittgenstein and Heidegger*. Cambridge, MA: MIT Press.

Bultmann, Rudolf. 1960. "Neues Testament und Mythologie: Das Problem der Entmythologisierung der neutestamentlichen Verkündigung." In *Kerygma und Mythos*, vol. 1, 4th ed., edited by Hans-Werner Bartsch, 15–48. Hamburg: Reich.

Bultmann, Rudolf. 1961. "New Testament and Mythology: The Mythological Element in the Message of the New Testament and the Problem of its Re-interpretation." In *Kerygma and Myth: A Theological Debate*, edited by Hans Werner Bartsch, translated by Reginald H. Fuller, 1–44. New York: Harper & Row.

Buren, John van. 1994a. "Martin Heidegger, Martin Luther." In *Reading Heidegger from the Start: Essays in His Earliest Thought*, edited by Theodore Kisiel and John van Buren, 159–74. Albany, NY: SUNY Press.

Buren, John van. 1994b. *The Young Heidegger: Rumor of the Hidden King*. Bloomington: Indiana University Press.

Carroll, Thomas. 2008. "The Traditions of Fideism." *Religious Studies* 44 (1): 1–22.

Deleyre, Alexandre. 1756. "Fanatisme." In *Encyclopédie ou Dictionnaire raisonné des sciences, des arts et des métiers*, vol. 6, edited by Denis Diderot and Jean le Rond d'Alembert, 393–401. Paris: Briasson, David, Le Breton & Durand.

Deleyre, Alexandre. 1967. "Fanaticism." In *Denis Diderot's The Encyclopedia: Selections*, translated and edited by Stephen J. Gendzier, 104–7. New York: Harper & Row.

Derrida, Jacques. 1996. "Foi et savoir: Les deux sources de la 'religion' aux limites de la simple raison." In *La religion: Séminaire de Capri*, edited by Jacques Derrida and Gianni Vattimo, 9–86. Paris: Seuil.

Derrida, Jacques. 1998. "Faith and Knowledge: The Two Sources of 'Religion' within the Limits of Mere Reason." Translated by Samuel Weber. In *Religion*, edited by Jacques Derrida and Gianni Vattimo, 1–78. Stanford, CA: Stanford University Press.

Harman, Graham. 2011. *Quentin Meillassoux: Philosophy in the Making*. Edinburgh: Edinburgh University Press.

Hegel, Georg Wilhelm Friedrich. 1985. *Gesammelte Werke*, vol. 21: *Wissenschaft der Logik: Die objektive Logik*, vol. 1.1: *Die Lehre vom Sein (1832)*. Edited by Friedrich Hogemann and Walter Jaeschke. Hamburg: Meiner.

Hegel, Georg Wilhelm Friedrich. 2010. *The Science of Logic*. Translated by George di Giovanni. Cambridge: Cambridge University Press.

Heidegger, Martin. 1968. *What Is Called Thinking?* Translated by Fred D. Wieck and J. Glenn Gray. New York: Harper & Row.

Heidegger, Martin. 1976. *The Piety of Thinking*. Edited and translated by James G. Hart and John C. Maraldo. Bloomington: Indiana University Press.

Heidegger, Martin. 1977. *The Question Concerning Technology and Other Essays*. Translated by William Lovitt. New York: Harper & Row.

Heidegger, Martin. 1979. *Gesamtausgabe*, vol. 20: *Prolegomena zur Geschichte des Zeitbegriffs*. Edited by Petra Jaeger. Frankfurt am Main: Klostermann.

Heidegger, Martin. 1980. *Gesamtausgabe*, vol. 39: *Hölderlins Hymnen "Germanien" und "Der Rhein."* Edited by Susanne Ziegler. Frankfurt am Main: Klostermann.

Heidegger, Martin. 1985. *History of the Concept of Time: Prolegomena*. Translated by Theodore Kisiel. Bloomington: Indiana University Press.

Heidegger, Martin. 1989. *Gesamtausgabe*, vol. 65: *Beiträge zur Philosophie (Vom Ereignis)*. Edited by Friedrich-Wilhelm von Herrmann. Frankfurt am Main: Klostermann.

Heidegger, Martin. 1991a. *Nietzsche*, vol. 1: *The Will to Power as Art*. Translated by David Farrell Krell. San Francisco: HarperSanFrancisco.

Heidegger, Martin. 1991b. *Nietzsche*, vol. 2: *The Eternal Recurrence of the Same*. Translated by David Farrell Krell. San Francisco: HarperSanFrancisco.

Heidegger, Martin. 1991c. *Nietzsche*, vol. 3: *The Will to Power as Knowledge and as Metaphysics*. Translated by Joan Stambaugh, David Farrell Krell and Frank A. Capuzzi. San Francisco: HarperSanFrancisco.

Heidegger, Martin. 1991d. *Nietzsche*, vol. 4: *Nihilism*. Translated by Frank A. Capuzzi, edited by David F. Krell. San Francisco: HarperSanFrancisco.

Heidegger, Martin. 1994. *Gesamtausgabe*, vol. 55: *Heraklit*. 3rd ed. Edited by Manfred S. Frings. Frankfurt am Main: Klostermann.

Heidegger, Martin. 1996. *Wegmarken*. 3rd ed. Edited by Friedrich-Wilhelm von Herrmann. Frankfurt am Main: Klostermann.

Heidegger, Martin. 1997a. *Gesamtausgabe*, vol. 66: *Besinnung*. Edited by Friedrich-Wilhelm von Herrmann. Frankfurt am Main: Klostermann.

Heidegger, Martin. 1997b. *Was heisst Denken?* 5th ed. Tübingen: Niemeyer.

Heidegger, Martin. 1998a. *Nietzsche*, vol. 1. 6th ed. Stuttgart: Neske.
Heidegger, Martin. 1998b. *Nietzsche*, vol. 2. 6th ed. Stuttgart: Neske.
Heidegger, Martin. 1998c. *Pathmarks*. Edited by William McNeill. Cambridge: Cambridge University Press.
Heidegger, Martin. 2000a. *Vorträge und Aufsätze*. 9th ed. Stuttgart: Neske.
Heidegger, Martin. 2000b. *Zur Sache des Denkens*. 4th ed. Tübingen: Niemeyer.
Heidegger, Martin. 2001. *Sein und Zeit*. 18th ed. Tübingen: Niemeyer.
Heidegger, Martin. 2002a. *Identität und Differenz*. 12th ed. Stuttgart: Klett-Cotta.
Heidegger, Martin. 2002b. *Identity and Difference*. Translated by Joan Stambaugh. Chicago: University of Chicago Press.
Heidegger, Martin. 2002c. *Off the Beaten Track*. Edited and translated by Julian Young and Kenneth Haynes. Cambridge: Cambridge University Press.
Heidegger, Martin. 2002d. *On Time and Being*. Translated by Joan Stambaugh. Chicago: University of Chicago Press.
Heidegger, Martin. 2002e. "The Reply to the Third Question at the Seminar in Zurich, 1951." Translated by Laurence Paul Hemming. In *Heidegger's Atheism: The Refusal of a Theological Voice* by Laurence Paul Hemming, 291–92. Notre Dame, IN: University of Notre Dame Press.
Heidegger, Martin. 2003a. *The End of Philosophy*. Translated by Joan Stambaugh. Chicago: University of Chicago Press.
Heidegger, Martin. 2003b. *Holzwege*. 8th ed. Frankfurt am Main: Klostermann.
Heidegger, Martin. 2005. *Gesamtausgabe*, vol. 15: *Seminare*. 2nd ed. Edited by Curt Ochwadt. Frankfurt am Main: Klostermann.
Heidegger, Martin. 2006. *Mindfulness*. Translated by Parvis Emad and Thomas Kalary. London: Continuum.
Heidegger, Martin. 2010. *Being and Time*. Translated by Joan Stambaugh, revised by Dennis Schmidt. Albany, NY: SUNY Press.
Heidegger, Martin. 2012. *Contributions to Philosophy (Of the Event)*. Translated by Richard Rojcewicz and Daniela Vallega-Neu. Bloomington: Indiana University Press.
Heidegger, Martin. 2014. *Hölderlin's Hymns "Germania" and "The Rhine."* Translated by William McNeill and Julia Ireland. Bloomington: Indiana University Press.
Heidegger, Martin, and Hermann Noack. 1954. "Gespräch mit Martin Heidegger." *Anstösse: Berichte aus der Arbeit der Evangelischen Akademie Hofgeismar* 1: 30–37.
Hölderlin, Friedrich. 1951. *Sämtliche Werke*, vol. 2.1: *Gedichte nach 1800, 1. Hälfte: Text*. Edited by Friedrich Beissner. Stuttgart: Kohlhammer.
Hölderlin, Friedrich. 2002. *Hyperion and Selected Poems*. Edited by Eric L. Santner. New York: Continuum.
Janicaud, Dominique. 1991. *Le tournant théologique de la phénoménologie française*. Combas: Éditions de l'Éclat.
Janicaud, Dominique. 2000. "The Theological Turn of French Phenomenology." Translated by Bernard G. Prusak. In *Phenomenology and the "Theological Turn": The*

French Debate, by Dominique Janicaud et al., 1–103. New York: Fordham University Press.
John Paul II. 1998. "Encyclical Letter *Fides et Ratio* of the Supreme Pontiff John Paul II to the Bishops of the Catholic Church on the Relationship between Faith and Reason." Accessed January 11, 2016. http://w2.vatican.va/content/john-paul-ii/en/encyclicals/documents/hf_jp-ii_enc_14091998_fides-et-ratio.html.
John Paul II. 1999. "Acta Ioannis Pauli Pp. II litterae encyclicae cunctis catholicae Ecclesiae episcopis de necessitudinis natura inter fidem et rationem." *Acta apostolicae sedis* 91: 5–88.
Kant, Immanuel. 1996. *Practical Philosophy*. Translated and edited by Mary J. Gregor. Cambridge: Cambridge University Press.
Kant, Immanuel. 1998a. *Kritik der reinen Vernunft*. Edited by Jens Timmermann. Hamburg: Meiner.
Kant, Immanuel. 1998b. *Critique of Pure Reason*. Translated and edited by Paul Guyer and Allen Wood. Cambridge: Cambridge University Press.
Kant, Immanuel. 1998c. *Religion within the Boundaries of Mere Reason and Other Writings*. Translated and edited by Allen Wood and George di Giovanni. Cambridge: Cambridge University Press.
Kant, Immanuel. 2003a. *Kritik der praktischen Vernunft*. Edited by Horst D. Brandt and Heiner F. Klemme. Hamburg: Meiner.
Kant, Immanuel. 2003b. *Religion innerhalb der Grenzen der blossen Vernunft*. Edited by Bettina Stangneth. Hamburg: Meiner.
Kierkegaard, Søren. 1985. *Fear and Trembling: Dialectical Lyric by Johannes de silentio*. Translated by Alastair Hannay. London: Penguin Books.
Luther, Martin. 1883. *D. Martin Luthers Werke: Kritische Gesamtausgabe*, vol. 1. Weimar: Böhlau.
Luther, Martin. 1938. *D. Martin Luthers Werke: Kritische Gesamtausgabe*, vol. 56: *Die Vorlesung über den Römerbrief*. Weimar: Böhlau.
Luther, Martin. 2006. *Lectures on Romans*. Translated by Wilhelm Pauck. Louisville, KY: Westminster John Knox Press.
Luther, Martin. 2012. *Martin Luther's Basic Theological Writings*. Edited by Timothy F. Lull and William R. Russell. 3rd ed. Minneapolis, MN: Fortress Press.
Marion, Jean-Luc. 1991a. *Dieu sans l'être*. Paris: Presses Universitaires de France.
Marion, Jean-Luc. 1991b. *God Without Being*. Translated by Thomas A. Carlson. Chicago: University of Chicago Press.
Meillassoux, Quentin. 1997. "L'inexistence divine." Doctoral dissertation. Université de Paris I.
Meillassoux, Quentin. 2006a. *Après la finitude: Essai sur la nécessité de la contingence*. Paris: Seuil.
Meillassoux, Quentin. 2006b. "Deuil à venir, dieu à venir." *Critique* 62 (704–5): 105–15.

Meillassoux, Quentin. 2008a. *After Finitude: An Essay on the Necessity of Contingency.* London: Continuum.

Meillassoux, Quentin. 2008b. "Spectral Dilemma." In *Collapse*, vol. 4: *Concept Horror*, edited by Robin McKay, 261–75. Falmouth: Urbanomic.

Nielsen, Kai. 1967. "Wittgensteinian Fideism." *Philosophy* 42 (161): 191–209.

Nielsen, Kai, and D. Z. Phillips. 2005. *Wittgensteinian Fideism?* London: SCM Press.

Rorty, Richard, Gianni Vattimo and Santiago Zabala. 2005. "What Is Religion's Future After Metaphysics?" In *The Future of Religion* by Richard Rorty and Gianni Vattimo, edited by Santiago Zabala, 55–82. New York: Columbia University Press.

Sheehan, Thomas. 1979. "Heidegger's 'Introduction to the Phenomenology of Religion,' 1920–21." *The Personalist* 60 (3): 312–24.

Tillich, Paul. 1999. *The Essential Tillich: An Anthology of the Writings of Paul Tillich.* Edited by F. Forrester Church. Chicago: University of Chicago Press.

Toscano, Alberto. 2010. *Fanaticism: On the Uses of an Idea.* London: Verso.

Toscano, Alberto. 2011. "Against Speculation, or, A Critique of the Critique of Critique: A Remark on Quentin Meillassoux's *After Finitude* (After Colletti)." In *The Speculative Turn: Continental Materialism and Realism*, edited by Levi Bryant, Nick Srnicek and Graham Harman, 84–91. Melbourne: re.press.

Vainio, Olli-Pekka. 2010. *Beyond Fideism: Negotiable Religious Identities.* Farnham: Ashgate.

Vattimo, Gianni. 1999. *Belief.* Translated by Luca D'Isanto and David Webb. Stanford, CA: Stanford University Press.

Voltaire, François-Marie. 1764. *Dictionnaire philosophique portatif.* Geneva: Grasset.

Voltaire, François-Marie. 2011. *A Pocket Philosophical Dictionary.* Translated by John Fletcher. Oxford: Oxford University Press.

Wittgenstein, Ludwig. 1960. *Tractatus Logico-Philosophicus.* Translated by Charles Kay Ogden. London: Routledge & Kegan Paul.

Zuckert, Rachel. 2010. "Kant's Account of Practical Fanaticism." In *Kant's Moral Metaphysics: God, Freedom, and Immortality*, edited by Benjamin J. Bruxvoort Lipscomb and James Krueger, 291–318. Berlin: de Gruyter.

Part Two

Faith and Reason

4

"How we, too, are still pious":

The Status of Truth and the Irreducibility of Faith in the Work of Nietzsche

Carlotta Santini

As is well known, the critical process inaugurated by Nietzsche, beginning with *Human, all too Human* (1878), intended to call into question the dogmatic principles and maxims of modern Western culture, particularly in relation to the concept of truth, on which faith, morality, science and philosophy itself are based. Truth, in an absolute sense, is always understood in the *vulgata* of Nietzsche studies as a fictive word: that is, *truth* in quotation marks, as an empty concept, or as many truths in a relative sense. Truth would therefore seem to have no place in the work of Nietzsche. And yet, on closer inspection, it appears that there is no more widespread, assiduous and vexing a presence than that of truth in the philosopher's oeuvre; indeed, it cannot easily be expunged from its philosophical path and remains a frequently examined theme throughout. This constant insistence on truth, which does not exist, but without which not even the criticism of truth itself could be justified, may be considered in two ways: either as an irreducible element in the radical criticism of Nietzsche, and thus, as a constitutive lack in his philosophy, or—and that's the way I prefer—as the trace of a speculative unresolved core of his thought, which proves itself to be fraught with new developments over the years.

In this article, I discuss the problematical elements of Nietzsche's deconstruction of the concept of truth, highlighting unresolved moments within his argument. In order to do so, I focus on a central line of research within the copious edited works and fragments of the *Posthumous Fragments* (*Nachlass*), which constitutes the multifaceted analysis of truth in Nietzsche's work. This leading thread arises out of a particular formula that, in varying incarnations, appears in Nietzsche's earliest philological writings and continues into his later works: the concept of an instinct toward the truth, *Trieb der Wahrheit*. This formula emerged almost by accident within a nonphilosophical context, but it became hugely prominent throughout Nietzsche's work and would not suffer, unlike many of his more famous formulas, by being limited to a particular phase in his thinking. It is discernible in every period and in every genre, from his philological notes to the preparatory notes through to the philosophical works themselves. The concept of an instinct toward the truth owes its success to its periphrastic nature, meaning that it is able to replace the concept of truth without incurring, contrary to the latter, the pitfalls of the dogmatic use of the term. With this formula, Nietzsche can afford not to hypostatize the concept of truth and to make it a functional, operative concept, one with which he, the critical dismantler of truth, is also able to work. The history of this concept in Nietzsche's work can be traced throughout varying stages. These stages are sometimes seemingly contradictory and bear witness to his complex engagement with the concept of truth and its rightful place within the horizon of human experience.

1. *Trieb der Wahrheit*: Ethical and aesthetic aspects of the desire for knowledge

The very first time that Nietzsche broached the question of the instinct of truth was long before the so-called critical period. In 1871, as Professor of Greek Language and Literature in Basel, he gave a course on the *Encyclopedia of Classical Philology* (Nietzsche 1993, 339–437). This particular type of lesson was quite common among philologists of the time. In fact, in their academic classes, many of them began to discuss their own discipline, analyzing its tools, principles, pedagogical aspects and scientific aspirations.[1] The text by Nietzsche differs from that of his predecessors and contemporaries in the sense that it was devoted to an analysis of the figure of the philologist, including the instincts that dominate his nature, the reasons and principles governing his technical behavior, and

[1] The Philological Encyclopaedias (*Enzyklopädien*) are a German tradition of great scientific importance for the development of the classical philological discipline. After the pioneering work of Friedrich August Wolf (1807, 1831a, 1831b), one of the most famous and most accomplished studies is the lessons of August Boeckh (1877), though there are many others, conceived as a rule in the form of university courses by Otto Jahn, Gottfried Bernhardy (1832) and Friedrich Ritschl, Nietzsche's Professor in Bonn and Leipzig; unfortunately, these latter works have not survived in their entirety. The famous *Hermeneutik und Kritik* (1838) by Friedrich Schleiermacher also belongs to these ranks.

finally, his role as a teacher. Nietzsche acknowledges therefore that the instinct toward truth is one of the noblest qualities pertaining to the figure of the philologist, locating it within a more general instinct toward knowledge.[2] However, as will become clear, this instinct toward the truth does not end with the thirst for knowledge, and indeed, may even contradict it.

In Chapter 8 of his *Encyclopedia*, in which he discusses the *Propaedeutic to Hermeneutic and Critic*, Nietzsche judges the work of the philologist not so much from the point of view of science or epistemology, but according to an ethical standpoint. In Nietzsche's opinion, there is something ethical about the work of the philologist, especially in his instinct toward truth, as he enjoys critiquing and solving the linguistic riddles of the text (Nietzsche 1993, 374). In this passage of the *Encyclopedia*, we find the first textual occurrence of the instinct toward the truth (*Trieb der Wahrheit*). It was depicted as being in a sense both ethical and disinterested; therefore, we are not confronted with a sterile self-satisfaction achieved through the accumulation of knowledge, although the instinct toward truth is proper to the philologist as a scientist. At first glance, it seems philological science has nothing to do with pleasure or utility, but it is concerned with the desire for truth in its strictest and most abstract sense. It aspires indeed to the highest elevation of the ideal, the truth. On closer inspection, however, what this ethical component involves, more than the demands of science, is an aesthetic aspect: namely, that the philologist is interested in what is defined as moral and at the same time aesthetic and ideal, the truth.

Let us first consider briefly this aesthetic aspect of truth. The formula selected by Nietzsche to replace the concept of truth, *Trieb der Wahrheit*, takes us back to the world of the senses, to natural urges and instincts. All instincts, according to Nietzsche, are connected to pleasure and pain; in other words, an instinct toward a pure truth, completely empty of consequences and affects, cannot exist. There is, in fact, no instinct that does not necessarily anticipate desire in its satisfaction (Nietzsche 1980d, 632, 29[16]).[3] The instinct toward truth therefore is not a disinterested phenomenon, but has a physical, physiological quality. Its realization is linked to pleasure, namely, to that particular pleasure that is apparently the most spiritual and elevated, that is, the aesthetical one; for the

2 This is one of the three positions attributed to the professionals of antiquity; the others involve a love for antiquity and a pedagogical inclination. See Santini 2015.

3 Notations such as "29[16]" at the end of the reference indicate the fragment numbers.

truth, as well as being good, is also beautiful. We are faced almost with a real sense of the truth, which makes it part of the sensitive experiences of man.

As for the ethical nature of truth—which is what interests us most here—the philologist's role is characterized by both a continuous search for the truth and a continuous desire for honesty. The instinct toward truth manifests itself at every level of the philologist's work, most particularly in his most important task: reading well. "We must learn again how to read" (Nietzsche 1993, 373): This *motto* is at the center of Nietzsche's reflection on classical antiquity and the work of the philologist. It becomes a core element of his thought during his philosophical period, especially as a central theme in the *New Prefaces* to his writings in the years 1886–87. What does to "Learn *again* how to read" mean, then? You learn to read for the first time as a child, when you learn about the significance behind the symbols that at first seem to be meaningless. And then you learn to combine them, to connect them to sounds and to their meanings. We have all learned to read the content of books in this way. But at the same time, we have also learned to have confidence in what we read. The need to relearn how to read, or if you will, the need to learn how to read well, better than the normal mode of reading, arises once you lose confidence in the truth of what is written. A child does not wonder if what he or she reads is true or false: he or she learned to read and that was all. Discovering that what is written is not necessarily true symbolizes, in a sense, a loss of innocence: There exists for the first time the possibility of an underlying falsehood. The loss of innocence once associated with the simple task of reading and the subsequent entrance into the ethical life of reading well. This is the mission of the philologist, who is engaged in the reconstruction of ancient texts that have been corrupted by the ravages of time or the will of the individual forger. At the heart of this approach lies what Nietzsche calls the instinct toward the truth, which is characterized not as a cognitive instinct, but as an ethical one.

2. "Pathos toward the truth" as "living a lie"

As I have already mentioned, the instinct toward the truth (*Trieb der Wahrheit*) is a particularly effective formula, which in its various forms has played a significant role in Nietzsche's work. Incidentally, this expression, in its particular formulation, is a *hapax legomenon* in Nietzsche's corpus, appearing only once, as far as we can see, in these pages of the *Encyclopedia*. This is a minor *caveat* however because the formula recurs frequently in slightly differing variants (*Trieb zur Wahrheit, Wahrheitstrieb*). However, the first time the formula appears outside of a specifically philological context, it has already been transformed into "Pathos toward the truth" (*Pathos der Wahrheit* or its variant *Wahrheitspathos*). *On the Pathos of Truth* (*Ueber das Pathos der Wahrheit*) is the title of one of the 1872 *Five Prefaces to Five Unwritten Works* (Nietzsche 1980a, 755–63), imaginary introductions to five planned yet unwritten books. Regarding this particular preface, which had as its theme the interrogation of the concept of truth, we know that Nietzsche had advanced quite far in his designs for the publication.[4] This preface must also be viewed in conjunction with Nietzsche's unpublished work of 1873, *On Truth and Lie in an Extra-Moral Sense* (Nietzsche 1980a, 875–90), since the latter reflects the former in terms of composition, as is evident from the many textual quotations.

In these two texts, the *Preface* and *On Truth and Lie*, the pathos of truth is undermined by a rather foregone process concerning the basis of the unsustainability of the concept of truth itself. This destabilization of the pathos of truth follows two complementary lines of argument. First, because truth does not exist, pathos toward truth will necessarily engender disillusionment and despair (this is indeed the position adopted in *On the Pathos of Truth*). Second, via a turn—typical of the time—toward Arthur Schopenhauer's philosophy, this pathos will consist in maintaining an illusion of happiness beyond all reasonable doubt. Following this definition, pathos toward truth represents, instead of a tension, rather the desire for illusion and the will to be deceived. Man is destined for despair and destruction; he is condemned to untruth and to continuous deception throughout his entire life (Nietzsche 1980a, 760).

It is perhaps inevitable that during this period Nietzsche's formulation of this question was influenced by Schopenhauer. In fact, pathos toward the truth appears here as a form of hypocrisy or trickery of reason, which desires the truth against all evidence of its nonexistence. This pathos toward the truth is also a cunning of reason that contributes to the maintenance of life (*Selbsterhaltung*)

[4] In the drafts of tables of contents, we find the following titles: 3. *Pathos of Truth* (*Pathos der Wahrheit*) (Nietzsche 1980d, 463, 19[138]); *Introduction to Truth and Lie*. 1. *The Pathos of Truth* (*Pathos der Wahrheit*). 2. *Genesis of Truth* (Nietzsche 1980d, 478, 19[191]); *Analysis of the Common Sense of Truth* (*inconsequential*) 3. *The Pathos of Truth* 4. *Impossibility as Corrective of Man* 5. *The Fundament of the Man is the Lie, because it is Optimistic* 6. *The World of the Body* (Nietzsche 1980d, 623, 29[7]); II. *The Pathos toward the Truth* (*Pathos der Wahrheit*) *refers to the faith* (*Glaube*). III. *The Instinct toward the Lie is Fundamental*. IV. *The Truth is Unknowable. All what is Possible to Know is Appearance. Importance of the Art as Truthful Appearance* (Nietzsche 1980d, 633, 29[20]).

(Nietzsche 1980d, 497, 19[248]) by affirming as true that which is false. Pathos does not seek truth, then; it is instead satisfied with a lie, and it exists safe in the illusion that this lie is the truth. This idea is emphasized more clearly still in the preparatory notes to *On Truth and Lie in an Extra-Moral Sense*, written between 1872 and 1873. Here, the pathos toward the truth is explicitly associated with deception (*Lüge*) and illusion (*Illusion*); more explicitly, Nietzsche paradoxically defines the pathos of truth as a phenomenon that is strictly related to a world of lies (*Wahrheitspathos in einer Lügenwelt*) (Nietzsche 1980d, 488, 19[218]).[5]

This kind of judgment is radical insomuch as it does not serve as an alibi for the pathos of truth. It does not even fall short when Nietzsche discusses more consistent forms of desire for knowledge, such as those of the scientist or the philologist. Even in these cases, the same pathos that seeks the truth finishes by becoming the guarantor of truth itself. In all these applications of the pathos toward the truth, the path of knowledge becomes a spoiled, circular path in which deception seeks itself, and through itself, provides guarantees (Nietzsche 1980d, 444, 19[76]). This instinct for the truth—defined as a disease of logic, as "an optimistic Metaphysic of Logic" (*optimistische Metaphysik der Logik*) (Nietzsche 1980d, 453, 19[103]), as complacency in relation to knowledge or the search for truth in and of itself—will be a key focus of Nietzsche's criticism in the second *Untimely Meditation, On the Use and Disadvantages of History for Life* (Nietzsche 1980a, 243–334). However, what I would like to stress for the current discussion, is how this paradoxical position of an identity of purpose between pathos of the truth and the world of the lie should not be taken too seriously. It is indeed rather a paradoxical statement more than it is a strong speculative point in Nietzsche's argument. His reflection on truth, as I hope to demonstrate, is much more refined, and it does not stop at this aporetical statement.

3. The status of faith and the value of truthfulness

In texts from the period 1872 to 1873, indeed, the discussion on truth and lie is more nuanced. In many fragments produced during these years, but also in published texts such as *On Truth and Lie*, the afore-mentioned *On the Use and Disadvantages of History for Life* and the third *Untimely Meditation, Schopenhauer as Educator* (Nietzsche 1980a, 335–427), Nietzsche introduces distinctions, or at

5 See also Nietzsche 1980d, 475, 476, 19[180, 183].

least calls into question, the radical nature of his criticism. He writes now of an instinct toward the truth that can be called "claimed" (*angeblich*), presumably as opposed to an "actual" one, which is rather honest and pure (*ehrlich und rein*), although it is still produced in a world besieged by lies (Nietzsche 1980a, 394). Already in *On Truth and Lie*, together with these statements, Nietzsche tried to retrieve the relationship between the pathos of truth and the world of appearances. He highlights the truthful and nonfraudulent nature of those who, in spite of being driven by the pathos of truth, end up being deceived. If the result is a lie, this was not the original intent at the beginning of the journey. Nietzsche therefore attenuates the tone of the debate: The pathos of truth will, of course, lead only to a lie, but it will at least be an unconscious one.

Now, Nietzsche does not deny that those who seek the truth and claim to attain it do so in good faith, although it must be admitted that truth in itself does not exist. How, then, should we now define this pathos toward the truth, this "unconscious—and involuntary—illusion" (*Unbewusste Täuschung*) (Nietzsche 1980d, 486–87, 19[216])? What exists between the truth and the lie if not blind trust and faith? Where in the world can we find the pathos of truth? In Nietzsche's opinion, it is not so much the truth itself, as it is the belief and the faith in something that is sought (Nietzsche 1980d, 496, 19[244]). The pathos of truth is therefore related to faith, understood as a form of trust in the truth. But how can we move from this interpretation of the desire for truth as being in good faith to a definition of faith in the strong sense of a religious belief? Nietzsche relocates this appreciation of the pathos of truth—as faith in the existence of truth, and thus, as a truthful attitude that remains on this side of the truth—within all forms of modern man's privileged relationship with the truth: in science, philology, and unsurprisingly, religious faith and the Christian one in particular.

Nietzsche is not one to abstain from criticizing these systems, yet here, he affords them an unexpectedly high degree of respect. Let us take, for example, the most problematic of these relationships between man and the truth: religious faith, and in particular, Christianity. As already highlighted by Karl Jaspers (1947), Christianity in its purest form represents for Nietzsche, beyond any eventual criticism he levels at it, the most elevated and unchallenged expression of the will of truth. In this case, God is in fact the guarantor of truth, and it is the truth inherent to Him that is relentlessly sought by Christians throughout their lives. In this sense, devotion is the ethical mode of life par excellence because being pious, religious and devoted means first and foremost to search for God, who is Truth. As Nietzsche puts it in *The Gay Science*:

> §344. How we, too, are still pious.... But you will have gathered what I am driving at, namely, that it is still a *metaphysical faith* upon which our faith in science rests—that even we seekers after knowledge today, we godless anti-metaphysicians still take our fire, too, from the flame lit by a faith that is thousands of years old, that Christian faith which was also the faith of Plato, that God is the truth, that truth is divine.
>
> Nietzsche 1974, 280; 1980b, 574–75

In these important lines from *The Gay Science*, Nietzsche argues that philosophy, science and any other form of what might be termed lay knowledge is actually a form of faith, which is expressed at its highest level in the Christian faith: Truth is the god of philosophers, just as God represents truth for Christians.

To summarize, then, Nietzsche's elaboration of the impulse toward truth proceeds by successive exclusions and limitations of its lawful scope. We began with the paradox of the world of lies (*Lügenwelt*) that would delegitimize the pathos of truth. The second step is to show how the pathos of truth instead survives and legitimates itself as the belief in truth, despite the continuing backdrop of the world of lies. The third stage is to demonstrate how, even without such a faith in truth, the instinct of truth itself is not lost. At this point, Nietzsche introduces another category that allows him to deal with those intermediate attitudes that come into play when truth is lacking: truthfulness (*Wahrhaftigkeit*).

The ontological lack of truth stated with the admission of the world of lie, should not spoil the truthful nature of the search for the truth, and therefore, of honesty, which is what motivates the impulse toward truth itself. One primary form of honesty relates to the faithful individual, that is, to the one who gets it wrong but who does so in good faith. Now, however, Nietzsche reveals a higher form of truthfulness, a form that is completely independent from truth and from any belief in the truth. It is characterized by the persistence of the instinct to own the truth, which taken to the extreme, will result in an overcoming of the truth itself. He who seeks the truth to the end will eventually end up discovering the illusion behind the concept of truth itself: To want the truth to such an extent as to remain truthful to the end means that truth itself will be exceeded and surpassed. This instinct for truth can indeed persist beyond truth itself since it is no longer founded on or legitimated by the latter; instead, it is based on the practice of truthfulness and being truthful.

At this point, it is necessary to deploy other terminology to describe this approach, which is no longer merely a form of naive, blind faith, but a conscious will that survives even to the point of disillusionment. The terms used by

Nietzsche to signify these attitudes are *honesty* and *justice*. Honesty (*Ehrlichkeit*), which has already been encountered as a quality that Nietzsche attributes to the philologist, was understood as a moral discipline, that is, as the practice of a truthful attitude. Likewise, justice (*Gerechtigkeit*), in order to circumvent the risk of hypostatization if it were to replace the truth, is not considered to be static but dynamic. Justice is thus not employed to determine what is right or wrong on the basis of a stable criterion of truth. Rather, it consists in maintaining a truthful attitude that is imposed as a rule of conduct on man and the scientist: "Only insofar as the truthful man possesses the unconditional will to justice is there anything great in that striving for truth, which is everywhere so thoughtlessly glorified" (Nietzsche 1997, 88–89; 1980a, 287).[6]

Here, then, the very conflict between the pathos of truth and truth itself, out of which Nietzsche's critique emerged, is no longer a source of contradiction. The real instinct for truth cannot and must not result in truth itself, because its tension necessarily goes beyond any possible contingent truths. The instinct of truth, therefore, abandons the field of truth, going beyond it and surpassing it. In this way, Nietzsche demonstrates that the truth has the ability to overcome itself, and that the need for the truth will potentially result in the recognition of its falsity. At the basis of any belief in the truth there lies, therefore, this boundless need for honesty which, when pushed to the extreme, becomes a weapon that will undermine every faith sooner or later. And this is what will happen to the Christian religion, or rather, what would have happened if the passion for the truth of Christianity had not prematurely withered. Even a figure like Blaise Pascal could, according to Nietzsche, bring to completion the millennial education in relation to the truth of Christianity, thus overcoming Christianity itself.[7]

By withdrawing its horizon of truth, Nietzsche thus isolated the truthful attitude, legitimizing it on the basis of the practical concept of justice rather than on the dogmatic concept of truth. Such a process, which is the result of Nietzsche's critical project, is also functional in this same project. How can criticism of the false notion of truth be legitimated if one cannot muster up the same truth?

6 The concept of justice is functional in order to criticize the concept of objectivity in the scientific and historic-literary field (Nietzsche 1980a, 285). Against the hypostatization of objectivity, which pretended to be based on true fundaments, Nietzsche proposed the attitude of the fair judge, who suspends his judgment and accepts the limits imposed on him by circumstance, history and his subjectivity as individual.

7 For more information on Blaise Pascal as an individual capable of exceeding and going beyond Christianity, as well as material on the impulse toward the truth that forms part of Christianity and that moves beyond it, see the comprehensive analysis of Alberto Frigo (2010).

What can a critical issue insist on, if it does not hinge on the affirmation of a truth? The Nietzschean legitimacy of the will for truth responds to this at the expense of truth itself: Nietzsche replaces the positive truth with truthfulness and honesty, which are not intended as realized phenomena (what is honest, what is true), but rather as negative ones (recognition and unmasking of what is not true). And thus, if truth cannot be positively identified, one can nonetheless state what the truth is not. Gilles Deleuze, in *Nietzsche and Philosophy* (1962), faultlessly grasps this passage and provides a brilliant description paraphrasing the afore-mentioned aphorism §344 from *The Gay Science, How we, too, are still pious*:

> The concept of truth describes a "truthful" world.... But a truthful world presupposes a truthful man as its center. —Who is this man, what does he want? First hypothesis: he wants not to be deceived, not to let himself be deceived, because it is "harmful, dangerous, and inauspicious to be deceived." But this hypothesis presupposes the truthfulness of the world itself.... There remains another hypothesis: I want the truth means I do not want to deceive, and "I do no want to deceive comprises, as a special case, I do not want to deceive myself" (FW, 344)—If someone wills the truth it is not in the name of what the world is, but in the name of what the world is not.
>
> Deleuze 1983, 95; 1962, 109

4. The will to truth

Up to this point, we have seen how a reflection on the instinct of truth led Nietzsche to question the varying levels of man's relationship with the truth, from the lowest grade of illusion, to more complex forms of faith, truthfulness (weak, procedural and nondogmatic form of the concept of truth), honesty and justice. Nietzsche does not avoid attacking them with the instrument of his critic, but each of these relationships results to be justified in itself, and endowed, to some extent, with its internal consistency. Concerning the more complex relationships that humans have established with the alleged concept of truth, scientists, philologists, philosophers and people of faith move within the same sphere. They are all characterized by a deep sense of truth, which if pushed to extremes, is able to overcome the limits of truth itself.

At this stage, it is pertinent to move forward chronologically in order to resume the thread offered by our formula (*Trieb der Wahrheit*) and to examine a new development arising out of this reflection. Aphorism 344 from *The Gay Science*, first quoted and commented on by Deleuze, is part of the fifth book of the oeuvre. That means, this chapter has been added along with the second preface of the book only in 1887 (but written presumably in 1886, at the same time as *Beyond Good and Evil* [Nietzsche 1980c, 9–243] was published). If Nietzsche's reflection on the instinct of truth would again play a central role from 1886, it had already gone through a long period of latency in the underground *Nachlass*.[8] Since its reappearance, however, it underwent a further transformation: the interchangeable formulas of pathos and the instinct toward the truth (*Pathos/Trieb zur Wahrheit*) most frequently encountered up to this point were replaced by that of the will to truth (*Wille zur Wahrheit*). In this latter form, the reflection would also be a core topic in the notes of 1885, and would remain stable until 1888.

With the above reflections on the *Trieb der Wahrheit* and the *Wahrhaftigkeit* Nietzsche merely established a practice of suspicion, common to both philologists and philosophers alike. It allowed him to found his critique and its discriminatory practice on a negative concept of truth, that is, that which is not true. Following the texts around 1886 abovementioned, Nietzsche instead expresses a desire to move beyond the critical stage and to focus on a more constructive plan. In line with many Nietzschean scholars, I would venture that his transition to a constructive phase was never truly realized. The misgivings that influenced his thought were numerous and decisive, forcing him to regularly review, repeat and iterate its critical components. The case of the will to truth is very telling of the particular nature of this indecisive phase in Nietzsche's thought. Here, he endeavors to abandon his criticism of the concept of truth, or his assessment of it on an ethical and aesthetic level. He seems more concerned with illustrating how it operates, and in understanding how the will to truth actively functions in the world. In so doing, Nietzsche certainly does not move significantly away from a critical consideration of the phenomenon of the will to truth, but still seems to evaluate aspects mostly in terms of their future application.

If we are to identify the genesis of this particular formulation of the will to truth, it is necessary to return to the end of 1882 and the beginning of 1883. Some ten years after Nietzsche's analysis of the instinct for truth and truthfulness discussed above, the self-same core elements form the basis of his definition of

8 See Nietzsche 1980e, 54, 3[1]; Nietzsche 1980f, 231, 237, 26[301, 334]; 463, 34[129]; 617, 38[20]; 623, 39[13]); 699, 43[1].

the will to truth. Although the formula has changed, the term is defined once again as an instinct (*Trieb*), and the strongest instinct (*der stärkste Trieb*) (Nietzsche 1980e, 521, 16[63]), as Nietzsche puts it in a preparatory note to *Zarathustra*. In an attempt to further develop the definition and implementation of this concept, in the same Zarathustrian context Nietzsche dares again to restrict its scope: The will to truth corresponds to an extreme need for existing things to be thought and to be conceivable. People's need to understand, according to their logic, the whole of creation, and not least themselves, amounts to a general tendency for all beings to become visible, to be thinkable, and thus, to exist. In this sense, the will to truth is characterized as a will to conceivability (*Wille zur Denkbarkeit*), which is a feature of the identity of the world and of people in the world, according to the spirit of modern Cartesian philosophy (Nietzsche 1980e, 459, 13[10]). In this connection, the will to truth is the result of people's need to control the world and life itself, a control that passes through the enunciation of definitions and judgments.

If we stress this recognition of the voluntaristic nature of all knowledge, as well as the purpose of control and the recognition of each will to truth, the identification set out by Nietzsche in this period between the will to truth and the well-known will to power (*Wille zur Macht*) appears to be less abrupt. First, I want to say a few brief words on this formula, made famous by studies on Nietzsche. The formula does not appear in the *Nachlass* until 1876, and its first major appearance as a theme is during the years 1882–85, continuing sporadically until 1888, with further mentions in the *Nachlass* (instances of it in his published works are important, but not abundant). This particular chronology allows us to better understand the interdependence of the formulas that have thus far been examined. It is striking to see the discourse on the instinct for the truth returning in 1883 under the guise of a will to truth. Clearly, therefore, Nietzsche's reflection on the instinct toward the truth, with all its corollaries, is strongly influenced by his nascent discussion of the will to power; in coming into contact with the latter, and somehow being catalyzed by it, it is forever changed, even in name. In a fragment from 1885 (Nietzsche 1980f, 623, 39[13]), we find a mention of the will to truth, which is translated as: "I do not want to be deceived," "I will not deceive" and finally, "I want to convince myself and to be sure." In the same fragment, Nietzsche thus defines explicitly the will to truth as a form of the will to power, together with the "will to justice," the "will to beauty" and the "will to help." Justice (*Gerechtigkeit*) is mentioned here, belonging as it does to the realm of the instinct toward the truth circumscribed by Nietzsche; in other places justice

(*Gerechtigkeit*) and truthfulness (*Wahrhaftigkeit*) appear alongside their counterpoints, faith (*Glaube*), unconscious illusion (*unbewusste Fälschung*), illusion (*Illusion*), and falseness (Nietzsche 1980g, 352, 9[36]; 323, 8[1]).

The relationship between the will to truth and the will to power is revealed first and foremost as an expression of the logic of control and dominion that is central to the meaning of the will to the conceivability of the world. According to Nietzsche, the will to truth enables a certain kind of untruth to gain victory and longevity, and to establish a coherent set of untruths as the ongoing basis for a certain form of life (Nietzsche 1980f, 699, 43[1]).[9] This reference to the untruth (*Unwahrheit*) and to the illusion (*Fälschung*) required in the process of the will to power at the service of survival, closely recalls the mechanisms of the pathos toward the truth in its abovementioned Schopenhauerian connotation of artifice of reason. According to the path reconstructed so far in this article, this last could seem a step back in Nietzsche's reflection. Now again, I think this is nothing but a functional step, to go further in the reflection.

What is particularly interesting now is that Nietzsche poses questions concerning the value of the will to truth, and with it, of the will to power. The problem of value, and of values in general, forms the basis of *Genealogy of Morals* (Nietzsche 1980c, 245–412), in which Nietzsche's critical process assumes an explicit genealogical and historical structure. In the third essay of *Genealogy* (Nietzsche 1980c, 339–412), chapter 24, Nietzsche again calls into question the will to truth using the same objections we have discussed above[10]:

> But the *compulsion* towards it, that irresistible demand for truth, is the belief *in the ascetic ideal itself*, even if it takes the form of its unconscious imperatives—make no mistake about it, it is the belief, I repeat, in a *metaphysical* value, in an *intrinsic* value of *truth*, of a character which this ideal alone can furnish (it stands and falls with that ideal).
>
> Nietzsche 2013, 135; 1980c, 400

The truth would thus be a metaphysical value, just as God is for faith. The fact that until now the need for a justification of the concept of truth has been denied, is a consequence of the dogmatic attitude toward the truth, which was also central in the history of human knowledge, not excepted philosophy.

[9] See also Nietzsche 1980g, 303, 7[24], where *justice* is defined as will to power, and the will to truth as a "means of the will to power."

[10] Nietzsche quotes explicitly in this chapter some excerpts from his fifth book of the *Gay Science*, in particular, the Aphorism *§344. How we, too, are still pious* (Nietzsche 1980b, 574–75), which we are discussing in this article.

> Appealing to the most ancient and the most modern philosophies is of no avail, for they all fail to realize the extent of the need for a justification of the desire for truth—here is a lacuna in every philosophy—why does it exist? Because up to the present the ascetic ideal *dominated* all philosophy, because truth was established as Being, as God, as the Supreme Authority, because truth was not *allowed* to be a problem.
>
> Nietzsche 2013, 136; 1980c, 401

Hence, the need to call into question the notion of truth as a value:

> Once the belief in the God of the ascetic ideal is repudiated, there arises a new problem: the problem of the value of truth. The desire for truth needed a critique—let this critique be then our own task—the value of truth is tentatively to be called in question. . . . (If this seems too laconically expressed, I recommend the reader to peruse again that passage from the *Gay Science* entitled, *How we, too, are still pious* (Aphorism 344) and best of all the whole fifth book of that work, as well as the Preface to *The Dawn*.
>
> Nietzsche 2013, 136; 1980c, 401

It is possible to link the reference in the closing quotation to the afore-mentioned passage of the fifth book of *The Gay Science, How we, too, are still pious*. Even here, Nietzsche attempts to stigmatize the dogmatism of truth, but he further questions the legitimacy of the suspect, and the critique of the concept of truth itself. In practice, even though we claim to have freed ourselves from the concept of truth, in order to be able to exercise any form of scientific, critical or philosophical inquiry, we still require a supposition or a finality, which is deemed to be true. The truth is something original, a primitive feeling, which is essential in any action or thought. Even a discipline of suspicion such as that put forth by Nietzsche between 1872 and 1873, which is based on truthfulness (*Wahrhaftigkeit*) as a functional concept and as a regulative element in the progress of criticism, is necessarily based on an instinct toward the truth (*Trieb der Wahrheit*). The value of the will to truth (*Wille zur Wahrheit*) is therefore the most important value, as it founds all human experience in the world, and indeed, every moral, aesthetic and scientific mode of domination. At the same time, it is not an ideal, superhuman or supernatural value, but a historically defined phenomenon, immanent in the world of human experience, and therefore, a human phenomenon *par excellence*.

Once the nature of this instinct—which is now known as a will—had been defined, and its manifestation in the world had been clarified, the question that Nietzsche posed reads as follows. Should we fight this instinct, deny it if it is recognized, falsify its action? Or should we rather take note of and make use of it by entering into its logic and continuing its path? If we consider the main part of Nietzsche's work, precisely because of the ongoing critical analysis surrounding the instinct toward the truth, it seems that the response to the first question will have the priority. Nietzsche's survey of the nature, effects and implications of the instinct for the truth never reaches a conclusion, and instead, begins again as often as it appears to peter out. The polemical tone of his analysis is undeniable, as I have demonstrated, because it serves to highlight the historical and not the absolute, that is, the human and non-ideal origin of the principles of morality, religion and science.

On the other hand, this critical part cannot be considered alone. As was the case concerning the will to power, the will to truth is also subject to a dual consideration in Nietzsche's work. Even the will to power (as a more general form of what is expressed in the will to truth) has been pilloried to recall all human values and acts to their anti-idealistic origin. At the same time, however, Nietzsche investigated the possibility of establishing a new philosophical perspective via the will to power, which could promote a new form of conscious action in the world.[11]

As is the case with the will to power, then, the will to truth is not only criticized by Nietzsche, but also evaluated for its potential. This tendency to temporarily place to the side any criticisms he may have had, is apparent in much of Nietzsche's work. We can observe this method for example in his treatment of the concept of *Wahrhaftigkeit* and his reflection on the value of faith. In such cases, in fact, Nietzsche has always shown more interest in understanding and knowing the motives, which govern human thought and action, rather than condemning their illusory nature and absence of an absolute foundation. Even at this advanced stage in his thought, Nietzsche wonders whether it is not the task of the philosopher to replace the dogmas of metaphysics and philosophy with a faith based on the will to truth, as a form of will to power.

In 1886, in *Beyond Good and Evil*, Nietzsche dedicated one of his central aphorisms, the 211, to this question. According to this aphorism, the philosopher is distinguishable from all the other figures of knowledge I have analyzed (the philologist, the scientist and the man of faith) as he represents perhaps the highest embodiment of the will to truth. He has already experienced all stages of

[11] Thus far, focus on these constructive reflections on the will to power has led to a series of misunderstandings, according to which the will to power, which is only sporadically discussed in *Posthumous Fragments*, could be considered as the heart of Nietzsche's mature philosophy.

the will for truth—faith, skepticism, idealism and criticism—and therefore, he is highly attuned to each of these attitudes that partially express this instinct.

> But all these are merely preconditions of his task: this task itself demands something different—it demands that he create values. Those philosophical laborers after the noble model of Kant and Hegel have to determine and press into formulas, whether in the realm of logic or political (moral) thought or art, some great data of valuations—that is, former positings of values, creation of value, which have become dominant and are for a time called "truths."
>
> Nietzsche 1966, 136; 1980c, 144

We encounter now again in this quotation some important elements analyzed in this article. The goal of many philosophers, like the other figures observed of men of knowledge, is a certain form of world domination, which they exercise through the position of values. The philosopher is perhaps the highest expression of the will to truth, which, as per Nietzsche's own admission, is nothing more than a form of the more general will to power, which then responds to a logic of control and domination of existence on the existing beings themselves.

> The real philosophers, however, are commanders and law-givers; they say: "Thus shall it be!" They determine first the Whither and the Why of mankind, and thereby set aside the previous labour of all philosophical workers, and all subjugators of the past—they grasp at the future with a creative hand, and whatever is and was, becomes for them thereby a means, an instrument, and a hammer. Their "knowing" is creating, their creating is a law-giving, their will to truth is—will to power. —Are there at present such philosophers? Have there ever been such philosophers? Must there not be such philosophers some day?
>
> Nietzsche 1966, 136; 1980c, 144

How, then, should we interpret the final words of this important Nietzschean aphorism? Evidently, we have momentarily moved away from criticism, and we are faced with a rare moment in which Nietzsche attempts to project the fruits of his labor into the future. Did these philosophers, creators of worlds, and legislators perhaps never exist? The example of Hegel and Kant can only provide an idea of the systematic and creative outlook behind the work of the philosopher because, after all, as Nietzsche tells us, real creators in the field of philosophy have never existed. Could similar philosophers, whose character is dominated by the will for truth, exist in the future? And will this desire for truth end in the continuous creative action of new values, rather than in the conservation of ancient ones? And finally, is it possible that the will for the truth might go beyond itself not only to deny truth, but also to establish new values without basing them on truth itself, or indeed on the just or the unjust, on good and evil? This is the great challenge that Nietzsche seems to face in his more mature philosophy. If his refined 1872 analysis of the *Trieb zur Wahrheit* ended confidently in establishing a negative principle of truth on which to base criticism, his postcritical transition seems to require more effort. It is, therefore, no longer in the name of truth that the philosopher can establish new values, no longer in the name of what the truth "is not," but rather in the name of the will of truth itself.

References

Bernhardy, Gottfried. 1832. *Grundlinien zur Encyklopädie der Philologie*. Halle: Eduard Anton.

Boeckh, August. 1877. *Enzyklopädie und Methodologie der philologischen Wissenschaften*. Leipzig: Teubner.

Deleuze, Gilles. 1962. *Nietzsche et la philosophie*. Paris: PUF.

Deleuze, Gilles. 1983. *Nietzsche and Philosophy*. Translated by Hugh Tomlinson. New York: Columbia University Press.

Frigo, Alberto. 2010. "'La vittima più istruttiva del Cristianesimo': Nietzsche lettore e interprete di Pascal." *Giornale critico della filosofia italiana*. 6 (2): 275–98.

Jaspers, Karl. 1947. *Nietzsche und das Christentum*. Hameln: Seifert.

Nietzsche, Friedrich. 1966. *Beyond Good and Evil*. Translated by Walter Kaufmann. New York: Random House.

Nietzsche, Friedrich. 1974. *The Gay Science*. Translated by Walter Kaufmann. New York-Toronto: Random House.

Nietzsche, Friedrich. 1980a. *Sämtliche Werke. Kritische Studienausgabe in 15 Bänden*, vol. 1: *Die Geburt der Tragödie. Unzeitgemäße Betrachtungen I–IV*. Edited by Giorgio Colli and Mazzino Montinari. Berlin: De Gruyter.

Nietzsche, Friedrich. 1980b. *Sämtliche Werke. Kritische Studienausgabe in 15 Bänden*, vol. 3: Morgenroethe, Idyllen aus Messina, Die froehliche Wissenschaft. Edited by Giorgio Colli and Mazzino Montinari. Berlin: De Gruyter.

Nietzsche, Friedrich. 1980c. *Sämtliche Werke. Kritische Studienausgabe in 15 Bänden*, vol. 5: *Jenseits von Gut und Böse. Zur Genealogie der Moral*. Edited by Giorgio Colli and Mazzino Montinari. Berlin: De Gruyter.

Nietzsche, Friedrich. 1980d. *Sämtliche Werke. Kritische Studienausgabe in 15 Bänden*, vol. 7: *Nachgelassene Fragmente 1869–1874*. Edited by Giorgio Colli and Mazzino Montinari. Berlin: De Gruyter.

Nietzsche, Friedrich. 1980e. *Sämtliche Werke. Kritische Studienausgabe in 15 Bänden*, vol. 10: *Nachgelassene Fragmente 1882–1884*. Edited by Giorgio Colli and Mazzino Montinari. Berlin: De Gruyter.

Nietzsche, Friedrich. 1980f. *Sämtliche Werke. Kritische Studienausgabe in 15 Bänden*, vol. 11: *Nachgelassene Fragmente 1884–1885*. Edited by Giorgio Colli and Mazzino Montinari. Berlin: De Gruyter.

Nietzsche, Friedrich. 1980g. *Sämtliche Werke. Kritische Studienausgabe in 15 Bänden*, vol. 12: *Nachgelassene Fragmente 1885–1887*. Edited by Giorgio Colli and Mazzino Montinari. Berlin: De Gruyter.

Nietzsche, Friedrich. 1993. *Werke. Kritische Gesamtausgabe*, part 2, vol. 3: *Vorlesungsaufzeichnungen (SS 1870–1871)* Edited by Giorgio Colli and Mazzino Montinari. Berlin: De Gruyter.

Nietzsche, Friedrich. 1997. *Untimely Meditations*. Edited by Daniel Breazeale, translated by Reginald John Hollingdale. Cambridge: Cambridge University Press.

Nietzsche, Friedrich. 2013. *On the Genealogy of Morals*. Translated by Michael A. Scarpitti. London: Penguin.

Santini, Carlotta. 2015. "Eduquer la différence. Nietzsche et la tâche du philologue." *Conférence* 41: 265–88.

Schleiermacher, Friedrich. 1838. *Hermeneutik und Kritik*. Berlin: Reimer.

Wolf, Friedrich A. 1807. *Darstellung der Altertumswissenschaft nach Umfang, Begriff, Zweck und Wert*. Berlin: Lange & Sprinter.

Wolf, Friedrich A. 1831a. *Enzyklopädie der Philologie (1798–1799)*. Edited by G. M. Stodmann. Leipzig: Teubner.

Wolf, Friedrich A. 1831b. *Vorlesungen über die Altertumswissenschaft*. Edited by J. D. Gürtler. Leipzig: Teubner.

5

Dionysius, Apollo and Other *Göttliche*:

Denial and Excess of Meaning in Nietzsche, Heidegger and Wittgenstein

Tobias Keiling

One way of thinking about the radicality of experience is to ask by comparison to what an experience is radical: What is the "ordinary" in contrast to which an experience is radical? There needs to be what one "usually" perceives, does and says, some established set of meanings, a particular attitude, say, or conceptual scheme, an established frame of reference outside of which a radical experience will fall, with which it will break. A radical experience will transgress such framing to an extent that it can no longer count as what "normally" counts as experience.

This line of thought may seem insufficient, however. Given the contrast of the radical to the ordinary, there are at least two different ways of thinking about the relation of an established form of understanding to the experience we want to call radical: You may say that a radical experience is an *excess of meaning*; it goes beyond established interpretive patterns—and it is just this that makes it even *more* meaningful. A radical experience exceeds a particular reference frame, but it doesn't question the validity of the conceptual scheme with which it breaks or the meaningfulness of experience as such. What makes such an experience radical is simply that it means "more"; that it is, say, "higher" than an experience fully within the confines of our ordinary understanding. But such radical experience is still meaningful, and may even define what it is to have meaning. Such excess of meaning would be the ultimate given in experience, so that the conceptual or semantic norm we usually rely on, although exceeded, receives its strongest confirmation by what initially appears other to it. The particular movement of radical experience, thus understood, would be one from exclusion not to simple inclusion, but to the affirmation of the "normal" forms of understanding through the radical.

But one may also say that a radical experience is not excess but *denial of meaning*. Because it falls outside an established form of understanding, it has no meaning at all. What is experienced is, rather, something so unthinkable that it may well be something about nothing can be said. Yet, this unsayable is present nonetheless; it is and remains incomprehensible. Incapable of making sense of it, one may retort to deliberate exclusion, even to the denial of this very experience. But such thinking endangers the way of understanding people hold to be the ordinary, for it is now seen as limited. Seeing perceptual, conceptual and semantic norms as limited in their scope or regularity reveals their contingency. A radical experience, if it is taken to be a denial of meaning, would be radical precisely because it threatens to deny all meaning by denying the normality of or any regularity in meaning. To have such an experience would mean a continuous and enlarging, "abysmal" withdrawal of meaning.

Such a distinction between excessive and denied meaning, however, should not be taken to imply a valid alternative to determine what the correlate or content of a radical experience *is*, for the difference between excess and denial of meaning can be experiential without being ontologically determinative. Describing a radical experience as either excess or denial of meaning, or as both, is not claiming this to be a sufficient explanation. Instead of being taken as determinants of the content of a radical experience, one may think of such excess and denial rather as heuristic schemes themselves. In this vein, one would attempt to determine a hermeneutics of radical experience by asking how we *interpret* and *understand* such an experience (if we do understand it or to the extent that we understand it). One way to philosophically reflect such understanding would be precisely by putting it into perspective from the two opposite points of excess and denial. The hermeneutical project of understanding radical experience would thus continue the transcendental project of clarifying our grasp of meaning. In such a view, we may see our understanding both remain with one of excess or denial, or see it move or hover between the two alternatives.

When turning to Nietzsche, to Heidegger and to Wittgenstein now, and considering what can be learned about excess and denial of meaning from them, I want to make a similar point about not falling for false alternatives. In particular, I want to raise the question in what sense a radical experience could be a *religious* experience. What would it involve calling a radical experience a religious experience? I anticipate that what it would mean for an experience to be radical would be for it to forgo even its religious interpretation, if by *religion* we mean anything akin to what I have referred to (using these words interchangeably) as a particular "set of beliefs," a "form of understanding," a "frame of reference" or a "conceptual scheme." If that is true, then what we may call a religious experience is, in principle, not radical enough. Because its religious meaning results from an interpretation requiring a specific set of background assumptions into which a radical experience is to integrate, a radical experience is not reducible to its religious understanding. An interpretation of such experience, determining it as religious, doesn't allow for a denial of meaning, but can, at the utmost, only think of the radicality of experience as exceeding, yet ultimately, reaffirming religious beliefs. But there is nothing that forces us to remain with this way of understanding radicality alone. We may always regard a radical experience in its negativity, as a denial of meaning.

If such a line of thought is convincing, the radicality of an experience cannot imply that we may not think of it as a religious experience, but it must mean that we do not have to think of it in this way. Radical experiences are then of importance to hermeneutical philosophy only outside their religious interpretation: They reaffirm the human capacity for interpretation even in view of a denial of meaning, but such experiences do not bind interpretation to any of its established results. Radical experiences would rather determine understanding as inherently pluralistic, as the capacity to conceive of something, even the excessive, and possibly the meaningless, in *different* ways. It is the inescapability of understanding, not a fixed set of beliefs, that can reaffirm the universality of hermeneutics even in view of radical experience.

It is Nietzsche who, against his general intention, brings this plurality of understanding to the fore. And it is Heidegger who brings out, again in part against his intention, the necessity of interpretation in the moment of its greatest need. And it is Wittgenstein who reorients the interpretation of radical experiences toward our actual, possibly quite ordinary, speaking, locating radicality where it was not expected.

1. Dionysian and/or Apollonian meaning

Already on the first few pages, the whole argument of *The Birth of the Tragedy* is laid out: By joining the "distinct art worlds of dream and rapture" (Nietzsche 1980, 26; 1967, 33) represented by Apollo and Dionysus, respectively, tragedy was born as the unification of these two extremes, Greek tragedy, in turn, being the paramount example of art. The birth of art in such a birth of tragedy is a birth *from the spirit of music* (as the original subtitle of the essay reads) because music is the eminent form of Dionysian art, which Nietzsche believes is historically prior to its Apollonian counterpart. And it is through a further radicalization of the Apollonian into the Socratic that the balance of the two aesthetic principles is destroyed and Greek tragedy eventually dies again. After that, no form of art again reaches the climax of Attic tragedy, against which even Wagner is to be measured.

It is not hard to see how the Apollonian and the Dionysian represent phenomenologically distinguishable forms of radical experience. Explicitly prior to their aesthetic mediation, Nietzsche describes the Apollonian form of experience by comparing it to dreaming. Like dreaming, it is accompanied by a "diaphanous feeling of *seeming* [*durschimmernde Empfindung des Scheins*]" (Nietzsche 1980, 26; 1967, 34). This feeling is the same in contemplating images, where one remains removed from the object depicted. Seen from within the Apollonian conceptual scheme, everything appears removed from the observer and image-like. Such images do not contrast, however, to a supposed reality of what is but imagined. On the contrary: Such an iconic existence, in this conceptual scheme, is the actual and true existence of what there is, and the Apollonian observer is content with her distance to what she sees. Even in the "dangers and horrors of dreams," because she knows she cannot be affected, an Apollonian observer will say (with dreaming Nietzsche): "It is a dream! I want to continue dreaming!" (ibid.) Thus, integrating any experience into the interpretive scheme of the Apollonian allows one to look at it from a distance and consider it in its particularity. Referencing Schopenhauer, Nietzsche is tempted "to describe Apollo himself as the glorious godly image of the principium individuationis" (Nietzsche 1980, 28; 1967, 36). The Apollonian experience, considered phenomenologically, is marked by iconic distance, distinctness and individuality.

The third characteristic, the emphasis on both the individuality of the observer and the particularity of the observed, marks the strongest contrast to the Dionysian. Against the Apollonian "image world of the dream," which is meaningful because of its distinctness, the Dionysian experience "does not respect the individual but attempts to destroy it, redeem it in a mystical feeling of unity" (Nietzsche 1980, 30; 1967, 38). Such a conciliation of humans with each other and with nature is embodied by the "orgiastic frenzy" (Nietzsche 1980, 44; 1967, 49) in which Dionysus himself takes part. Yet, this moment of ecstasy, of Dionysian radicality, is limited, and if it were not, no art could come forth from it. In coming to grasp the Dionysian, Nietzsche imagines, "we see Dionysus and the maenads," but then, we see the poet as "intoxicated enthusiast fast asleep" (Nietzsche 1980, 44; 1967, 49). In this scene, art then originates on the return of the dreaming: "now Apollo approaches him [the poet Archilochus, T.K.] and touches him with his laurel: the Dionysian-musical bewitchment of the sleeper now, as it were, spraying images [*Bilderfunken*], lyrical poems that in their highest unfolding are to be called tragedies" (Nietzsche 1980, 44; 1967, 50). If the Dionysian is the exact opposite experience of the Apollonian by being immediate, indistinct and collective, art is determined through the reconciliation of these opposites.

What Nietzsche describes is, no doubt, how experience exceeds what we would consider a "normal" meaning: The Apollonian observer of life is not dealing with images among other things, but "the Apollonian" is the principle of the utter remoteness of the iconic; "the Dionysian," on the other hand, stands for an experience of sheer immediacy and indifference in everything. Both these forms of experience are certainly not what we would consider ordinary, but rather extreme. Yet these extremes are defined not in contrast to the ordinary, but by opposition to each other. Both descriptive patterns are products of generalization, and it is the conflict arising from generalizing such extreme positions that Nietzsche then uses to determine the emergence of true art, so vividly described in the scene of the poet awakening from his sleep (and in many similar passages in the text of *The Birth of the Tragedy*). Art appears as a rebound from two extremes, two forms of excess mediated, Nietzsche suggests, only here. The Aristotelian idea of art as *mimesis* is transformed into the reconciliation of oppositions (see Figal 2012).

Although *The Birth of the Tragedy* seems quite obviously to try to come to terms with phenomena out of the ordinary, if one attempts to say how Nietzsche would describe a radical experience, one is left with two conflicting answers. The two alternatives of Apollonian and Dionysian meaning mutually confirm each other, but so vanishes their experiential radicality. There is no room for anything not to be understood in either of these schemes, not any room in particular for a lack or denial of meaning. On the contrary, it is now against the measure of Apollonian-Dionysian art that other experiences, such as Socratic philosophizing or Modern art, can be compared. What is more, Nietzsche grants no place to the ordinary. Certainly, what Nietzsche describes is not what we may call our ordinary lives. But that this is so, already involves a critical distance to the text. An important implication of the extensive and vivid rhetoric of the Apollonian and the Dionysian is that the every-day is not worth talking about.

It is important to note at this point what exact status the Apollonian and the Dionysian have. For one, they are associated with Apollo and Dionysus as the "Gods of Art [*Kunstgottheiten*]" (Nietzsche 1980, 25; 1967, 33). But, Nietzsche takes these gods to be themselves only intellectual parallels of more fundamental metaphysical phenomena: The Apollonian and the Dionysian are "*Nature's drives to art* [*Kunsttriebe der Natur*]" (Nietzsche 1980, 31; 1967, 38), of which drives human existence is derivative. Thus, the gods Apollo and Dionysus are ultimately ideas to cope with the conflicting desires arising from the natural drives: "in order to live, the Greeks, in direst need, had to create these gods" (Nietzsche 1980, 36; 1967, 42). Thus, more fundamental than the "duplicity" (Nietzsche 1980,26; 1967,33) of the Apollonian and the Dionysian is the idea that experience must be *interpreted* and that both ancient religion and art achieve such an interpretation: turning the "metaphysical" experience of the drives in nature into a religious and aesthetic experience, understanding dream and rapture as features of what belongs to the doings of Apollo and Dionysus and then understanding their interaction as art, is such a double interpretation of the world as a whole. Yet, if there is a moment of interpretation involved in coping with radical experience, Nietzsche doesn't allow for interpretation to fail or even to hesitate.

Apollonian and Dionysian understanding both provide interpretations of what clearly transgresses what may count as a standard against which an experience may be called radical. But, this happens so as to reaffirm the universality of meaning and confirm the claims that meaning has its ground in art, the experience of which Nietzsche describes only indirectly, without any measure outside its description. Thus, to ask why there are exactly these two gods would in the context of *The Birth of the Tragedy* be akin to a heretical question. It undermines our capacity to survive through unfailing interpretation, which, so Nietzsche seems to think, can only operate if it doesn't know itself as such an interpretation. (It is worth noting that in this respect, Nietzsche's early writings greatly differ, for example, from *Thus Spoke Zarathustra*, where Nietzsche adapts his style to force his own reader into becoming an interpreter.)

2. Heidegger's last God and his *Göttliche*

Like Nietzsche, Heidegger sees a community between what one may call an aesthetic experience, a religious experience and an experience of history. The three are not distinguishable kinds of events, but dimensions of any experience one may well call radical. Yet, unlike Nietzsche in *The Birth of the Tragedy*, Heidegger in a very particular way describes the limits of understanding and attempts to address the denial of meaning involved in a truly radical experience. For all of this, not Greek tragedy but Hölderlin's poetry is the eminent example, which is itself, however, in part significant because it reaches back to the Greek origin of culture. The exemplary role of Hölderlin is most pertinent in *The Origin of the Work of Art*, in which after Heidegger's own philosophy has been laid out, the closing lines call attention to Hölderlin's poetry as an event remaining to be recognized in its historical import for the German people and for a philosophical estimation of art. Heidegger positions his own questioning for the origin of art in relation to this narrative:

> But this reflective knowledge is the preliminary and therefore indispensable preparation for the becoming of art. Only such knowledge prepares its space for art, their way for the creators, their location for the preservers. . . . Are we in our existence historically at the origin? Do we know, which means do we give heed to, the essence of the origin? Or, in our relation to art, do we still merely make appeal to a cultivated acquaintance with the past? For this either-or and its decision there is an infallible sign. Hölderlin, the poet—whose work still confronts the Germans as a test to be stood—named it in saying:
>
> *Schwer verlässt / was nahe dem Ursprung wohnet, den Ort.*
> Reluctantly / that which dwells near its origin abandons the site.
>
> Heidegger 1977, 66; 1993, 202–3

It is striking how in this passage Heidegger describes the heightened attention for art and the questioning for its origin as both provisional and unavoidable, urging to think about art, but denying that any particular results may be gained from it. Bordering on paradox, this idea undermines the decision between alternatives sketched just afterward, the decision whether "we give heed to . . . the essence of the origin" (Heidegger 1977, 66; 1993, 202) of art or instead remain with cultivated but meaningless knowledge of it. Despite the rhetoric, however, such a decision is quite empty, for the turn to art and to the experience of poetry, in particular, is a turn to what is necessary to achieve the envisaged transformation, but it is also a turn to the utterly unexpected. Like the ideal of resolute existence, it is a decision *against* something (educated ignorance), but it is no decision *for* anything particular. The experience of art is to be transformed itself in a manner quite unknown, so it is unclear what one opts for if one chooses to confront it.

Given the ambivalence of this only apparent decision, of knowing and not knowing the meaning of radical experience, Heidegger's appeal to the Germans as possible readers of Hölderlin can itself be interpreted in two ways. Such an experience of eminent poetry is an excess of a supposedly "normal" understanding of art to be integrated into a renewed, genuinely philosophical understanding of it. Hölderlin's poetry, the eminent example of what art can be, would then serve as excessive conformation of the philosophy of art Heidegger outlines in the artwork essay, revealing art in its true aesthetic/historical/national importance. Alternatively, that very experience is taken to be, first and foremost, as a denial of meaning, as that which breaks with any trivializing denial of the radicality of art, replacing it with but a "preparation for the becoming of art" (Heidegger 1977, 66; 1993, 202). Not even Heidegger would then have a grasp of what the genuine experience of art consists in. In this second reading, there is no doubt *that* Heidegger imagines Hölderlin's poetry to be a radical experience; but, it is unclear *how* this experience is to be understood if it is indeed to transform our understanding of art and of philosophy, and through the transformation of philosophy, transform a people. Where Nietzsche is giving an inherently double and paradox meaning to art, Heidegger's stance toward the radicality of aesthetic experience is paradoxical in a different way: He attributes to Hölderlin's poetry a meaning of utmost importance, and at the same time, denies the possibility of such attribution, calling for utter openness to its experience instead. Although the problem of interpreting art is not explicitly addressed, it is what the paradoxical combination of both excess and denial of meaning, like Nietzsche's two forms of excess, presuppose.

Unlike in the Nietzschean dyad, the problem of interpretation is central to Heidegger's detailed reading of Hölderlin: Not only because it proceeds by close, if not always careful, interpretation of his later hymns, but also because Heidegger sees Hölderlin as the poet of poetry, the eminent poet who can elucidate the nature of poetry as such. Here, the religious dimension of poetry becomes thematic: Heidegger emphatically subscribes to Hölderlin's poetology, and thus, the importance Hölderlin attributes to poetry as given by the gods carries over into Heidegger's emphatic understanding of poetry and his discussion of the appearance of the divine. The divine appears through a *Winken* (a beckoning or hinting), and it is this indirect appearance poetry attests to, that is in turn to be interpreted by the reader of poetry. At all of these different stages, some form of interpretation must occur.

The idea of a beckoning of the divine takes up verses from Hölderlin's poem *Rousseau*: "und Winke sind / Von Alters her die Sprache der Götter," "and beckonings are, / From time immemorial, the language of the gods" (Hölderlin 1992, 238; my translation). In the essay *Hölderlin and the Essence of Poetry*, which gathers the central moments of his reading of Hölderlin, Heidegger relates these verses to two stanzas from the hymn *The Voice of the People*, and then summarizes Hölderlin's poetology: "the poet's saying is the intercepting of these hints, in order to pass them on to this people. This intercepting of the hints is a reception, and yet at the same time a new giving.... Thus the essence of poetry is joined into the laws of the hints of the gods and the voice of the people—laws that strive both apart from, and toward each other." The poet "is one who has been cast out—out into that between, between gods and humans. But only in this between is it decided who the human is and where his existence settles." Quoting another Hölderlin verse, Heidegger continues: "'Poetically the human dwells on this earth.'" (Heidegger 1981, 46–47; 2009, 127–28).

From this context, *Wink*, literally meaning a beckoning, but also, more generally, a hint or an intimation, becomes a concept that is operative in many of Heidegger's texts, indicating both something important to be understood and a need for interpretation. Thus, if Heidegger believes Hölderlin believing (at least saying) he passes on the beckonings of the gods, this does not mean simply relaying a message of determinate content. It rather renews the need for interpretation of what the radical or religious dimension of experience could be, something not decided in advance. At the same time, however, Heidegger sees himself as anticipating at least the great importance of Hölderlin's poetry at this particular moment of history, and thus, prefigures any interpretation. It is this integration into a historical narrative that gives to Heidegger's interpretations an eschatological dimension that contrasts the appeal to a mere receptiveness toward the radical. Heidegger's turn to art in the 1930s thus is an indeterminate appeal to the expected radicality of certain experiences unexpected in content and at the same time giving some concrete determinations of these very experiences. At some moments, these amount to a stunning overdetermination of the unknown or not-yet-known, displaying a peculiar insecurity as to their precise meaning in the attempt to conceal that very insecurity.

A similar, double account of religious experience as excess and denial is patent in *Contributions to Philosophy*. In the part devoted to *the last God*,[1]

1 On the notion of the last God, see Figal 2001.

Heidegger describes the "hints of the last God" as both the "intrusion and remaining absent of (...) the gods." (Heidegger 1989, 408; 2012a, 323, transl. mod.) And on "the essence of hinting [*Wesen des Winkens*]" he comments that in it "lies the mystery of the unity of the innermost nearing in the most extreme distance" (ibid.). Again, this appears to be a particular description of interpretation that attends to both what is near and what is far, both brought close in understanding and kept at a distance at what may not (yet) be understood. Given this trouble in understanding the meaning of the divine, it is unclear how Heidegger (or his interpreters, see Wrathall and Lambeth 2011) could think to be certain that the coming of the last God is the inaugural event of a no longer secular or metaphysical age. If the appearance of the divine occurs through hinting, it is necessarily indirect and our understanding of it is both given over to interpretation and necessarily partial. It is true that Heidegger anticipates a most radical event. But, to define it as an appearance "of the gods," "of the last God," or "of the divinities" is already part of an encompassing process of interpreting experiences that are in some way or other exceptional, reaffirming, first of all, our capacity to attempt such an interpretation. Despite his emphasis on this excessive-but-denied meaning, in the way Heidegger develops these ideas, the primary focus of such an interpretation is its own status as a genuinely philosophical engagement with poetry as the exemplary radical experience.

This primacy of interpretation over any religious message or expectation of a coming fulfillment comes to the fore in Heidegger's shift from "the gods" and "the last God" to "the divinities" in the second half of the 1940s. There are two aspects in his understanding of the divine that are decisive. First, the religious interpretation of experience is to be taken as only one possible implication of "nearness" among others, the four dimensions of the so-called fourfold being the most perspicuous aspects for the constitution of world through the gathering character of things. Second, the interpretability of life with respect to its religious implications is not guaranteed through a discourse on the coming and passing of any god or gods, but it is rather integrated into a discussion of the appearing of things that may always be taken to bear religious meaning.

In Heidegger's writings from the 1950s, the radical meaning of experience can only be grasped in relation to its seemingly most uncontroversial description as experience of things in this world. It is such an understanding of the beckoning, freed from the burden of its supposed historical import, that allows the much more liberal discourse on *die Göttlichen* to develop; thus, in *Building, Dwelling, Thinking*: "The divinities are the beckoning messengers of the godhead. Out of the holy sway of the godhead, the god appears in his presence or withdraws into his concealment" (Heidegger 2000, 151; 1993, 351–52). And in the Bremen lecture *The Thing*: "the divinities are the hinting messengers of the godhood. From the concealed reign of these there appears the god in his essence, withdrawing from every comparison with what is present" (Heidegger 1994, 17; 2012b, 16).

In both essays, the experience of the divinities is described with respect to a particular thing (a bridge, a jug) as it is understood in the world of the fourfold. The religious dimension of experience thus continues to be one of indirect appearance and a denial of divine meaning. But it is explained not as a transgression of the ordinary understanding of the world for the sake of something outside it, or as anticipation of a future or as coming and passing of a god or of the gods. Rather, the anticipation of religious meaning is something within the ordinary world of things. It may be inconspicuously present in it, but it is nowhere but there. It is not to provide some radical, but ultimately external confirmation of the ordinary as such. The experience of the divinities, understood as a possible meaning of the things of this world, doesn't exceed this world.

3. Talking (or not talking) about what may (or may not) be radical: Wittgenstein

In describing the world as a world of things and locating even religious experience within such a world, Heidegger's account, in some respect, converges with that of the later Wittgenstein. To conceive of the world as a world of things does not rule out the idea of an intertwining of world and language as such (see Cavell 2006 243–44); the mediation between the two just cannot be described (as Wittgenstein envisaged in the *Tractatus*) through propositions picturing facts. If this marks a pivotal insight in the philosophy of the later Wittgenstein, it also has important consequences for how he would conceive of a radical experience: If language is in order as it is, the language we use to describe such experiences also is in order as it is. A radical experience doesn't need radical (say, poetic) language or radical interpretation. Although there is no singular language for these experiences, and although such speaking may not be made fully transparent, there is no need to avoid speaking.

In the *Tractatus*, however, what Wittgenstein says about what one may take as radical experience displays a particular movement from the description of an excess to a denial of meaning, leading up to the demand not to speak about what one cannot speak about, to the well-known articulation of not understanding at the very end of the *Tractatus*: "what we cannot speak about we must pass over in silence" (Wittgenstein 1963, §7). It has often been commented, and rightly so, that this is both a description of a necessity of silence in philosophical language and an imperative itself quite articulate. As such, it brings to some sort of silent conclusion the remarks already made in the previous sections of the *Tractatus* about "what we cannot speak about." I will put three of these remarks included in the explanation of paragraph 6 (about the "general form of a truth-function" and "the general form of a proposition") in reverse order:

"6.522 There are, indeed, things that cannot be put into words. They *make themselves manifest*. They are what is mystical" (Wittgenstein 1963, 151).

"6.44 It is not *how* things are in the world that is mystical, but *that* it exists" (Wittgenstein 1963, 149).

"6.45 To view the world sub specie aeterni is to view it as a whole—a limited whole. Feeling the world as a limited whole—it is this that is mystical" (ibid.).

In this perspective, reading from paragraph 7 back into the earlier sections, Wittgenstein's final demand not to talk about what cannot be talked about loses its coercive force. It is rather itself an exception, given the earlier elaboration of mystical experience and the questions it spurs, or at the very least, it is not the only possible interpretation of the feeling of the mystical. For sure, the discussion of the mystical, of the fact *that* the world exists, itself transgresses the system of claims set forth in the earlier sections of the *Tractatus*, violating the demand "to say nothing except what can be said, i.e. propositions of natural science" (Wittgenstein 1963, §6.53). It should not be talked about the mystical, but something can and has already been said. In reading along, the urge to remain silent seems to complete philosophical discourse precisely by ending it. But, even describing the unsayable as "the mystical" remains a way of understanding.

With the distinctions used here, one may say that it is only with the very last paragraph of the *Tractatus* that a denial of meaning is expressed and performed. Yet, this denial, as it were, comes too late. Given the context of its claim to the impossibility of description, the experience of the mystical can no longer remain meaningless. In particular, there is always the possibility to reread and to reverse one's reading. If one does follow Wittgenstein's text, it moves from the articulation of a philosophical theory to something akin to its ultimate, although transgressive confirmation. This is certainly not simply making a philosophical claim, but more akin to performative speech, or itself an enactment of the mystical "feeling." Among the texts examined here, the *Tractatus* is certainly the most performative in this sense. But this performance cannot proceed differently than by first at least adumbrating what it would mean to know the world *sub specie aeterni*, and then to offer a name for this experience by referring to a word with implications and a history of its own: "the mystical." Thus, the text moves from a description of the mystical experience of the world and to the denial that such confirmation can be achieved. It may be that this brings out an ultimately ethical point Wittgenstein wants to make (see McManus 2006), but in view of how he conceives of radical experience, it amounts to a paradoxical estimation, both attributing to it the status of an affirmative-though-transgressive experience and at the same time denying the possibility of such attribution. Wittgenstein's version of this paradox consists in having said something about what cannot (or must not) be talked about. Thus, Wittgenstein in his discussion of the mystical grants centre stage in philosophy to what we may call a radical experience, but this exposes his conception of philosophy to the seemingly exclusive constraints of grasping this experience as both excess and denial of meaning, depending on where in the text you are reading.

If it is plausible to see the text of the *Tractatus* as attempting to move from an account of the radical as excess to an account of the radical as utter denial of meaning (although this doesn't prevent its readers from reading it in the reverse), this may put into perspective Wittgenstein's later description of radical experience too. The relation of the *Tractatus* to his later philosophy has been extensively discussed, but one thing that has become clear is that it involves a complex movement that cannot be easily separated into two or more subsequent stages (see Conant 2011). One way to comment on this movement from the perspective on possible determinations of radical experience is to look more closely at a text from between the *Tractatus*-period and *Philosophical Investigations*, a text referred to as Wittgenstein's *Lectures on Religious Belief* (Wittgenstein 1970), dating from "roughly" 1938 (ibid., i) and accessible only through an edition of notes taken by Wittgenstein's students. While in the major part of these lectures Wittgenstein takes the utterance of particular Christian beliefs as examples, asking how belief in the Last Judgment or belief in an afterlife can be articulated and defended, he also gives the example of the interpretation of a miracle in the second lecture. It is here that Wittgenstein comes most closely to a description of what one may take as a radical religious experience:

> Suppose I went to somewhere like Lourdes in France. Suppose I went with a very credulous person. There we see blood coming out of something. He says: "There you are, Wittgenstein, how can you doubt?" I'd say: "Can it only be explained one way? Can't it be this or that?" I'd try to convince him that he'd seen nothing of any consequence. I wonder whether I would do that under all circumstances. I certainly know that I would under normal circumstances.
>
> Wittgenstein 1970, 60–61

Wittgenstein does not attempt to refute the fact of "blood coming out of something" established by shared experience, but insists on there being several possible explanations of its evidence. Such explanations are subject to a particular form of disagreement Wittgenstein goes on to describe. It is not quite clear if he truly takes the religious interpretation to be an explanation at all, but he goes on to question the import this interpretation gives to the experiential fact of "blood coming out of something" in Lourdes. Despite the seemingly overwhelming contextual evidence (a "typical" miracle, at a place of pilgrimage), a simple "how can you doubt?" can never be a reasonable demonstration of any particular way of understanding this event. In particular, its meaning is not determined by a specific interpretation of its context, nor is this context self-interpreting, as it were, such that Lourdes and "blood coming out of something" can have only one meaning.

From the manner in which Wittgenstein develops this example, it becomes clear that he is willing to accept the circumstantiality of understanding: it would be absurd to try to formulate different understandings of this event in propositional form and attempt to determine the truth-value of some proposition or set of (elementary) propositions regarding this event. Rather, it is the actual development of the conversation about this experience that both discovers and determines its meaning. If there is a schematism to determine the truth of this description, such as the *Tractatus* would seem to offer, it would fail to do so (Diamond 2005, 102). Given the way Wittgenstein dismisses the religious pre-understanding, it seems most important that what an experience one may want to consider a miracle means cannot be determined in advance, taking it as a (certainly excessive) confirmation of one's creeds, but as confirmation of a particular set of beliefs nonetheless.

In discussing the imagined conversation with his friend, Wittgenstein invokes a contrast between "normal circumstances" and "all circumstances," saying that he is certain he will try to convince his interlocutor and fellow witness of the inconsequentiality of his beliefs "under normal circumstances," but says he is unsure whether he would attempt this "under all circumstances." It is unclear how exactly this contrast is to be spelled out, but it obviously concerns the very disputability of religious beliefs. Thus, to the renewed initiative of his believer to defend his creed ("'Oughtn't one after all to consider this?'") Wittgenstein imagines himself replying nothing but "'Come on. Come on.'" Then he comments on this dismissal: "I would treat the phenomenon in this case just as I would treat an experiment in a laboratory which I thought badly executed" (Wittgenstein 1970, 60–61).

If "under normal circumstances" means as long as the believer is receptive of rational discourse and argument, Wittgenstein is unwilling to discuss his interlocutor's religious explanation at all as long as he believes him to be sane. So a circumstance in which Wittgenstein would engage in a discussion of a religious meaning of this event might be one in which he continues with some therapeutic engagement with his friend. But at that point, it would become a very special discourse that is no longer concerned with the true meaning of such experience. The analogy to the experiment in a laboratory, however, seems to reorient the discussion toward finding the meaning inherent in this event despite previous failure to do so. But, the analogy also very openly suggests that a gross error in the interpretation of that event has been made. There is no use to philosophically discuss a fact that is empirically disputed, like a fact resulting from an experiment badly executed.

In many respects, the example of the miracle confirms the remarks Wittgenstein makes about a belief in the Last Judgment or in an afterlife: It is impossible for a nonbeliever to "contradict" (Wittgenstein 1970, 53) a believer, although he may react with incomprehension and doubts about the reliability of his interlocutor. If, Wittgenstein imagines, one answers to a statement of religious belief by saying "Well, I'm not so sure. Possibly" (ibid.), the similarity to a quite ordinary case in which one considers the possibility of an event (a German airplane flying above one's head) is utterly superficial. Answering someone who believes in the Last Judgment by saying that it may "possibly" be true isn't considering it a real possibility at all, and despite appearances, it is quite unclear whether both partners in the conversation are talking about the same modality at all. Rather, "it isn't a question of my being anywhere near him, but on an entirely different plane, which you could express by saying: 'You mean something altogether different, Wittgenstein'" (ibid.).

But if the distance between a believer and a nonbeliever is not to be measured on a single logical space such as the *Tractatus* puts forward, the alternative is not that these beliefs are random or irrational as such, and not to be measured against what we usually hold, for there are different things it can mean to be near or far from each other (see Diamond 2005, 100–108). Both the analogy to the laboratory experiment and the comparison to the airplane case bring out that what happens in the discussion between a religious believer and an atheist or agnostic is that their common ground dissolves as the different preconditions for mutual understanding emerge, preconditions for gaining even a circumstantial understanding of what a particular shared experience may or may not mean. The "pictures" both overwhelm the interpretation of that situation and lead to a reflection on how one should lead one's life, rather than to a more comprehensive account of that particular experience at least one of the two contestants may want to call radical. Here, the religious becomes important for the constitution of subjectivity (see Bax 2011, 102–5).

Although it is not entirely clear what alternative to mere dismissal Wittgenstein offers in the *Lectures on Religious Belief*, one essential point is that the actual conversation, even on such seemingly indisputable experiences as a miracle happening where everything suggests a miracle may/could/should happen, cannot be avoided, and that there is no way to force someone into believing one's own interpretation of that event. Thus, if a given experience has a meaning one wants to call religious, it is discovered nowhere else but in the actual discussion of its significance, a discussion always open to disagreement. This disagreement arises, however, not only because we may have completely disagreeing world views, but insofar as we are interpretive beings, concerned with understanding a particular event we are confronted with, even if it is most unusual.

Commenting on these ideas from the question how to describe or interpret a radical experience, this emphasis on the factual discussion to be had seems Wittgenstein's way to avoid the alternative of excess and denial: Even the experience of "blood coming out of something" does not have to either be an excessive confirmation of some pre-understanding nor must it be dismissed as completely meaningless, something about nothing should be said. Both these extremes of thinking about such experience, much like the two patterns of radical experience that Nietzsche described, have been revealed as being themselves doubtful exaggerations in view of what might actually be said in view of such an experience. Even a radical experience, in other words, may be talked about into the most ordinary ways. What you may want to take as a hint of a

Göttliches occurs nowhere but within the world of our ordinary language and of ordinary things.

4. Hermeneutical ideas on a theory of radical experience

Wittgenstein's example underscores the necessity of interpretation, indirectly acknowledged, too, in Nietzsche's idea of the creation of Gods for the sake of understanding, and accepted by Heidegger, too, in his description of how we can understand poetry as radical (aesthetic/religious/national) experience. Yet, Wittgenstein also brings to the fore the eminent possibility of disagreement and dispute in establishing the meaning of a radical experience. Nietzsche, on the other hand, undercuts the description of factual disagreement through his scheme of opposite extremes, and Heidegger, when envisioning some most fundamental confrontation with poetry, also downplays the possibility of actual disagreement, paradoxically exposing this experience as both eminently meaningful and at the same time withdrawn in its meaning, foreclosing, like Nietzsche, a conflict of interpretations. It is only when Heidegger's discourse on radical experience is reoriented toward the (phenomenologically accessible) interpretation of meaning in determining the appearance of things that a more complex way of understanding is offered. Yet, although Heidegger's *Göttliche* are less determinate than the "duplicity" (Nietzsche 1980, 26; 1967, 33) of Apollo and Dionysus, they are to be understood in no other context than the fourfold. Both the early Nietzsche and the Heidegger of the fourfold subscribe to a particular metaphysical "picture" that a radical experience would affirm rather than destroy, foregoing a true philosophical confrontation with this experience (Wittgenstein 1958, §115). And although Heidegger discovers the place of the radical in the ordinary, he still takes the radical, though inconspicuous, experience of a thing as confirmation of a philosophical understanding of the world, converting a discourse on the denial of meaning into an understanding of excessive meaning as being part of the supposedly most ordinary way we understand the world. Something similar would hold true of the *Tractatus*: The mystical affirms what can be talked about precisely by (de)limiting it.

If Heidegger's emphatic insistence on the denial of meaning counters describing radical experience simply as excessive confirmation in service of a particular "picture" or conceptual scheme, what is attractive about later Wittgenstein's treatment of radical experience is that, by bringing into view the unavoidable disagreement in its interpretation, he all the more explicitly avoids putting the supposed excessive meaning in service of denying the plurality of conceptual schemes. Especially in view of radical experiences, forcing agreement by disallowing disagreement already on the level of worldviews or conceptual schemes would seem an all the more problematic move (see Forster 1993) and would mean to treat radical experiences unphilosophically from the very beginning of their interpretation. To treat them philosophically, however, involves awareness of the problems involved in taking radical experiences to be either denial or excess of meaning, for both these alternatives may conceal the necessity of interpretation, even if such interpretation must not be based on a particular reference frame or conceptual scheme. For it to be a philosophical account of radical experience rather requires that one relinquishes such foundation.

Interpretation does have a hold, however, in both the actual discourse on experience and in the meaning of things and events as they appear. The texts studied here, among many others, testify to the human capacity to make at least some sense of such experiences and to the wish to communicate their meaning to others. In such a way, they are fragments of a *phenomenological* account of radical experience, and such an account would begin nowhere but in the life-world. If these texts are accounts of radical experience, they will be read and understood in a world that is by and large independent of whatever may be discovered in interpreting radical experiences. The quite ordinary world in which a dispute about the interpretation of radical phenomena will take place, is not dependent on the formation of a particular conceptual scheme, which would, in turn, need confirmation through its excess.

Whether one conceives of hermeneutics as description of hermeneutical space (Figal 2010), as the philosophy concerned with the emergence of meaning in nonmeaning (Angehrn 2011) or simply as the philosophical study of how we understand texts (Forster 2007), it situates itself as prior to any particular assumption about how radical experience should be understood. This is why the distinction of denial and excess of meaning may serve as a hermeneutical key to understanding radical experience and how interpretations of their meaning have been articulated in (philosophical) texts. These interpretations, however, will always rival in view of the phenomenon that they are ultimately directed at.[2]

[2] I am indebted to Jussi Backman, Andrew Benjamin and Antonio Cimino for helpful discussion and comments.

References

Angehrn, Emil. 2010. *Sinn und Nicht-Sinn: Das Verstehen des Menschen*. Tübingen: Mohr Siebeck.

Bax, Chantal. 2011. *Subjectivity after Wittgenstein: The Post-Cartesian Subject and the "Death of Man."* London: Bloomsbury.

Cavell, Stanley. 2006. *Philosophy the Day after Tomorrow*. Cambridge, MA: Harvard University Press.

Conant, James. 2011. "Wittgenstein's Method." In *The Oxford Handbook of Wittgenstein*, edited by Oskari Kuusela and Marie McGinn, 620–45. Oxford: Oxford University Press.

Diamond, Cora. 2005. "Wittgenstein on Religious Belief: The Gulfs Between Us." In *Religion and Wittgenstein's Legacy*, edited by D. Z. Phillips and Mario von der Ruhr, 99–138. Aldershot: Ashgate.

Figal, Günter. 2001. "Forgetfulness of God: Concerning the Centre of Heideggers Contributions to Philosophy." In *Companion to Heidegger's Contributions to Philosophy*, edited by Charles E. Scott, Susan M. Schoenbohm, Daniela Vallega-Neu and Alejandro Vallega, 198–212. Bloomington: Indiana University Press.

Figal, Günter. 2010. *Objectivity: The Hermeneutical and Philosophy*. Albany, NY: SUNY Press.

Figal, Günter. 2012. "Nietzsche liest Aristoteles." *Internationales Jahrbuch für Hermeneutik* 11: 51–63.

Forster, Michael N. 1993. "On the Very Idea of Denying the Existence of Radically Different Conceptual Schemes." *Inquiry* 41 (2): 133–85.

Forster, Michael N. 2007. "Hermeneutics." In *The Oxford Handbook of Continental Philosophy*, edited by Brian Leiter and Michael Rosen, 30–74. Oxford: Oxford University Press.

Heidegger, Martin. 1977. *Gesamtausgabe*, vol. 5: *Holzwege*. Edited by Friedrich-Wilhelm von Herrmann. Frankfurt am Main: Klostermann.

Heidegger, Martin. 1981. *Gesamtausgabe*, vol. 4: *Erläuterungen zu Hölderlins Dichtung*. Edited by Friedrich-Wilhelm von Herrmann. Frankfurt am Main: Klostermann.

Heidegger, Martin. 1989. *Gesamtausgabe*, vol. 65: *Beiträge zur Philosophie (Vom Ereignis)*. Edited by Friedrich-Wilhelm von Herrmann. Frankfurt am Main: Klostermann.

Heidegger, Martin. 1993. *Basic Writings*. Edited and translated by David Farrell Krell. New York: Harper Collins Publishers.

Heidegger, Martin. 2000. *Gesamtausgabe*, vol. 7: *Vorträge und Aufsätze*. Edited by Friedrich-Wilhelm von Herrmann. Frankfurt am Main: Klostermann.

Heidegger, Martin. 2009. *The Heidegger Reader*. Edited with an introduction by Günter Figal, translated by Jerome Veith. Bloomington: Indiana University Press.

Heidegger, Martin. 2012a. *Contributions to Philosophy (Of the Event)*. Translated by Richard Rojcewicz and Daniela Vallega-Neu. Bloomington: Indiana University Press.

Heidegger, Martin. 2012b. *Bremen and Freiburg Lectures.* Insight Into That Which Is *and* Basic Principles of Thinking. Translated by Andrew J. Mitchell. Bloomington: Indiana University Press.

Hölderlin, Friedrich. 1992. *Sämtliche Werke und Briefe*, vol. 1: *Gedichte.* Edited by Jochen Schmidt. Frankfurt am Main: Deutscher Klassiker Verlag.

McManus, Denis. 2006. *The Enchantment of Words: Wittgenstein's Tractatus Logico-Philosophicus.* Oxford: Clarendon Press.

Nietzsche, Friedrich. 1967. *The Birth of Tragedy and The Case of Wagner.* Translated by Walter Kaufmann. New York: Random House.

Nietzsche, Friedrich. 1980. *Sämtliche Werke. Kritische Studienausgabe in 15 Bänden*, vol. 1: *Die Geburt der Tragödie, Unzeitgemäße Betrachtungen I–IV, Nachgelassene Schriften 1870–1873.* Edited by Giorgio Colli and Mazzino Montinari. Berlin: De Gruyter.

Wittgenstein, Ludwig. 1958. *Philosophische Untersuchungen / Philosophical Investigations.* Translated by G. E. M. Anscombe. 2nd ed. Oxford: Blackwell.

Wittgenstein, Ludwig. 1963. *Tractatus Logico-Philosophicus.* Translated by D. F. Pears and B. F. McGuinness. London: Routledge & Kegan Paul.

Wittgenstein, Ludwig. 1970. *Lectures and Conversations on Aesthetics, Psychology, and Religious Belief.* Edited by Cyril Barrett. Oxford: Basil Blackwell.

Wrathall, Mark, and Morganna Lambeth. 2011. "Heidegger's Last God." *Inquiry* 54: 160–82.

6

"A way of living, or a way of assessing life":

Wittgenstein on Faith, Reason and Philosophy

Chantal Bax

Like Nietzsche and Heidegger, Wittgenstein is known as a fierce critic of traditional metaphysics, or even of metaphysics *tout court*. He is famous for taking issue with the philosophical attempt to unearth the ultimate essence of, for example, mind and meaning, as well as for proposing to stop doing philosophy in favor of a therapeutic dismantling of philosophical pseudo-problems. Even if Wittgenstein does not explicitly point the blame to pernicious historical predecessors, this is not unlike the undertakings of the afore-mentioned critics of metaphysics. Yet, whereas Nietzsche's and Heidegger's negative appraisals of traditional philosophy cannot be separated from their criticisms of religion and theology, Wittgenstein had a life-long interest in religious belief, both on a personal and on a philosophical level. In addition to his well-known remarks on matters such as logic and language, Wittgenstein's *Nachlass* contains numerous entries in which he reflects on the specific nature of faith and tries to safeguard religion from distorting misinterpretations. From earlier writings such as the *Notebooks* to later ones such as the *Lectures on Religious Belief*, this was an ongoing concern of Wittgenstein.

If we follow Heidegger in explaining metaphysics as onto-theology, this may raise the question as to how fundamental Wittgenstein's critique of traditional philosophy can, in fact, be said to be. For can a thinker really herald in the end of metaphysics when he does not properly dissociate himself from the all too intimate relation between philosophy and theology? Should Wittgenstein's persistent interest in religion not at least make us wary of mentioning him in the same breath as Nietzsche and Heidegger? Or is this perhaps precisely where an important, though inadvertent, similarity between all three thinkers lies? It has, after all, been argued that Heidegger himself was unable to fully break with philosophy's onto-theological heritage, just as he had claimed that Nietzsche was the last metaphysician rather than the first to move beyond that tradition. The main difference between Nietzsche, Heidegger and Wittgenstein would then simply lie in the latter's wearing his religious interests more plainly on his sleeve.

In what follows, I take my lead from these questions and have a closer look at Wittgenstein's reflections on faith and religion. I will not explicitly compare his thoughts (and/or "unthoughts") with those of Heidegger and Nietzsche, but will simply examine Wittgenstein's consecutive writings on the topic of religious belief. I will subsequently discuss—albeit necessarily briefly—the *Notebooks* and *Tractatus*, the *Remarks on Frazer's* "Golden Bough," the *Lectures on Religious Belief*, and *Culture and Value*. This discussion will show that earlier works such as the *Tractatus* and later ones such as the *Lectures on Religious Belief* all make a similar point: They unfailingly emphasize the categorical distinction between faith and reason.[1] That is not to say that there are no differences between Wittgenstein's successive writings on religion, far from it. I will, however, precisely make use of these (seeming) tensions in order to tease out what Wittgenstein more exactly means when he argues that faith and reason should be strictly distinguished. It is this insight, I will argue, that Wittgenstein does not tire of defending and that accordingly safeguards him from an all too intimate relation with (onto-)theology.

Wittgenstein's interest in religion, in other words, did not bring him to explain everything in religious terms. Indeed, as will become clear below, he repeatedly takes issue with certain religious orthodoxies. However, this does not yet mean that Wittgenstein is entirely safe from each and every onto-theological suspicion, as I will point out in the penultimate section of my essay. For Wittgenstein's very last collection of remarks, published as *On Certainty*, may seem to suggest that he ultimately gave up the faith–reason dichotomy. *On Certainty*, after all, argues that reason is dependent on something that can perhaps only be explained as faith: a whole set of beliefs that one does not subscribe to on the basis of investigation and experimentation, but rather on the basis of a kind of trusting. In order to fully understand the relation between Wittgenstein and religion, I will therefore also comment on *On Certainty*. After showing that the Wittgensteinian concept of certainty should not be equated with faith, I will end

[1] Hence, I will show that there is a clear continuity in Wittgenstein's philosophy when it comes to his reflections on religion. Apart from this, however—and even though the debate about the continuity in Wittgenstein precisely concerns the antimetaphysical nature of (either just the later part or the entirety of) his oeuvre—I refrain from taking an explicit stand either for or against "mono-Wittgensteinianism" (Conant 2007).

this essay by arguing that my explorations nonetheless give reason to rethink the widespread picture of Wittgenstein as an uncompromising antiphilosopher. Not because he failed to keep religion out of philosophy, but because his religious reflections show him to be a constructive thinker rather than one that only dismantles the confused views of others.

1. The *Notebooks* and *Tractatus*

Wittgenstein's earliest reflections on faith and religion can be found in his famous first—and only—book, the *Tractatus Logico-Philosophicus*, as well as in the *Notebooks* that he wrote between 1914 and 1916, and that already explore important Tractarian topics. With their entries on truth tables and the basic structure of propositions, these works may seem to be purely about logic and language. On closer inspection, however, Wittgenstein's earliest writings can be said to ultimately concern what the *Tractatus* rules out from being talked about, namely, ethics and religion.[2] Indeed, Wittgenstein precisely consigns the ethico-religious to the realm of the ineffable in order to safeguard its absolute significance. What we can speak of—to very briefly summarize the Tractarian account—are (possible) states of affairs; the effable and the factual, in other words, coincide.[3] States of affairs are, however, arbitrary and accidental: No fact exists necessarily, and all that is might just as well have been different.[4] According to the early Wittgenstein, therefore, that ethics and religion cannot be spoken of need not be deplored. It has to do with their being, far from arbitrary and accidental, of the most valuable nature. Or as one of the Tractarian theses states: "Propositions can express nothing that is higher" (Wittgenstein 1963, §6.42).

Yet, even if Wittgenstein thus supports a strict distinction between random fact and absolute value, this does not come at the cost of cutting the ethico-religious off from our life on earth completely. That is to say, as the *Notebooks* explain, "the world in itself is neither good nor evil," but good and bad "enter

[2] Wittgenstein, for instance, made this explicit in the letters he wrote to his hoped-for publisher Ludwig von Ficker (Wittgenstein 1969, 35–36). Let me also use this opportunity to explain my terminology: here and throughout these pages, I use the words *ethics* and *religion* interchangeably. I permit myself this liberty because Wittgenstein—as will become clearer soon—takes ethics and religion to both concern something like the meaning of life, and accordingly does not make a strict distinction between the ethical and the religious himself.

[3] See, for example, Wittgenstein 1963, §§1, 4.01, 4.05, 4.1 and 7.

[4] See, for example, Wittgenstein 1963, §§5.634, 6.3, 6.37, 6.41, and Wittgenstein 1961, 80.

through the *subject*" (Wittgenstein 1961, 79)—or the willing subject, to be precise, for as Wittgenstein continues: "If the will did not exist, neither would there be that center of the world, which we call the I, and which is the bearer of ethics" (Wittgenstein 1961, 80). This means that if we want to understand Wittgenstein's positive account of the ethico-religious—in addition to his negative characterization of it as ineffable and nonfactual—we need to have a closer look at his notion of the will.[5]

Now the early Wittgenstein uses the word *will* in a rather idiosyncratic way; the Wittgensteinian will relates to our actions very differently than what we normally call by that name. In everyday parlance, our activities are considered to be both the effect and the instrument of the will: We say that a person performs actions as a result of her willing them and in order to make what she desires come about. According to the Tractarian system, however, only logical relations are truly necessary. What may look like cause and effect—like my willing to raise my arm and my raising my arm—are merely two events that happen to succeed each other.[6] If the ethico-religious will is to preserve its nonarbitrariness, therefore, it cannot enter into the world by means of activities that just happen to follow it. Similarly, the will cannot be directed at concrete and contingent objects like an everyday intention, on pain of being contaminated by their utter insignificance. Wittgenstein accordingly reserves the term *wish* for what we would normally call an intention, and defines the ethical *will* by means of its contrast to the everyday wish. Unlike the latter, the will "is not the cause of the action but is the action itself," and if the will furthermore "has to have an object in the world, [it] can be the intended action itself" (Wittgenstein 1961, 87). Or as Wittgenstein summarizes the will–wish distinction: "Wishing is not acting. But willing is acting" (ibid.).

Suggesting that the ethico-religious will wholly coincides with our doings and sayings, this move may seem completely fruitless in safeguarding the noncontingency of ethics and religion. At this point, however, it should be noted that Wittgenstein actually operates with more than one notion of the world. According to the *Tractatus*, that is, the world can on the one hand be considered to be a specific constellation of facts, and in this sense, it is a place of accident

5 Or at his notion of the willing subject, to be exact, which would, in fact, also require a closer look at Wittgenstein's distinction between different kinds or senses of subjectivity. For lack of space, however, I will not discuss the difference between, for example, the willing and the metaphysical subject here; see either Stokhof 2002 (chapter 4) or Bax 2011 (chapter 4) for an explanation thereof.

6 See Wittgenstein 1963, §6.374; Wittgenstein 1961, 73, 77 and 86.

and arbitrariness. One can however also look at the world as a whole, or at the existence of the world as such. From this perspective, Wittgenstein maintains, one can see "that the facts of the world are not the end of the matter" (Wittgenstein 1961, 74), or that it does not really matter "*how* the world is," but rather "*that* it is" (Wittgenstein 1963, §6.44) in the first place. That is not an inner-worldly fact among others but can be explained in supra-factual terms: "the miracle is that the world exists" (Wittgenstein 1961, 86).

It is the world in this sense at which the will is directed, Wittgenstein makes clear: "my will enters into the world completely from outside as into something that is already there" (Wittgenstein 1961, 74). Lest we forget that the will is different from the everyday wish, however, it does not enter into the world in order to manipulate it and to "bend the happenings of the world to my will" (Wittgenstein 1961, 73). For as Wittgenstein continues, because the will enters completely from the outside, "we have the feeling of being dependent on an alien will . . . and what we are dependent on we can call God" (Wittgenstein 1961, 74). According to Wittgenstein, to briefly unpack what he is implying here, we humans always already find ourselves in a world that is not of our own making and most of which is beyond our power to change. Combined with the assumption that the existence of the world is of inherent and absolute value, this means that all human beings face one fundamental existential task: We have to accept the world as we happen to find it and live in peace with whatever life throws our way. Hence, only someone who no longer tries to alter or avoid anything, whether of a pleasant or of an unpleasant nature, can genuinely say: "I am doing the will of God" (Wittgenstein 1961, 75), Wittgenstein maintains.

The will is thus distinguished from the wish by being directed at the world as such rather than at concrete objects, as well as by being of an accepting rather than of an instrumental nature. This also distinguishes what Wittgenstein calls the "good" or "happy" from the "bad" or "unhappy"[7] will, for not everyone will be up to this existential task. In line with the will not concerning particular facts, the difference between the happy and the unhappy person is not one of concrete states of affairs but of the world in its totality: "If good or evil willing affects the world," Wittgenstein explains, "it can only affect the boundaries of the world, not the facts. . . . The world must, so to speak, wax or wane as a whole. As if by accession or loss of meaning" (Wittgenstein 1961, 73). The happy person, in other words, is able to reverently see the world as a meaningful whole, whereas

[7] See Wittgenstein 1963, §6.43; Wittgenstein 1961, 73, 74, 75, 77, 78 and 81.

the unhappy individual only constantly struggles to bend particular states of affairs her way.

It can now also be explained how willing is not of the same factual nature as concrete doings and sayings, even if the way Wittgenstein distinguishes it from the everyday wish may suggest that willing wholly coincides with acting. For just as the will is not directed at particular facts but concerns the world as a whole, it does not consist of a momentary attitude to the world but is rather a matter of how a person leads his or her entire life. "The will is an attitude of the subject to the world" (Wittgenstein 1961, 87), as Wittgenstein accordingly also puts it. This means that when Wittgenstein writes: "One cannot will without acting" (ibid.), he does not have isolated activities in mind, but is instead referring to someone's doings and sayings as they testify to his or her overall outlook on existence. Whether a particular action conforms to the will of God thus depends on the kind of life it belongs to, and the will can conversely be said to be an intrinsic part of a person's every word and deed. Instead of being fact-like itself, it should rather be understood as the ethico-religious dimension of human conduct.

This, then, to bring my discussion of the early writings to a close, is how Wittgenstein explains that the ethico-religious will pertains to the world without being of the world. According to the *Notebooks* and *Tractatus*, religion is a worldly affair in the sense that it concerns an attitude toward existence that is manifested in everything a person says and does. It can, however, not be reduced to discrete words and deeds because a person's ethico-religious attitude only shows itself from the perspective of his or her life as a whole. Moreover, rather than being directed at isolated inner-worldly facts, religious belief concerns the way a person does—or does not—lead his or her life in appreciation of the world in its entirety.

2. The *Remarks on Frazer's* "Golden Bough"

If the *Notebooks* and *Tractatus* already suggest that the ethico-religious cannot be captured in language and thought, the *Remarks on Frazer's* "Golden Bough" makes the distinction between faith and reason into one of its main topics. Written partly in 1931 and partly in 1948, the title refers to a sizeable study by the once well-known anthropologist Sir James Frazer. The latter's twelve-volume study *The Golden Bough*—the first part of which was published in 1890—details numerous rites and rituals, ranging from ancient Rome until nineteenth-century

Europe, but does not merely rest content with giving a descriptive account of these ceremonies. In or through *The Golden Bough*, Frazer also advances a specific interpretation of ritualistic behavior, according to which it simply constitutes a form of proto-scientific activity. Unacquainted with the blessings of modern science, to reconstruct Frazer's train of thought, presecular persons find themselves at the mercy of nature. In an attempt to control these forces, they accordingly postulate hypotheses about the workings of the world, such as the conjecture that "any effect may be produced by imitating it" (Frazer 1994, 9). This explains why they would stick pins into dolls resembling their enemies, or sprinkle some of the scarce water on the ground in times of drought. Yet as hypotheses about natural mechanisms, "primitive" beliefs have been disproved by modern science. It is therefore only a matter of time before all religious behavior will have disappeared from contemporary life, as Frazer's final prediction holds.

According to *The Golden Bough*, then, religion boils down to a false theory of nature and rituals are the instruments by means of which this pseudo-science is put into practice. Given Wittgenstein's earlier objections to a factual and instrumental view on faith, it should come as no surprise that he takes issue with Frazer's explanation. In the various *Remarks on Frazer*, Wittgenstein gives several arguments against and counterexamples to the anthropologist's account. He, for instance, points out that the same person who pierces a doll resembling his enemy does not construct a miniature house when he needs a home, but immediately builds a life-size one.[8] Similarly, people always perform rites of daybreak right before sunrise, but when they need light at other times during the night, they simply burn lamps.[9] This goes to show, Wittgenstein argues, that rituals cannot be explained as forms of misguided proto-science. For if they would be based on a theory about the workings of nature, we would expect these (purported) hypotheses to inform all of someone's activities. That is however not necessarily the case.

It is not even the case for rituals themselves, Wittgenstein furthermore observes. Think of the ritualistic or rite-like behavior that even (alleged) modern persons sometimes engage in, like caressing a photo of one's absent spouse or pursing one's lips when one wants someone else to stop being so loud.[10] When we perform such activities, we do not do so on the basis of a quasi-scientific

[8] See Wittgenstein 1993, 125.
[9] See Wittgenstein 1993, 137.
[10] See Wittgenstein 1993, 123 and 141.

theory, so why would this be any different for (so-called) primitive persons? Wittgenstein concludes that neither presecular rituals nor contemporary ones originate in empirical conjectures: "Burning in effigy. Kissing the picture of one's beloved. That is *obviously not* based on the belief that it will have some specific effect on the object which the picture represents" (Wittgenstein 1993, 123).

Frazer is thus wrong to claim that primitive beliefs are false hypotheses because he is wrong to claim that they are hypotheses in the first place. Rituals cannot be said express misguided proto-science because those who engage in them are not trying to get right about natural mechanisms at all. The fault, Wittgenstein sneers, is accordingly Frazer's rather than the believer's: "An error only arises when magic is interpreted scientifically" (Wittgenstein 1993, 125). Far from forming a kind of erroneous pseudo-science, religious belief cannot be considered to be a type of science in the first place.

There are some striking similarities between this analysis and the account of religion offered in the *Notebooks* and *Tractatus*. Like the early Wittgenstein's holding that the ethico-religious transcends the factual sphere, he takes Frazer to task for explaining religion as a theory about the workings of the natural world. And like the Tractarian claim that human behavior cannot be seen as the instrument of the will, Wittgenstein argues that Frazer is wrong to present rituals as the means for manipulating natural forces. Yet, there are also noticeable differences between the earlier works and the *Remarks on Frazer*, some that may even seem to overrule the similarities that I have just identified.

After dismissing Frazer's account, Wittgenstein reflects on the reasons people might have for performing rituals if these cannot be said to flow from a desire to understand and control nature. And as Wittgenstein observes, someone engaged in ritualistic behavior perhaps simply tries to vent certain all too human emotions.[11] Instead of conducting a scientific experiment, after all, a person sprinkling water over dried-out soil can be said to express hope or despair. Someone kissing a picture of his or her beloved is similarly manifesting yearning or affection rather than putting a theory into practice. This brings Wittgenstein to propose that rituals have no other goal than being an outlet for our feelings, if

[11] See Wittgenstein 1993, 123, 125 and 157; cf. Cioffi 1998 (155–82) and Clack 2001. For example, Phillips (2003) takes issue with Clack, yet while I have my doubts about the latter's analysis too, mine are different from Phillips's. I do not hold that Wittgenstein cannot be ascribed any positive account whatsoever, but rather wonder whether Clack's alternative explanation of rituals meets his own goal: avoiding the dangers of the expressivist account. For while Clack opposes that account for making religion into a language game "neither requiring justification nor susceptible to criticism" (2001, 12), he concludes that ritualistic behavior cannot be explained or understood and should simply be looked on in awe.

that can be considered to be a proper goal in the first place: "It aims at satisfaction and achieves it. Or rather: it *aims* at nothing at all; we just behave this way and then we feel satisfied" (Wittgenstein 1993, 123). As opposed to saying that rituals originate in empirical conjectures, Wittgenstein accordingly continues: "Such actions may be called Instinct-Actions" (Wittgenstein 1993, 137).

If this expressivist perspective forms a welcome antidote to Frazer's overly intellectualist view, it also makes for a difference with Wittgenstein's own earlier writings, no matter the similarities I already mentioned. For in contrast to the earlier claim that a person's doings and sayings are indicative of her general outlook on life, some of the *Remarks on Frazer* suggest that rituals serve no higher purpose than the channeling of emotions: That the believer simply acts for the sake of acting, or perhaps for the sake of her psychological well-being, but is at any rate not conveying her acceptance of the world as she happens to finds it.

Yet, regardless of this seeming contrast, the *Remarks* cannot be said to unambiguously defend an expressivist account. In response to Frazer's over-intellectualization of a specific ancient ritual, for instance, Wittgenstein does not claim that religious behavior has no intellectual component whatsoever, but simply replies: "where that practice and these views occur together, the practice does not spring from the view, but they are both just there" (Wittgenstein 1993, 119). Wittgenstein may similarly observe that "the characteristic feature of ritualistic action is not at all a view, an opinion," but immediately goes on to add: "although an opinion—a belief—can itself be ritualistic or part of a rite" (Wittgenstein 1993, 129).

This suggests that even though Wittgenstein fundamentally disagrees with Frazer's taking religion to be a quasi-scientific theory, he does not therefore embrace a diametrically opposed, purely expressivist account. When Wittgenstein talks of instincts and emotions, he is not claiming that ritualistic behavior always serves to give vent to our feelings and can never be indicative of a larger existential outlook. In such remarks, Wittgenstein does not show himself to be a full-blown expressivist, but is simply offering a number of counterexamples to Frazer's account. This means that the differences between the *Remarks on Frazer* and the earlier works do not automatically overrule the similarities between these parts of Wittgenstein's oeuvre. In his objections to Frazer, Wittgenstein can accordingly even be said to elaborate on ideas already present in the *Notebooks* and *Tractatus*. For like these earlier works, the *Remarks* first and foremost argue that religion does not concern the world in a factual or instrumental sense, and that faith can therefore not be approached purely theoretically or scientifically.

3. The *Lectures on Religious Belief*

With the *Lectures on Religious Belief*, we have arrived in 1938. These particular fragments were not written by Wittgenstein himself but consist of notes taken down by his Cambridge students during three lectures that he gave on the topic of faith and religion. In the transcripts of his students, we can see Wittgenstein trying to understand the specific nature of religious belief, mainly by contrasting it with nonreligious beliefs and statements. And not unlike the *Remarks on Frazer*, the *Lectures* look to science as one of the main realms or spheres from which religion should be distinguished.

The religious believer, for instance, differs from the scientist, Wittgenstein points out, in the evidence he gives—or rather does not give—for his convictions. Take a person who has the "unshakable belief" (Wittgenstein 1997, 55) that there will be a Last Judgment and who is willing to forgo everything on account of that. While we would expect him or her to have extraordinarily good grounds for such a life-altering conviction, he or she may not be able to give any reasons for his or her belief, or may offer evidence that is actually far from persuasive. The believer could, for instance, say he or she was informed about the coming of Judgment Day in a dream he or she once had. Normally, however, we would not consider that to be a proper proof at all, and might accordingly reply with a remark such as: "You are basing your belief on extremely slender evidence, to put it mildly" (Wittgenstein 1997, 61).

Yet it would be a mistake, Wittgenstein continues, to conclude that the believer is not yet entitled to his conviction and should look for further evidence in support of his faith. That religious persons base enormous things on the slightest grounds indicates that evidence and experimentation do not play the same role in religion as in science, and that terms such as *evidence* and *know* do not have the exact same meaning in these different contexts.[12] "It is for this reason," Wittgenstein reminds his students, "that different words are used" for religious as opposed to scientific convictions: "'dogma,' 'faith'" (Wittgenstein 1997, 57), for instance. Indeed, this goes to show that ultimately, religious belief does not have anything to do with knowledge and evidence at all. For a mere list of established facts, no matter how conclusive, "wouldn't be enough to make me change my whole life" (Wittgenstein 1997, 57), and "a religious belief might" conversely "fly in the face of [a scientific] forecast" (Wittgenstein 1997, 56). So

[12] See Wittgenstein 1997, 54, 56, 57 and 59.

when a self-proclaimed religious believer does approach his or her convictions scientifically, he or she is not anchoring his or her faith ever more firmly but actually undermines the very nature of religion.[13] True faith, Wittgenstein holds, is not only "not reasonable, but … doesn't pretend to be" (Wittgenstein 1997, 58).

This should not be taken to mean that religious belief is wholly irrational; Wittgenstein is rather saying that instead of being either reasonable or unreasonable, no reason-related qualifications apply to religion.[14] Why this is the case becomes clearer in his discussion of the contrast, not between the believer and the scientist, but between the believer and the atheist or agnostic. Wittgenstein imagines a conversation in which someone professes his belief in a Last Judgment and his interlocutor responds by saying: "Well, I'm not so sure. Possibly" (Wittgenstein 1997, 53). We would say, Wittgenstein notes, that there is "an enormous gulf" (ibid.) between these persons, which is remarkable, because if they would be discussing, say, whether there is a German airplane overhead, we would not be speaking of gulfs or divides. In such a case, after all, the uncertainty is (relatively) easy to resolve: The discussion partners know which object is under discussion and only need to have a closer look to see whether it is of German or of British making.

That we speak of an enormous gulf when someone is not so sure about the religious conviction of another is precisely due to the fact that they lack such common ground, Wittgenstein explains: "I give an explanation: 'I don't believe in …,' but then the religious person never believes what I describe" (Wittgenstein 1997, 55). The believer, in other words, does not affirm certain facts that the agnostic goes on to doubt or deny. Their discussion is not a matter of the nonbeliever contradicting the believer or of believing the opposite to the believer.[15] The difference is rather one, Wittgenstein suggests, between a person who always thinks of Judgment Day and a person for whom this simply never crosses his or her mind: "Here believing obviously plays much more this role: … a certain picture might play the role of constantly admonishing me, or I always think of it. Here, an enormous difference would be between those people for whom the picture is constantly in the foreground, and the others who just didn't use it at all" (Wittgenstein 1997, 56).[16]

13 See Wittgenstein 1997, 56, 59 and 61.
14 See Wittgenstein 1997, 58 and 59.
15 See Wittgenstein 1997, 53 and 55.
16 See also Wittgenstein 1997, 54, 55 and 71.

If the *Lectures on Religious Belief* are of a kind with the *Remarks on Frazer* in arguing against a scientific interpretation of religion, the latter suggestion stands in sharp contrast with the emphasis the *Remarks* place on the unreflective and expressive nature of rituals. In the *Lectures*, Wittgenstein precisely explains religious belief in terms of thoughts and pictures, and even states: "The expression of belief may play an absolutely minor role" (LRB p. 55). Yet, just as the *Remarks* do not unambiguously reject each and every role for views or attitudes, the *Lectures* cannot be said to present religion as a strictly intellectual affair. In fact, what Wittgenstein means when he talks of a religious picture is similar to what he defended in the *Notebooks* and *Tractatus*.

Now, the later Wittgenstein does not often have positive things to say about pictures, about how we are in the grip of pictures and misunderstand what pictures themselves are;[17] this topic even pops up in the *Lectures* as well.[18] Yet, as these notes also make clear, religious pictures should be distinguished from ordinary ones: "The word 'God' is amongst the earliest learnt—pictures and catechisms, etc. But not the same consequences as with pictures of aunts" (Wittgenstein 1997, 59). Wittgenstein recalls that he was never shown what or whom pictures of God exactly depict, and that questions about God's existence were also discouraged. This goes to show that religious pictures play a very different role in human life than other kinds of images. And in contrast to his reservations about pictures more generally, Wittgenstein holds that religious pictures do have a positive or constructive role to play. For as Wittgenstein explains, the person who believes in Judgment Day more precisely makes this picture into a "guidance for his life" (Wittgenstein 1997, 53). His faith, in other words, is not a matter of simply having repeated thoughts about the Last Judgment, or of merely thinking about and not acting on it. That the believer always has a certain picture in mind "will show, not by reasoning or by appeal to ordinary grounds for belief, but rather by regulating for in all his life" (Wittgenstein 1997, 54). He will, for instance, "take everything that happened to him as a reward or punishment" (ibid.), Wittgenstein points out.

The *Lectures* use the term *picture*, then, to underscore that the lives of the faithful do not form a mere succession of events. With the idea of there being a Last Judgment, say, believers place everything they do and undergo in a specific light and accordingly make their lives into a meaningful whole. Like the happy person

17 See, for example, Wittgenstein 1953, §§1, 115, 139–42, 295, 305, 422–27 and 526.
18 See Wittgenstein 1997, 66 and 67.

from Wittgenstein's earlier work, the believer from the *Lectures* is first and foremost characterized by his or her leading a life of unity and significance. This means that there is ultimately not an enormous gulf between the *Lectures* and the *Remarks on Frazer*. For even though the former mention thoughts and pictures when explaining religious belief, and the latter precisely stress the non-intellectualist nature of religion, the *Lectures* do not defend a purely theoretical account. As these notes make clear, after all, someone declaring his or her belief in Judgment Day is not making a statement about certain isolated reflections; he or she is rather saying something about the meaning and structure in his or her actual existence.

To also elaborate in a little more detail on the similarities with Wittgenstein's very first reflections on religion, this again repeats key elements from the *Notebooks* and *Tractatus*. For similar to these earlier writings, the *Lectures* hold that faith does not concern the same kind of facts that science deals with, and that it moreover manifests itself, not in discrete doings and sayings, but rather in the believer's life as a whole. If there is a difference with the earlier works, this lies in the *Notebooks* and *Tractatus* reserving the label "religion" for a very specific outlook on existence—namely, one of acceptance and appreciation—whereas the *Lectures* seem more liberal as to how the believer can make his or her life into a meaningful whole. When it comes to the basic structure of religious belief, however, Wittgenstein still appears to subscribe to the same view.

4. *Culture and Value* and *On Certainty*

This is confirmed when we look at *Culture and Value*, a collection of remarks on various sociocultural topics written between 1914 and 1951, thus spanning all of Wittgenstein's working life. In the consecutive entries that address religious matters, Wittgenstein unsurprisingly defends insights similar to those in the *Notebooks*, the *Tractatus*, the *Remarks* and the *Lectures*.

In *Culture and Value*, too, he underscores that religion does not concern facts for which proofs can be given and that it can accordingly not be explained in scientific or theoretical terms. Writing in 1937, for instance, Wittgenstein remarks that "Christianity is not a doctrine" (Wittgenstein 1984, 28) and that "the Gospels might, historically speaking, be demonstrably false and yet belief would lose nothing by this" (Wittgenstein 1984, 32).[19] *Culture and Value*

[19] See also Wittgenstein 1984, 29, 30, 63 and 81.

moreover offers the same reason as the earlier writings as to why there is no room for reason or theory in faith. "Amongst other things Christianity says," Wittgenstein notes in 1946, "that sound doctrines are all useless. That you have to change your *life*. (Or the *direction* of your life)" (Wittgenstein 1984, 53). No theory, in other words, has the existential impact of a religious belief and can direct the believer's entire existence. As Wittgenstein accordingly declares: "although it's *belief*, it's really a way of living, or a way of assessing life" (Wittgenstein 1984, 64).

This latter quote can be used to sum up Wittgenstein's account of religion from the earliest to the latest writings. It after all succinctly captures both how faith differs from reason and how it is about existence as a meaningful whole: The two main elements of Wittgenstein's religious reflections in the *Notebooks*, the *Tractatus*, the *Remarks* and the *Lectures*, even though these different collections do not always explain these insights in the exact same way, as I have pointed out in the foregoing.

Yet, in addition to recapitulating the earlier analyses, *Culture and Value* identifies an important implication of the idea that faith is a way of living that I have not yet discussed. For if religion is a matter of making one's life into a meaningful whole, it is up to individual believers themselves to take on this existential task and chose their very own direction in life. As Wittgenstein accordingly remarks in 1930—and in contrast to the much milder tone in the (somewhat later) *Remarks on Frazer*—"Everything ritualistic . . . must be strictly avoided, because it immediately turns rotten" (Wittgenstein 1984, 8). Or as he explains in 1950: "A theology which insist on the use of *certain particular* words and phrases, and outlaws others, does not make anything clearer" (Wittgenstein 1984, 85). In Wittgenstein's view, in other words, faith cannot consist in simply imitating certain pregiven doings and sayings. Consistently going to church on Sundays, say, is neither a necessary nor a sufficient condition for true belief. Whether (verbal) behavior is religious depends on the kind of existence it is part of, and someone might also choose a highly unorthodox direction in life.

Indeed, as *Culture and Value* furthermore makes clear, this means that religious education is or at least should be different from a child's upbringing in other respects. On declaring belief to be a way of living, Wittgenstein writes: "Instruction in religious faith . . . would have to take the form of a portrayal . . . of [the instructor's] system of reference, while at the same time being an appeal to conscience. And this combination would have to result in the pupil himself, of his own accord, passionately taking hold of the system of reference" (Wittgenstein

1984, 64).[20] Hence, in contrast to, say, teaching a child to speak his or her mother tongue, it is not up to his or her parents or community which rules the child ends up following or which direction he or she gives to life. That is ultimately an individual choice, Wittgenstein maintains.

Having touched on Wittgenstein's earlier as well as later reflections on religion, let me briefly return to the questions that I raised in the introduction to this essay before underscoring the significance of Wittgenstein's individualistic account of belief. To come back to the issue of Wittgenstein and onto-theology, even though his criticism of metaphysics goes together with a sustained interest in religion rather than with a thoroughgoing critique thereof, this does not mean that the comparison with Nietzsche and Heidegger does not hold. For throughout his religious writings, Wittgenstein defends a strict distinction between faith and reason. In all of his reflections on religion, he argues against confusing these different spheres of life and thought. What is more, as was for instance hinted at in the above discussion of the *Lectures on Religious Belief*, Wittgenstein takes issue with accounts of God that take him to be a special kind of entity, different from other entities, yet still representable in pictures, for instance. On a Wittgensteinian view, religious matters should never be taken to be fact-like or thing-like. His interest in religion moreover did not prevent him from being highly dismissive of dogmatic and orthodox theology, as can be seen from some of the *Culture and Value* remarks that I just quoted.

All of this however does not yet safeguard Wittgenstein from each and every onto-theological suspicion, though it is another part of his oeuvre that might still arouse such suspicions. I am referring to *On Certainty*, Wittgenstein's very last collection of remarks, in which he argues that our intellectual pursuits—*pace* both the skeptic and the antiskeptic—are made possible by our always already taking a host of unquestioned presuppositions for granted. Even though *On Certainty* primarily addresses epistemological rather than religious topics, it has been brought into connection with Wittgenstein's interest in religion nonetheless.

Some interpreters, namely, argue that faith falls in the same category as the unspoken assumptions that Wittgenstein takes to underlie our everyday practices: That faith, in Wittgensteinian terminology, falls in the same category as certainty.[21] Such interpretations are inspired by the fact that there are several interesting similarities between Wittgenstein's writings on religion and his

[20] See also Wittgenstein 1984, 81 and 86.
[21] See, for example, Kober 1993 and Schönbaumsfeld 2007.

arguments in *On Certainty*. He, for instance, observes that both in the statement "I know there is a God" and in the statement "I know I have a hand," *know* is not used in its ordinary sense, and explains that in the former as well as in the latter case, this (quasi-)claim is not based on evidence like a scientific statement.[22] This seems to suggest that Wittgenstein came to see religious belief as a form of certainty—which would mean that at the end of his life, he let go of the strict distinction between faith and reason in the sense that he came to make reason dependent on faith. For on this interpretation, faith and reason are not two distinct domains or discourses, but faith has on the contrary infiltrated the former domain.

An investigation into the relation between Wittgenstein and onto-theology is therefore not complete if it does not also take *On Certainty* into account. Yet despite appearances to the contrary, these remarks do not automatically establish an intimate relation between Wittgenstein and the philosophico-religious tradition.

For even if Wittgenstein holds that both professions of faith and certainties differ from ordinary knowledge claims, he does not give the same arguments in both cases. Whereas he claims that certainties cannot be proven right or wrong because they form the preconditions for knowledge and investigation to begin with, Wittgenstein maintains, as I have argued, that religious belief does not lend itself to empirical testing because it is an existential rather than an empirical matter.[23] As a result—and in contrast to a person's certainties—the pictures that guide the faithful are often in the front rather than in the back of their minds.[24] As Wittgenstein was furthermore all too familiar with himself, once one has passionately committed to a particular existential direction, this does not mean that one's religion is always already exempt from doubt.[25] The question whether one is really being true to it, that is, might arise at any point.[26] Moreover, to come back to the last *Culture and Value* entry that I quoted, whereas Wittgenstein maintains that a person always already shares his or her certainties with other

22 See, for example, Wittgenstein 1997, 59, 54, 56, 57; and Wittgenstein 1972, §§84, 103, 138, 205.

23 Cf., for example, Wittgenstein 1972, §§105, 115, 308 and 509.

24 Cf., for example, Wittgenstein 1972, §§87, 103, 147 and 159.

25 As I however argue in Bax 2013, it is not the case that what we currently take to be certain can never become the topic of discussion. Being confronted with someone who challenges some of our basis presuppositions might for instance trigger the long and difficult process of changing our outlook on particular things (like race or gender, say). If there is a parallel between certainty and faith, it is perhaps at this stage (though the "certainties" at issue no longer function as certainties here).

26 See, for example, Wittgenstein 1984, 26, 56, 57 and 86.

members of the community, and that children simply "swallow them down" (Wittgenstein 1972, 143) in the course of their upbringing,[27] he holds that a person ultimately has to chose his or her direction in life all by him- or herself. Or as he urged his friend Maurice O'Drury: "Make sure that your religion is a matter between you and God only" (Drury 1981, 117). Far from equating religious belief and certainty, then, Wittgenstein takes faith to be rather precarious and highly individual affair.

5. Concluding remarks

As my reading of both Wittgenstein's religious writings and his reflections in *On Certainty* makes clear, Wittgenstein's continuing interest in religion did not bring him to explain everything in religious terms or to disregard differences such as that between certainty and faith. From his earliest to his latest writings, he argued that religion is an immensely important issue that should not be described in terms foreign to it—which seems to go as much for reason as for certainty. According to Wittgenstein, faith is "a way of living, or a way of assessing life" (Wittgenstein 1984, 64), and can therefore not be approached as a purely factual or empirical matter. Yet even if something similar holds for certainties, faith is unlike the latter in that one's way of assessing life can be an uncertain affair in which the (religious) community ultimately plays a minor role.

Hence, Wittgenstein's writings are not more onto-theological than those of Nietzsche and Heidegger, at least, not in his own definition of faith.[28] My explorations in the foregoing, however, point to another way in which one might question the customary picture of Wittgenstein as a fierce antimetaphysician or even outright antiphilosopher, aiming to bring philosophy to a stop rather than hoping to constructively (albeit differently) contribute to the work of his philosophical predecessors. For in his reflections on religion, Wittgenstein does not merely rest content with dismantling mistaken views on religious belief; he also uses these analyses to formulate a more appropriate account of faith, namely,

[27] See also Wittgenstein 1972, §§94, 100, 144, 159, 279 and 472.

[28] This is not necessarily refuted by Wittgenstein's once remarking "I am not a religious man but cannot help seeing every problem from a religious point of view" (Drury 1981, 94). For as he emphasizes in the first part of this statement, Wittgenstein is not religious in the traditional sense of the word, and the religious point of view he refers to is, in line with what I argued above, a matter of not letting oneself be guided by received conventions and of not reducing everything one philosophizes about to clear and distinct facts or things.

as a meaningful existential direction. This suggests that Wittgenstein, although he has important qualms about philosophy as it is traditionally undertaken, does not necessarily think that philosophers should entirely refrain from trying to understand the nature of, for example, religious belief. He merely maintains that they should be careful not to lose sight of important details and distinctions while doing so.[29] Regardless of the fact that his sustained interest in religion does not yet make him into an onto-theologian, then, Wittgenstein's ongoing reflections on faith and religion still give food for thought as to the supposed antiphilosophical nature of his oeuvre.

References

Bax, Chantal. 2011. *Subjectivity after Wittgenstein: The Post-Cartesian Subject and the "Death of Man."* London: Continuum.

Bax, Chantal. 2013. "Reading *On Certainty* through the Lens of Cavell: Scepticism, Dogmatism and the 'Groundlessness of Our Believing.'" *International Journal of Philosophical Studies* 21 (4): 515–33.

Cioffi, Frank. 1998. *Wittgenstein on Freud and Frazer.* Cambridge: Cambridge University Press.

Clack, Brian R. 2001. "Wittgenstein and Magic." In *Wittgenstein and Philosophy of Religion*, edited by Robert L. Arrington and Mark Addis, 12–28. London: Routledge.

Conant, James. 2007. "Mild Mono-Wittgensteinianism." In *Wittgenstein and the Moral Life: Essays in Honor of Cora Diamond*, edited by Alice Crary, 31–142. Cambridge, MA: MIT Press.

Drury, Maurice O'Connor. 1981. "Conversations with Wittgenstein." In *Ludwig Wittgenstein: Personal Recollections*, edited by Rush Rhees, 112–89. Totowa: Rowman & Littlefield.

Frazer, James. 1994. *The Golden Bough: A Study in Comparative Religion, Volume I* (first edition 1890). Richmond: Curzon Press.

Kober, Michael. 1993. "On Epistemic and Moral Certainty: A Wittgensteinian Approach." *International Journal of Philosophical Studies* 5: 365–81.

Phillips, Dewi Zephaniah. 2003. "Wittgenstein, Wittgensteinianism, and Magic: A Philosophical Tragedy?" *Religious Studies* 39: 185–201.

Schönbaumsfeld, Genia. 2007. *A Confusion of the Spheres: Kierkegaard and Wittgenstein on Philosophy of Religion.* Oxford: Oxford University Press.

[29] See the second chapter of Bax (2011) for a more detailed reading of Wittgenstein as an "alter-philosopher" rather than an antiphilosopher.

Stokhof, Martin. 2002. *World and Life as One: Ethics and Ontology in Wittgenstein's Early Thought*. Stanford, CA: Stanford University Press.

Wittgenstein, Ludwig. 1953. *Philosophical Investigations*. Translated by Elizabeth Anscombe. Oxford: Blackwell.

Wittgenstein, Ludwig. 1961. *Notebooks 1914–1916*. Edited by Georg Henrik von Wright and Elizabeth Anscombe, translated by Elizabeth Anscombe. New York: Harper & Row.

Wittgenstein, Ludwig. 1963. *Tractatus Logico-Philosophicus*. Translated by David Pears and Brian McGuinness. London: Routledge.

Wittgenstein, Ludwig. 1969. *Briefe an Ludwig von Ficker*. Edited by Georg Henrik von Wright. Salzburg: Otto Müller Verlag.

Wittgenstein, Ludwig. 1972. *On Certainty*. Edited by Elizabeth Anscombe and Georg Henrik von Wright, translated by Denis Paul and Elizabeth Anscombe. New York: Harper & Row.

Wittgenstein, Ludwig. 1993. "Remarks on Frazer's *Golden Bough*." In *Ludwig Wittgenstein: Philosophical Occasions 1912–1951*, edited by James Carl Klagge and Alfred Nordmann, 118–55. Indianapolis: Hackett.

Wittgenstein, Ludwig. 1997. "Lectures on Religious Belief." In *Lectures and Conversations on Aesthetics, Psychology and Religious Belief*, edited by Cyril Barrett, 53–72. Berkeley: University of California Press.

Wittgenstein, Ludwig. 1984. *Culture and Value*. Edited by Georg Henrik von Wright, translated by Peter Winch. Chicago: University of Chicago Press.

7

A Question of Faith:

Heidegger's Destructed Concept of Faith as the Origin of Questioning in Philosophy

Vincent Blok

Heidegger always had an ambiguous relationship to the domain of faith and religion. From the outset of his career, he already characterized philosophy as questioning—for instance, as "a proper stance within questioning itself, in the actualization of questionability"—and excluded religion from this questionability of philosophy (Heidegger 1994a, 197; 2001, 147–48). However, while his early destruction of the concept of religion can be seen as an attempt to conceive it as a characteristic of philosophical method (Blok 2011a), in his *Introduction to Metaphysics,* for instance, it becomes clear that faith is radically excluded from the questionability of philosophy (Heidegger 1983a, 9).[1] The reason for this is that faith already has an *answer* to the questionability of philosophy, and therefore, isn't able to have any relation to this questionability at all: "Faith has no place in thought" (Heidegger 1977, 372; 2002, 280).

In this essay, we raise the question whether the concept of faith can be radically excluded from Heidegger's method of questioning, as Heidegger claims in his *Introduction to Metaphysics.* In his phenomenology of questioning, for instance, Edmund Husserl characterized questioning precisely as a modality of faith (1985, 117–19). In the 1930s, Heidegger himself provided a formal analysis of thought as faith or belief; belief is *holding-to-be-true* (cf. 1986, 131–42; 1991, 121–32 and 1994b, 368–70; 1999, 257–59). Our hypothesis is that Heidegger's

[1] The concept of destruction can be seen as one of the main characteristic of Heidegger's philosophical method (Heidegger 1982; cf. Blok 2009). It does not only concern the destruction of metaphysical concepts such as "idea" or "ousia," but also the destruction of the metaphysical meaning of philosophical concepts such as will "logic," "world" or "God" in order to articulate a nonmetaphysical meaning of these concepts (cf. Heidegger 1976). In this respect, we can also speak about a destruction of the concept of religion in his early work (cf. Blok 2011a).

concept of holding-to-be-true is a necessary condition for the "original stance of inquiry [*Fragehaltung*] of philosophy" (1986, 110; 1991, 104–5) because only in a philosophical questioning that is characterized by faith as holding-to-be-true, the "truth of being" can originally resonate.

After our exploration of Heidegger's characterization of philosophy as questioning in the first part of this essay, we articulate three characteristics of Heidegger's concept of questioning in the second part. It becomes clear that Heidegger's method of philosophical questioning concerns the exploration (*Entfaltung*) of questioning in which the truth of being originally resonates (Heidegger 1986, 110; 1991, 104–5). After our exploration of Heidegger's concept of the *Entfaltung der Frage* in the second part, we inquire into the relation between philosophical questioning and Heidegger's destructed concept of faith in the third part.[2]

1. Philosophy as questioning

From the outset of his career, Heidegger characterized philosophy as questioning (Blok 2011a; Derrida 1989, 9). In his *Introduction to Metaphysics*, questioning is characterized in the following way: "Questioning is the genuine and the right and the only way of deeming worthy that which, by its highest rank, holds our Dasein in its power. This understanding of being of ours, and being itself altogether, is therefore what is most worthy of questioning in all questioning" (Heidegger 1983a, 89; 2000b, 87–88). Heidegger distinguishes however between two specific types of questioning: the "guiding question" (*Leitfrage*) of the metaphysical tradition and the "grounding question" (*Grundfrage*) that is inaugurated by himself. Let us focus on Heidegger's characterization of the method of questioning in the guiding and grounding question first.

According to Heidegger, metaphysics is the name for the questioning of philosophy. Although there are several philosophical questions, these questions are guided by one single question, namely, the question of last grounds (*archē*). This ground is unusual, because it is not a cause that we can locate somewhere in the world. It concerns the essence of things, that is, their *Wesensgrund*. The

[2] Parts of this article are already published in Blok (2015). While in that article we focus on the Heidegger and Derrida controversy about the nature of questioning in order to rehabilitate questioning as an essential characteristic of contemporary philosophy, in this article, we focus on Heidegger's concept of questioning in relation to his destructed concept of faith.

archē of things is found in their essence, that is, in the what-is of this being. All metaphysical questions can be reduced to this question of last grounds. It is this question that, according to Aristotle, was raised long ago, is still and always will be asked and continues to baffle us. The only endeavor of philosophy is therefore to find an answer to the question "what is being?" (Aristotle, *Metaphysics* 7.3.1028b2-8). For this reason, Heidegger calls this question the *guiding* question, the question that guides all our questioning in the metaphysical tradition.

The distinction between the guiding question of metaphysics and Heidegger's own method of questioning becomes clear if we consider the following remark[3]: "The more this question becomes the guiding question, and the longer it remains such, the less the question itself becomes an object of inquiry. Every treatment of the guiding question is and remains *preoccupied with the answer,* preoccupied with finding the answer" (Heidegger 1986, 212; 1991, 106–7). According to Heidegger, the primary aim of metaphysical questioning is to find an answer to this guiding question what being is and to secure this answer. This answer had several configurations in the metaphysical tradition—being appeared as *phusis,* as *ens creatum,* as *Wille zur Macht* and so on—but all these answers appeared within the framework of the guiding question; being appears for instance *as* will to power, and this concept of the will to power is an answer to the guiding question what being is. With the answer to the guiding question, the questioner adopts a certain stance or position toward the whole of being (Heidegger 1986, 212–13; 1991, 107–8). According to Heidegger, therefore, the guiding question is characterized by the preoccupation with the answer, while the nature of this questioning itself remains undeveloped and unexplored.

For Heidegger, philosophy consists in questioning as well. But contrary to the metaphysical tradition, Heidegger's method of questioning does not primarily consist in finding an *answer* to the questionability of philosophy: "Actually asking . . . means venturing to exhaust, to question thoroughly, the inexhaustible wealth of this question, by unveiling what it demands that we question. Whenever

[3] In this essay, we consider Heidegger's work not as a new philosophy with a new content compared with the metaphysical tradition, but as an effort to develop a new method of philosophical thought that is able to reflect on the hegemony of representation (*Vorstellung*) without itself being subjected to representation (cf. Oudemans 1990; Van Dijk 1991; Blok 2005). To the extent that Heidegger's thought has to be understood as a *methodical thinking*, it is legitimate to consider his *grounding* question as another *method* of questioning, compared with the guiding question of the metaphysical tradition. In this chapter, the *Entfaltung der Frage* concerns another method of questioning, compared with the *Beantwortung der Frage* (cf. section 2).

such a venture occurs, there is philosophy" (Heidegger 1983a, 10; 2000b, 8).[4] What demands us to question is the possibility that beings have of being "what they are and how they are" but also "*of not being*" and Heidegger's questioning consists in opening up beings in their question-worthiness (*Fragwürdigkeit*), that is, in their wavering between nonbeing and being (Heidegger 1983a, 32; 2000b, 31). For Heidegger, therefore, being is not the answer to the question of being as in the guiding question, but what is most question-worthy: "Henceforth an essential differentiation and clarification can be brought into the question of being. Such clarification is never an answer to the question of being but rather only a thorough grounding of questioning, awakening and clarifying the *power* to question this question—which always arises out of Dasein's distress and upward swing" (Heidegger 1994b, 75; 1999, 52). If we restrict ourselves to Heidegger's characterization of the *method* of questioning in the guiding question and the grounding question—rather than the *content* of both questions—we receive an indication of the difference between the two methods of questioning. The main difference between the metaphysical and the Heideggerian method of questioning has to be situated in the difference between the focus on finding and securing an answer (guiding question) and the openness of every possible answer (grounding question), that is, the openness to the "inexhaustible wealth of this question."[5]

In his *Introduction to Metaphysics*, it becomes clear that religious faith is radically excluded from this questionability of philosophy, which is at stake in the grounding question. Heidegger argues: "One who holds on to such faith as a basis can, perhaps, emulate and participate in the asking of our question in a certain way, but he cannot authentically question without giving himself up as a believer" (Heidegger 1983a, 9; 2000b, 7–8). The reason for this is that faith already has an *answer* to the questionability of philosophy—being as a whole appears *as ens creatum*, which is created by God *as ens increatum*. Therefore, faith has no relation to the questionability of philosophy at all. This is confirmed in an early lecture on *Phenomenology and Theology* from 1927, in which Heidegger conceives faith as the natural enemy of philosophy: "This peculiar relationship does not exclude but rather includes the fact that faith, as a specific possibility of existence, is in its

4 This doesn't mean that Heidegger's method of questioning rules out the possibility of an answer: "An answer is no more than the final step of the very asking; and an answer that bids adieu to the inquiry annihilates itself as an answer. It can ground nothing like knowledge. It rests content with the sheer opinions it traces and in which it has ensconced itself. A question—especially a question that involves being as a whole—can be appropriately answered only if it is adequately posed in the first place" (Heidegger 1986, 214; 1991, 192).

5 The overcoming of the guiding question consists therefore in the "Überwindung des bisherigen Fragens" (Heidegger 1986, 230).

innermost core the mortal enemy of the form of existence that is an essential part of philosophy and that is factically ever-changing" (1976, 66; 1998, 53).

But why is it the case that "what is asked for in our question, is for faith foolishness" (Heidegger 1983a, 9; 2000b, 8). Why is a "Christian philosophy a round square and a misunderstanding," as Heidegger argues in his *Introduction to Metaphysics*? Is it likely that faith is completely excluded from philosophical questioning, which constitutes the piety (*Frömmigkeit*) of thinking (Heidegger 2000a, 36)? If we focus our analysis on the nature of questioning in relation to faith, we can conclude that Heidegger's rejection of faith has nothing to do with the *content* of Christian faith. On the contrary, Heidegger rejects Christian faith here because it is preoccupied with finding answers. Only because of its preoccupation with finding and securing an answer does Christian faith fail to have a relation to the questionability of philosophy, *just like the guiding question of philosophy.* In this respect, we can conclude that, according to Heidegger, not only a Christian philosophy but also a metaphysical philosophy is a round square and a misunderstanding.

More important, Heidegger doesn't exclude the concept of faith from his method of questioning, but only a metaphysical concept of faith that is preoccupied with finding answers. In his *Contributions to Philosophy* from 1936 to 1938, on the one hand, Heidegger calls the ones who question *genuine believers* (Heidegger 1994b, 12; cf. also the third section of this essay). On the other hand, he even seems to be quite positive about questioning as a proper relation to God: "It remains to be considered whether the god possesses more divinity in the question concerning him or in the situation where we are sure of him and are able, as it were, to brush him aside or fetch him forward, as our needs dictate" (Heidegger 1986, 71; 1991, 68). If Heidegger excludes faith from his method of questioning, therefore, it is only faith that is concerned with finding and securing answers. A destructed concept of faith still may be associated with the questionability of philosophy.

Before we can explore this relation between Heidegger's method of questioning and a destructed concept of faith, in the next section, we first turn to a radical criticism of Heidegger's privilege of questioning.

2. Three characteristics of Heidegger's destructed concept of questioning

In this section, we explore three characteristics of Heidegger's method of questioning. In *What is Metaphysics?* we find a first characteristic of Heidegger's method of questioning: "First, every metaphysical question always encompasses the whole range of metaphysical problems. Each question is itself always the whole. Therefore, second, every metaphysical question can be asked only in such a way that the questioner as such is also there within the question, that is, is placed in question" (Heidegger 1976, 103; 1998, 82). The question of being concerns the "whole" of being. Our inclusion in the question of being makes clear that the "whole" of being cannot be understood in a metaphysical way, that is, as the principle, *archē* or ground of beings which is found in the essence of these beings (ontology) and in a highest being (theology).[6] Contrary to this onto-theological framework of traditional metaphysics, in which the being of *beings* is the point of departure, Heidegger's question of being concerns the whole of being or *being as such:* "According to the usual interpretation, the 'question of being' means asking about beings as such (metaphysics). But if we think along the lines of *Being and Time,* the 'question of being' means asking about being as such" (Heidegger 1983a, 21; 2000b, 20–21). It is this whole of being that is question-worthy (*das Fragwürdige*) according to Heidegger.

As a consequence of Heidegger's question concerning the whole of being, the questioner is *included* in this question; that which is asked—the question of being—in return affects the one who asks.[7] The primacy of questioning therefore doesn't testify to a humanistic tendency, as Derrida suggests (Derrida 1984, 125–26; Blok 2015), but is motivated by the *Sache*:

> The question of who man is must in its very formulation include in its approach man in and with his relations to beings as a whole; it must include in its inquiry the question of being as a whole. But we have just now heard that being as a whole can only be interpreted by human beings in the first place—and now man himself is to be interpreted in terms of being as a whole. Everything here is spinning in a circle. Of that there can be no doubt. The question is whether and

6 "Once we had explained the fact in this way, we characterized it as the unshaken point of departure for all the traditional metaphysical questioning about 'Being.' It begins with *beings* and is directed toward them. It does *not* begin with *Being* in the questionworthiness of *ist* openness" (Heidegger 1983a, 91; 2000b, 90).

7 "Yet what accounts for the fact that with this thought it is precisely thinking, and the conditions of thinking, that are emphasized so essentially? What else could it be but the thought's 'content,' what it gives us to think? Accordingly, the content does not really go into abeyance, as it seemed to; rather, it comes to the fore in a singular way. For now the conditions of the thought-process as such thrust their way to the forefront. With the thought in question, *what* is to be thought recoils on the thinker because of the *way* it is to be thought, and so it compels the thinker. Yet it does so solely in order to draw the thinker into what is to be thought" (Heidegger 1986, 204; 1991, 183; cf. 1983a, 7; 1986, 237).

in what way we can succeed in taking this circle seriously, instead of continually closing our eyes in the face of it.

Heidegger 1986, 110; 1991, 104–5

The whole of being cannot be understood in a metaphysical way and calls for a radical new method of questioning in which the questioner is included.

Heidegger calls his method an *exploration* of questioning. Already in *Being and Time*, Heidegger does not claim to answer the question of being, but to explore (*ausarbeiten*) this question.[8] The objective of this exploration (*Ausarbeitung*) of the question of being is to prepare *(ausarbeiten)* for a question, that is, the grounding question with regard to the sense (*Sinn*), or in his later work, the truth of being.[9] What is the nature of this exploration of questioning? Heidegger's answer is: "to explore the question as it is formulated, is to pose the question more essentially: in asking the question one enters explicitly into those relationships [*Bezüge*] that become visible when one assimilates virtually everything that comes to pass in the enactment of asking [*Vollzug*] the question" (Heidegger 1986, 214; 1991, 192 [my emphasis]).[10] In the enactment (*Vollzug*) of the exploration of the question of being, we experience the *relation* between being and thinking, that is, the sense or truth as the un-concealment of being.[11]

Which *relation* is opened by the *exploration* of the guiding question? The exploration of the guiding question first of all draws our attention to the *direction* of questioning and demands that we follow this direction, as is said in *Being and Time*. Every questioning is a seeking and every seeking takes its direction beforehand from what is sought (Heidegger 1993, 5). When we explore

8 "*Being and Time* can be evaluated only by the extent to which it is equal or unequal to the question it raises. There is no standard other than the question itself; only the question, not the book, is essential. Furthermore, the book merely leads us to the threshold of the question, not yet into the question itself" (Heidegger 1985, 23; 1991, 20–21).

9 "Rather, the determining ground of the development of the guiding question is to be sought in a renewed posing of the question, indeed, in a more original asking of that question" (Heidegger 1986, 214; 1991, 192). Also, the title of the "introductory remarks" of the aim of *Being and Time*—"*The exposition of the question of the sense of being*"—cannot be understood as an introduction to this book. Its aim is to explore questioning itself in view of the exposition ("exponere") of the question about the sense of being: "Quite apart from the fact that if we were to follow up the problem of the ontological structure of world-historical historizing, we would necessarily be transgressing the limits of our theme, we can refrain from this all the more because the very aim of this exposition is to lead us face to face with the ontological enigma of the movement of historizing in general" (Heidegger 1993, 389; 2008, 441).

10 See also the following remarks: "Henceforth as essential differentiation and clarification can be brought into the question of being. Such clarification is never an answer to the question of being but rather only a thorough grounding of questioning, awakening and clarifying the *power* to question this question—which always arises out of Dasein' distress and upward swing" (Heidegger 1994b, 75; 1999, 52).

11 For Heidegger's concept of the truth of being, see Blok 2011b.

(*auseinanderfalten*) what is at stake in the guiding question—what is being—it becomes clear that it is about being (*Gefragte*). This is not just any being, but the being of beings. But because all questioning is somehow a questioning of something—a being—this *Gefragte* is, second, dependent on that which is interrogated (*Befragte*). We call that which is interrogated the field of the question. This field is not a neutral domain of questioning of which we can take notice in an arbitrary way. Asking the guiding question has a specific aim because beings are asked about *insofar* as they are. That which is asked for (*Gefragte*) is in other words the essence of that which is interrogated (*Befragte*).[12] With this, questioning aims at the "being" of these beings. The "being" of these beings is that which is asked about (*Gefragtes*) of that which is interrogated (*Befragte*). The fact that beings are interrogated in their relation to being means, third, that beings themselves are already accessible and sufficiently determined; they are not question-worthy (*fragwürdig*).

In order to become that which is asked about (*Gefragte*), that which is interrogated (*Befragte*) is questioned in certain respects. These respects are determined by the aim or goal of our questioning; in this case, the definition of the being of beings as an answer to the guiding question "what" being is. Heidegger indicates that this being has been understood in a very specific way since the beginning of the metaphysical tradition.

Greek science (*epistēmē*) asks about *phusis*. Based on an example from Aristotle, Heidegger shows that for the Greeks *phusis* does not have the narrow meaning of a natural being. Furthermore, the *epistēmē phusikē* does not yet designate a scientific discipline directed toward the facts within a specific area of research only. The Aristotelian *epistēmē phusikē* is reflection primarily on the question of what life, time, space and so on are as that in which the variable, and therefore, the moved (*phusis*) is what it is, namely, the whole of being: "This ἐπιστήμη φυσική has as its object everything that in this sense belongs to φύσις and that the Greeks designate as τὰ φυσικά. The questioning proper to these sciences dealing with φύσις is the supreme question of the Prime Mover, of what this whole of φύσις is in itself as this whole" (Heidegger 1983b, 49; 1995b, 32–33).

12 In *Being and Time*, Heidegger does not only speak about the *Gefragte*, but also about the *Erfragte*. This *Erfragte* concerns the specific scientific-theoretical way the *Gefragte* is articulated: "In investigative questions—that is, in questions which are specifically theoretical—what is asked about is determined and conceptualized. Furthermore, in what is asked about there lies also *that which is to be found out by the asking* [*das Erfragte*]; this is what is really intended: with this the inquiry reaches its goal" (Heidegger 1993, 5; 2008, 24). In his later work, Heidegger seems to take these two moments of questioning—*das Gefragte* and *das Erfragte*—together (cf. Blok 2011a).

Aristotle asks about the whole of being through the question about the prime mover. This question about the prime mover, which is understood by Aristotle as the Divine without any specific religious doctrine, belongs to the *epistēmē phusikē*.

Phusis however not only designates nature in this sense. *Phusis* also concerns the *nature* of things, that is, nature in the sense of the essence of beings. The metaphysical question concerning being *as such* (*ousia*) is called the *ontological* question. In Aristotle's work, the different questions concerning *phusis* as the whole of being (theology) and as being as such (ontology) belong together in the *first philosophy* (*protē philosophia*). The beginning of Greek science is therefore the beginning of onto-theology.

What Heidegger tries to show with his *exploration* of the guiding question is that questioning is not neutral, but has a certain onto-theological arrangement (*Fügung*). This arrangement originates from the mode of questioning itself. What is asked about is the beingness (*Seiendheit*) of beings, which is understood as the whole of being (theology) and as being as such (ontology). In this specific arrangement of questioning, the interrogating relation between questioning and that which is asked about in questioning remains forgotten, according to Heidegger.[13]

Our exploration of Heidegger's concept of the *Entfaltung der Frage* makes clear that the exploration of questioning is something completely different than traditional questioning. It is not preoccupied with finding answers to the guiding question, but explores the self-evident relation between questioning and the interrogated. The exploration of questioning is indeed circular, but not a *circulus vitiosus*. Why? Characteristic of the exploration of questioning is that this questioning *withdraws* from beings without letting them go completely. The exploration of questioning "challenges beings as a whole, so to speak, outstrips them, though never completely. But this is precisely how the questioning gains its distinction. What is asked in this question rebounds on the questioning itself, for the questioning challenges beings as a whole but does not after all wrest itself

[13] "During the course of a facticallly experienced day, I deal with quite different things; but in the factical course of life, I do not become aware of the different *hows* of my reactions to those different things. Instead, I encounter them at most in the content I experience itself: factical life experience manifests an *indifference* with regard to the manner of experiencing. It does not even occur to factical life experience that something might not become accessible to it" (Heidegger 1995a, 12). The reason for this is the tendency of life to be absorbed by the world it is engaged in: "Living is caring and indeed is so in the inclination toward making things easy for oneself, in the inclination toward flight. Thereby arise a directionality toward possible mistakes as such, mistakability, decline, making things easy, fooling oneself, fanaticism, and exuberance" (Heidegger 1994a, 109; 2001, 81).

free from them" (Heidegger 1983a, 6; 2000b, 6). The exploration of the question doesn't ask about *beings*, but withdraws from these *beings* in order to have an indirect view of the *relation* between being and thinking, that is, the whole of being. In this respect, the circularity of Heidegger's exploration of questioning doesn't involve a "circular argument," but the "laying bare the ground" for any question and answer (Heidegger 1994a, 8; 2001, 7–8; cf. Heidegger 1993, 153). The *exploration* of questioning concerns the whole of being, that is, the relation between being and thinking which encircles every question and answer.

The exploration of questioning cannot be compared with the guiding question according to Heidegger: "Certainly, giving up the ordinary and going back into questioning interpretation [*Auslegung*] is a leap" (Heidegger 1983a, 185; 2000b, 188). Only a completely different mode of questioning has access to the *whole* of being. In *Being and Time*, Heidegger therefore argues:

> The being of beings "is" not itself a being. If we are to understand the problem of being, our first philosophical step consists in not μῦθόν τινα διηγεῖσθαι, in not "telling a story"—that is to say, in not defining beings as beings by tracing them back in their origin to some other being, as if being had the character of some possible being. Hence being, as that which is asked about, must be exhibited in a way of its own, essentially different from the way in which beings are discovered.
>
> Heidegger 1994a, 6; 2001, 6

Heidegger's other method of questioning consists precisely in the *exploration* of questioning with respect to the whole of being. The exploration of questioning withholds the answer and commits itself to the *relation* (*Bezug*), which is opened up by the *enactment* (*Vollzug*) of questioning.

In order to see what this method comprises, we focus for a moment on a specific thesis in Heidegger's *Introduction to Metaphysics*, in which he argues that a human being doesn't receive any particular emphasis:

> For what is this being, after all! Let us consider [*Vorstellen*] the Earth within the dark immensity of space in the universe. We can compare it to a tiny grain of sand; more than a kilometer of emptiness extends between it and the next grain of its size; on the surface of this tiny grain of sand lives a stupefied swarm of supposedly clever animals, crawling all over each other, who for a brief moment have invented knowledge. . . . Within beings as a whole there is no justification to be found for emphasizing precisely *this* being that is called the human being and among which we ourselves happen to belong.
>
> Heidegger 1983a, 6; 2000b, 4

Heidegger's aim here is not to utter an informative proposition about a being that is called human, but in an *indirect* way, he tries to show how human being is already understood, which *relation* between being and thinking is already presupposed in our proposition about beings.[14] This self-evident relation shows itself in an indirect way in our propositions *about* beings, so also in Heidegger's proposition we cited a moment ago. "*Stellen wir uns vor*" means that the self-evident relation between being and thinking is one of presentation and re-presentation, in which also human being is represented. "No justification [*Rechtsgrund*] can be found" means that the representing relation is self-evidently determined by the truth as *recht* and *richtig*, by the *rectitudo* between representation (thinking) and the represented (being). Philosophical thought only has access to this *relation* by its withdrawing from beings without its losing contact with these beings. Only because of the fact that we are included in representation (thinking) does the exploration of questioning have access to the representing relation between being and thinking that marks the whole of being.

With this, we encounter the philosophical meaning of the circularity of questioning the grounding question. Because questioning the grounding question withdraws from beings without losing contact, the risk is always that our questioning of the grounding question is still bound up to the representation of an *archē* or principle as an answer to the question of being[15]: "Our questioning is not yet the leap; for that, it must first be transformed; it still stands, unknowing, in the face of beings" (Heidegger 1983a, 8; 2000b, 6–7). The actual *enactment* of the grounding question presupposes a *Rückstoß* of that which is asked for in our questioning; being *itself* comes up and that we are touched by the hidden power of the question of being (cf. Heidegger 1983a, 15). And yet, our questioning cannot be understood in a passive way: "Thus the leading into the asking of the grounding question is not a passage over to something that lies or stands around somewhere; instead, this leading-to must first awaken and create the questioning. Leading is a questioning going-ahead, a questioning-ahead" (Heidegger 1983a,

14 "Philosophy is essentially untimely because it is one of those few things whose fate it remains never to be able to find a direct resonance in their own time, and never to be permitted to find such a resonance.... Philosophy, then, is not a kind of knowledge which one could acquire directly, like vocational and technical expertise, and which, like economic and professional knowledge in general, one could apply *directly* and evaluate according to ist usefulness in each case" (Heidegger 1983a, 10; 2000b, 9 [my emphasis]).

15 "Why the why? What is the ground of this why question itself, a question that presumes to establish the ground of beings as a whole? Is this Why, too, just asking about the ground as a foreground, so that it is still always a *being* that is sought as what does the grounding?" (Heidegger 1983a, 6–7; 2000b, 5).

22; 2000b, 21). Our questioning is only confronted with being when it *creates* the grounding question, "compelling oneself into the state of this questioning" (Heidegger 1983a, 3; 2000b, 1). With regard to our *questioning* of this question, Heidegger remarks: "The scope of our question is *so* broad that we can never exceed it" (Heidegger 1983a, 4; 2000b, 2). The grounding question concerns the whole of being in which thought is included and the scope of this whole is so broad that our questioning will never exceed it. Questioning the grounding question then means "venturing to exhaust, to question thoroughly, the inexhaustible wealth of this question, by unveiling what it demands that we question. Whenever such a venture occurs, there is philosophy" (Heidegger 1983a, 10; 2000b, 8). Our questioning of the grounding question always remains *finite* compared with the whole of being. With this, it is said that human thinking may compel oneself into the state of this questioning, but that the grounding question is in the end not achieved by *thinking* (Heidegger 1994b, 84–87; cf. 90–95). Our questioning of the grounding question is our being opened *to* this question *by* a demand of being, *if* it takes place (cf. Heidegger 1983a, 151). A philosophical thinking that really wants to be open to being touched by the hidden power of the grounding question must be able to *wait* for the awakening of this question as well. In this sense, Heidegger argues that that which is asked for in the grounding question in return affects the one who asks. Only thanks to this circularity of questioning does our questioning of the grounding question enable us to ask for the whole of being.

When the grounding question is really enacted, then it is a "distinctive occurrence," a "happening" which *comes* over *us*, which *visits* our thought (Heidegger 1983a, 7; 2000b, 6). Until that happens, our questioning is bound up with the representation of a being (principle, *archē*) as the answer to our question. With this, it becomes clear why human thinking may compel itself into the state of this questioning, but that this questioning is in the end opened *by* a call of being, or not: "being able to question means being able to wait, even for a lifetime" (Heidegger 1983a, 215; 2000b, 221).[16]

[16] See also the following remarks: "The thinking attempted in *Being and Time* (1927) sets out on the way to prepare an overcoming of metaphysics, so understood. That, however, which sets such thinking on its way can only be that which is to be thought" (Heidegger 1976, 368; 1998, 279). With regard to the coming generation of philosophers, Heidegger therefore argues: "The question of being is *the* leap into be-ing which man as seeker of be-ing enacts, insofar as he is one who creates in *thinking*. . . . But we of today have only this one duty: to prepare for that thinker by means of a grounding that reaches far ahead, of a secure preparedness for what is most question-worthy" (Heidegger 1994b, 11; 1999, 9).

When this *Rückstoß* actually takes place, then it disrupts our way of questioning, it disrupts ourselves as the ones who question. It results in a "leap away from all the previous safety of their Dasein, be it genuine or presumed" (Heidegger 1983a, 8; 2000b, 6), the farewell of the guiding question and the establishment of the grounding question with regard to the relation between being and thinking. Questioning the grounding question only *is* in this leap, which is not an act of human thought, but "attains its own ground by leaping, performs it in leaping [*er-springt, springend erwirkt*]. According to the genuine meaning of the word, we call such a leap that attains itself as ground by leaping an originary leap [*Ur-sprung*]: an attaining-the-ground-by-leaping" (Heidegger 1983a, 8; 2000b, 7). Contrary to the guiding question of the metaphysical tradition, Heidegger's grounding question is characterized by the questioning confrontation (*fragende Auseinandersetzung*) with the whole of being, and this questioning confrontation consists precisely in the exploration of questioning that we discussed in this section.[17]

3. Faith and the questionability of philosophy

In the previous section, we articulated three essential characteristics of Heidegger's method of questioning: (1) Dasein is included in the question of being, in which primarily (2) the relation (*Bezug*) between being and thinking or the whole of being is explored. (3) In our enactment (*Vollzug*) of the exploration of the question of being, the sense or truth of being in return affects the one who asks. This means that the question of being only *is* in the case of a call of being and at the same time, that this call of being only *is* in our exploration of the question of being. With this, we are sufficiently prepared to raise the final question, whether the concept of faith can be radically excluded from Heidegger's method of questioning, as he claims in his *Introduction to Metaphysics,* or not.

In his *Contributions*, Heidegger argues that the abandonment of the guiding question of metaphysics and the shift toward the grounding question presupposes that the truth of being becomes *distress*. According to Heidegger, the only one who can succeed in this is the one who questions: "It is only through the ones who question that the truth of be-ing becomes a distress. They are the genuine *believers,* because, in opening themselves up to what is essential to truth, they

[17] For Heidegger's method of confrontation, see Blok 2009.

maintain their bearing to the ground" (Heidegger 1994b, 12; 1999, 10). So contrary to his *Introduction to Metaphysics,* Heidegger argues here that the ones who question are the genuine believers. Why? "[B]ecause, in opening themselves up to what is essential to truth, they maintain their bearing to the ground" (Heidegger 1994b, 12; 1999, 10). Heidegger continues: "Those who *question* ... establish the new and highest rank of inabiding in the midpoint of be-ing, in the essential swaying of be-ing (enowning) as the midpoint" (Heidegger 1994b, 12–13; 1999, 10). It is important to notice that Heidegger, in his characterization of this specific type of questioning of the grounding question, precisely refers to the concept of *faith* or *belief.* Why is Heidegger referring here to the concept of belief, contrary to our findings in the previous section?

We follow Heidegger's *Contributions* for a moment in order to understand what is meant by this concept of belief and why the one who questions is positively seen as the true believer here. Belief or faith is not understood here in a confessional way, that is, "faith ... is not the particular form of belonging to a 'confession'" (Heidegger 1994b, 368; 1999, 357). He introduces a "destructed" concept of faith here, namely, "the essence of faith, grasped from within what is essential to truth" (Heidegger 1994b, 368; 1999, 357). This essence of faith is found in holding-for-true (Heidegger 1994b, 368; cf. Heidegger 1986, 132–42). In this destructed concept of faith, it is not the appropriation (*Aneignung, Zustimmung*) of what is "true" that is stressed.

Faith or believing is normally understood in opposition to knowing. In opposition to knowing, "faith ... means holding-to-be-true that which withdraws from knowing in the sense of explaining intuition [*erklärende Einsichtnahme*]" (Heidegger 1994b, 368; 1999, 258). Because faith is understood here from its opposition to knowing, Heidegger first asks what knowing actually means: "It is the knowing that knows what is essential to truth and accordingly determines it primarily in the turning [*Kehre*] from within this essence" (Heidegger 1994b, 368; 1991, 258 (modified). In Heidegger's characterization of knowing, we recognize our characterization of questioning in section 2: Philosophical questioning concerns the exploration of questioning, in which the truth of being originally resonates. Knowing "is originarily *holding oneself within the essential sway of truth*" (Heidegger 1994b, 369; 1999, 258).

On the one hand, it is clear for Heidegger that his concept of knowing is more originary than any faith, "which always refers to *something* that is true" (Heidegger 1994, 369; 1999, 258 [my emphasis]). But since his own *destructed* concept of faith as holding-to-be-true grasps from within what is the essence of truth,

Heidegger can on the other hand conceptualize the essence of knowing in terms of his destructed concept of faith:

> Thus, if one takes "knowing" in the heretofore sense of representation and possession of representation [*Vorstellung und Vorstellungsbesitzes*], then of course essential knowing is not a "knowing" but a "faith." However, this word then has an entirely different meaning, no longer that of holding-to-be-true, whereby truth is already known—even if confusedly—but rather that of holding-oneself-in-truth. And this holding oneself, having the character of a *projecting-open,* is always a questioning, nay *the* originary questioning as such by which man exposes himself to truth and puts what is essential up for decision.
>
> Heidegger 1994b, 369; 1999, 258

The essence of knowing is understood here as faith, namely, as holding-oneself-in-the-essence-of-truth, and this destructed concept of faith has the character of questioning.

A critical reader could argue that according to this quote, essential knowing is understood as faith only *if* we oppose knowing as representation and essential knowing (holding oneself within the essence of truth). This doesn't mean that essential knowing as such can be understood in terms of faith; faith is holding-for-true, and therefore, refers always to something—a being—which is true.[18] And yet, Heidegger argues that "holding-for-true changes according to what is true (and finally foremost according to truth and what is its ownmost)" (Heidegger 1994b, 368; 1999, 257). In this respect, the essence of faith is grasped from within what is essential to truth according to Heidegger. The connection between the essence of faith and the essence of knowing is found in the fact that in faith, not only a relation to what is believed in is at stake, but also to the one who believes him- or herself; *holding oneself.* According to Heidegger, knowing as "*holding oneself* within the essential sway of truth" can be understood as faith as "*holding-oneself*-in-truth," and this destructed concept of faith is characterized by questioning (Heidegger 1994b, 368–69; 1999, 257–58). Such a *positive* interpretation of the essence of knowing as faith and questioning is legitimate, since Heidegger already in the beginning of his *Contribution* stated that "the ones who question" are "the genuine *believers*" (Heidegger 1994b, 12; 1999, 10). This positive relation between Heidegger's destructed concepts of faith or belief as holding-oneself-in-truth and questioning is also confirmed toward the end of

18 I am very grateful for the critical discussions with my colleague Antonio Cimino regarding my interpretation of this passage in Heidegger's *Contributions.*

the *Contributions*, where he defines the "originary believer" once again in a comparable way:

> *Those who question* in this manner are the originary and actual believers, i.e., those who take *truth* itself—and not only what is true—seriously and from the ground up, who put to decision whether what is essential to truth holds sway and whether this essential swaying itself carries and guides us, the knowing ones, the believing ones, the acting ones, the creating ones—in short, the historical ones.
>
> Heidegger 1994b, 369; 1999, 258

More important for our objective in this chapter is the question why, according to Heidegger, is it the case that questioning is always a holding-oneself-in-the-truth? In order to answer this question, we consult another passage in which Heidegger conceptualizes faith or belief as holding-to-be-true, from a lecture course on Nietzsche's *Eternal Recurrence of the Same* from 1937.[19]

In this lecture course, the "formal essence" of faith is characterized as holding-to-be-true as well:

> From these words we derive one thing alone, but the most important thing: to believe means to take what is represented as true, and thus it also means to hold fast to the true and hold firm in the true. In belief there lies not only a relation to what is believed but above all to the believer himself. Taking to be true is holding firm in the true, hence holding in a dual sense: having a hold on something *and* preserving the stance one has. Such holding receives its determination from whatever it is that is posited as the true.
>
> Heidegger 1986, 134; 1991, 124

In the case of Nietzsche, it is clear that truth refers to something—a being—that is true according to Heidegger (cf. Heidegger 1986, 139), and therefore, that Nietzsche's concept of faith is embedded in the metaphysical representation of the beingness of beings. Although Heidegger primarily interprets Nietzsche's concept of faith in this passage, we can read this passage also *against the grain* as a formal indication of his own destructed concept of faith we developed before.[20]

Like in the *Contributions*, the "formal essence" of faith is characterized as holding-to-be-true in his lecture course from 1937. According to Heidegger, this

[19] See Derrida (2002, 97) for his discussion of this passage. Derrida wasn't able to read this passage in light of Heidegger's *Contributions to Philosophy.*

[20] For Heidegger's concept of the formal indication, see Oudemans 1990, Van Dijk 1991, Blok 2005. For the ambiguous relation between interpretation and confrontation in Heidegger's lecture courses on Nietzsche, see Blok 2009.

essence of faith depends on our concept of truth. In the case of Heidegger, what is posited as the truth is the truth of being. In a formal way and contrary to Nietzsche's concept of faith, therefore, we can characterize *Heidegger's* holding firm in the truth as a holding-oneself-within-the-truth of being (cf. Heidegger 1994b, 368–70). This concept of truth has also consequences for the nature of this *holding oneself.* Faith as holding-oneself-in-the-truth of being is formally characterized by (1) holding firm in the truth of being *and* (2) a holding oneself in the questioning stance in this questioning of the truth of being.

Here, it becomes clear why, according to Heidegger, questioning is always a *holding*-oneself-in-the-truth. Questioning is always such a holding-oneself-in-the-truth-of-being, because questioning the grounding question presupposes a holding firm in the truth of being *and* a holding oneself in the questioning stance in this questioning of the truth of being: "this holding oneself, having the character of a projecting-opening, is always a questioning" (Heidegger 1994b, 369; 1999, 258).

Our foregoing analysis of the exploration of questioning can help us to understand the necessity of faith or belief for questioning the truth of being. In order to enact the exploration of the question of being, what is asked (the truth of being) should in return affect the one who asks the question. On the one hand, the exploration of questioning as projecting-opening *holds* onto the truth of being; the exploration of questioning presupposes our disclosedness *for* the call of being *by* the call of being, if it takes place. This last condition is important, as we have seen, because the truth of being doesn't automatically have a hold on us in the age of the abandonment of being (*Seinsverlassenheit*). There is no call of being, nothing to hold oneself in. For this reason, Heidegger argues: "This originary believing, of course, has nothing in common with accepting that which offers immediate support and renders courage superfluous. Rather, this believing is persevering in the utmost deciding. This alone can once again bring our history to a grounded ground" (Heidegger 1994b, 369–70; 1999, 258–59). In this respect, it is clear that Heidegger's destructed concept of faith or belief cannot be understood, as Derrida suggests (Derrida 2002, 95), as trust in or conviction of (*fides, pistis*) the truth of being. This "persevering in the utmost deciding" consists in a holding-oneself-in-the-truth-of-being *without any hold*[21]: "Such holding firm and the stance it implies will be more genuinely successful the more

[21] Derrida's argument that Heidegger presupposes faith, namely, the understanding of being (*Seinsverständnis*) (Derrida 2002, 94–95), has to be rejected therefore.

originally they are determined by the stance, and the less exclusively they are defined purely by the hold they have on things; that is to say, they will be more genuinely successful if they are essentially able to revert back to themselves and not lean on things, not depend on them for support" (Heidegger 1986, 135; 1991, 124–25). This holding-oneself-in-the-truth of being concerns a specific *Haltung* or attitude that enacts a *possible* projection of the truth of being, a *possible* hold (Heidegger 1986, 140; 1994b, 368–70).[22] It is this *projecting-opening* attitude (*Haltung*) that holds onto its projection of the truth of being, holds onto the truth that discloses our questioning. Both ways of faith or belief as holding-oneself-in-the-truth of being essentially belong together in our philosophical questioning in the age of the abandonment of being. In the age of the abandonment of being, faith or belief is a necessary condition for the original stance of inquiry (*Fragehaltung*) of philosophy because the truth of being can only resonate in a philosophical questioning that is characterized by this *holding*-oneself-in-the-truth.

References

Aristotle. 1989. *Metaphysics*. Translated by H. Tredennick. Cambridge, MA: Harvard University Press.

Blok, Vincent. 2005. *Rondom de Vloedlijn. Filosofie en kunst in het machinale tijdperk. Een confrontatie tussen Heidegger en Jünger.* Soesterberg: Aspekt.

Blok, Vincent. 2009. "Communication or Confrontation: Heidegger and Philosophical Method." *Empedocles. European Journal for the Philosophy of Communication* 1: 43–57.

Blok, Vincent. 2011a. "Der 'religiöse' Charakter von Heideggers philosophischer Methode: *relegere, re-eligere, relinquere.*" *Studia Phaenomenologica* 11: 285–307.

Blok, Vincent. 2011b. "Establishing the Truth: Heidegger's Reflections on *Gestalt.*" *Heidegger Studies* 27: 101–18.

Blok, Vincent. 2015. "Heidegger and Derrida on the Nature of Questioning: Towards the Rehabilitation of Questioning in Contemporary Philosophy." *Journal of the British Society for Phenomenology* 46 (4): 307–23.

Derrida, Jacques. 1984. *Margins of Philosophy*. Translated by Alan Bass. Chicago: University of Chicago Press.

[22] See also the following passage: "Creation is communication—it is important to listen here in the right way. Every creating is a sharing with others. This implies that creation in itself grounds new possibilities of Being—erects them or, as Hölderlin says, founds them. Creation as such, and not only in its utilization, is a gift-giving. . . . To create is to share—the most genuine service we can think of, because the most reticent" (Heidegger 1986, 136–37; 1991, 127–28).

Derrida, Jacques. 1989. *Of Spirit: Heidegger and the Question*. Translated by Geoffrey. Bennington and R. Bowlby. Chicago: University of Chicago Press.
Derrida, Jacques. 2002. *Acts of Religion*. Translated by Gil Anidjar. New York/London: Routledge.
Dijk, R. J. A. van. 1991. "Grundbegriffe der Metaphysik. Zur formalanzeigenden Struktur der philosophischen Begriffe bei Heidegger." *Heidegger Studies* 7: 89–109.
Feher, Istvan M. 1987. "Religion, Theologie und Philosophie auf Heideggers Weg zu *Sein und Zeit*." *Heidegger Studies* 3: 103–45.
Heidegger, Martin. 1976. *Gesamtausgabe*, vol. 9: *Wegmarken*. Edited by Friedrich-Wilhelm von Herrmann. Frankfurt am Main: Klostermann.
Heidegger, Martin. 1977. *Gesamtausgabe*, vol. 5: *Holzwege*. Edited by Friedrich-Wilhelm von Herrmann. Frankfurt am Main: Klostermann.
Heidegger, Martin. 1982. *Gesamtausgabe*, vol. 31: *Vom Wesen der menschlichen Freiheit*. Edited by Hartmut Tietjen. Frankfurt am Main: Klostermann.
Heidegger, Martin. 1983a. *Gesamtausgabe*, vol. 40: *Einführung in die Metaphysik*. Edited by Petra Jaeger. Frankfurt am Main: Klostermann.
Heidegger, Martin. 1983b. *Gesamtausgabe*, vol. 29/30: *Die Grundbegriffe der Metaphysik. Welt-Endlichkeit-Einsamkeit*. Edited by Friedrich-Wilhelm von Herrmann. Frankfurt am Main: Klostermann.
Heidegger, Martin. 1985. *Gesamtausgabe*, vol. 43: *Nietzsche: Der Wille zur Macht als Kunst*. Edited by Bernd Heimbüchel. Frankfurt am Main: Klostermann.
Heidegger, Martin. 1986. *Gesamtausgabe*, vol. 44: *Nietzsches metaphysische Grundstellung im abendländischen Denken*. Edited by Marion Heinz. Frankfurt am Main: Klostermann.
Heidegger, Martin. 1991. *Nietzsche. Volumes One and Two*. Translated by David Farrell Krell. New York: HarperCollins.
Heidegger, Martin. 1993. *Sein und Zeit*. Tübingen: Max Niemeyer.
Heidegger, Martin. 1994a. *Gesamtausgabe*, vol. 61: *Phänomenologische Interpretationen zu Aristoteles. Einführung in die phänomenologische Forschung*. Edited by Walter Bröcker and Käte Bröcker-Oltmanns. Frankfurt am Main: Klostermann.
Heidegger, Martin. 1994b. *Gesamtausgabe*, vol. 65: *Beiträge zur Philosophie. Vom Ereignis*. Edited by Friedrich-Wilhelm von Herrmann. Frankfurt am Main: Klostermann.
Heidegger, Martin. 1995a. *Gesamtausgabe*, vol. 60: *Phänomenologie des religiösen Lebens*. Edited by Claudius Strube. Frankfurt am Main: Klostermann.
Heidegger, Martin. 1995b. *The Fundamental Concepts of Metaphysics. World, Finitude, Solitude*. Translated by William McNeill and Nicholas Walker. Bloomington: Indiana University Press.
Heidegger, Martin. 1998. *Pathmarks*. Edited by William McNeill. Cambridge: Cambridge University Press.
Heidegger, Martin. 1999. *Contributions to Philosophy (From Enowning)*. Translated by Parvis Emad and Kenneth Maly. Bloomington: Indiana University Press.

Heidegger, Martin. 2000a. *Gesamtausgabe*, vol. 7: *Vorträge und Aufsätze*. Edited by Friedrich-Wilhelm von Herrmann. Frankfurt am Main: Klostermann.

Heidegger, Martin. 2000b. *Introduction to Metaphysics*. Translated by Gregory Fried and Richard Polt. New Haven & London: Yale University Press.

Heidegger, Martin. 2001. *Phenomenological Interpretations of Aristotle. Initiation into Phenomenological Research*. Translated by Richard Rojcewicz. Bloomington: Indiana University Press.

Heidegger, Martin. 2002. *Off the Beaten Track*. Translated by Julian Young and Kenneth Haynes. Cambridge: Cambridge University Press.

Heidegger, Martin. 2008. *Being and Time*. Translated by John Macquarrie and Edward Robinson. New York: HarperPerennial.

Husserl, Edmund. 1985. *Husserliana*, vol. 28: *Vorlesungen über Ethik und Wertlehre (1908–1914)*. Edited by Ullrich Melle. Dordrecht/Den Haag: Kluwer.

Oudemans, Th. C. W. 1990. "Heideggers 'logische Untersuchungen.'" *Heidegger Studies* 6: 85–106.

Part Three

Pauline Resonances

8

Heidegger on Religious Faith:

The Development of Heidegger's Thinking about Faith between 1920 and 1928[1]

Ezra Delahaye

1. Introduction

In his 2014 Gifford lectures, Jean-Luc Marion stated that the faith-reason opposition that characterizes much of our thinking about both faith and reason stems from the traditional opposition between natural and revealed knowledge of God. The basic contention was that natural knowledge could be reached through thinking, but revealed knowledge only through faith. This emphasizes the opposition between faith and reason. In the work of Martin Heidegger, this is not the case. Heidegger opposes both the faith-reason opposition as well as the epistemological interpretation of faith. In this essay, I want to thematize the concept of faith in Heidegger.

Faith is, in itself, a varied and multifaceted concept. It can mean anything from trusting a person to the solipsistic belief that nothing exists except you. In this essay, I focus exclusively on Heidegger's concept of religious faith, which for Heidegger, is Christian faith. In a number of different texts, Heidegger deals with the concept of religious faith. Heidegger does not have a single account of faith. He uses faith in different ways throughout his oeuvre. For Heidegger, this faith follows an experience of conversion. Although faith is an important theme in many of his works, there are two texts in which Heidegger gives a more substantial

1 The present essay results from my PhD research project *Why Present-Day Philosophers Turn to Paul: Event, Comportment and Time*, financed by the Netherlands Organisation for Scientific Research (NWO). It is part of a larger project, *Overcoming the Faith-Reason Opposition: Pauline* Pistis *in Contemporary Philosophy* (project nr. 360-25-120), carried out at Radboud University and the University of Groningen.

account of Christian faith, namely, *Introduction to the Phenomenology of Religion* of 1920–21 and *Phenomenology and Theology* (Heidegger 1998, 39–62) of 1928. I will compare these texts in this contribution.

In the eight years between these two texts, Heidegger significantly changes his views on faith. In both cases, he discusses Christian faith. However, there are remarkable differences between his two accounts. In this essay, I want to discover why Heidegger evaluates faith so differently in these two texts. What has changed in his analysis between 1920 and 1928?

2. The phenomenology of religious life

In Heidegger's 1920–21 lecture course on Paul, faith plays an important role. This course thematizes the question of how primordial Christian life was lived; how did the earliest Christians live their Christianity? Heidegger does not read Paul as a dogmatic or a theoretician. For Heidegger, Paul gives an account of primordial Christian life as it was actually lived. The concept of faith in Heidegger's text can only be understood in this regard. Faith concerns how the early Christians lived.

Heidegger begins his reading of the letters of Paul with a methodological introduction. In this introduction, Heidegger discusses his method of phenomenology. In this early Freiburg period, Heidegger had a very specific approach to phenomenology, which differs from his later accounts. About phenomenology Heidegger states:

> What is phenomenology? What is phenomenon? Here this can be itself indicated only formally. Each experience—as experiencing, and what is experienced—can "be taken in the phenomenon," that is to say, one can ask: 1. After the original "what," that is experienced therein (*content*). 2. After the original "how," in which it is experienced (*relation*). 3. After the original "how," in which the relational meaning is *enacted* (*enactment*). But these three directions of sense (content-, relational-, enactment-sense) do not simply coexist. "Phenomenon" is the totality of sense in these three directions. "Phenomenology" is explication of this totality of sense.
>
> Heidegger 2004, 43

Thus, for Heidegger, phenomenology entails characterizing a phenomenon in a threefold way. Every phenomenon has a content, relation and an enactment. Only through asking the questions regarding the content, relation and enactment can a phenomenon be fully understood. Now, what do these three questions, these three sense-directions entail?

What is important in this phenomenological method for this present essay is the distinction Heidegger makes among content, relation and enactment. The content of a phenomenon is what is experienced therein. The relation is, in Heidegger's view, how one relates to the content of the phenomenon. It is the question of how the content is experienced. The enactment, finally, is how this relation is enacted in the life of the one experiencing it (see Cimino 2011, 217). This distinction is needed to understand precisely how Heidegger understands faith in his lectures on St. Paul. Faith is, as I argue, only the relation. This leads to the questions: Of which content is this a relation? How is this relation enacted?

After the methodological introduction, Heidegger starts to read Paul. Initially, he asks the question of Paul's self-understanding. How did Paul see himself and his own religious life? To this end, Heidegger starts out by reading the letter to the Galatians because it contains Paul's own report about his conversion (see Heidegger 2004, 47). In reading this letter, Heidegger comes to a number of conclusions.

Heidegger discovers that the proclamation of the *parousia* is central for Paul. For Paul, a new world has started after the death of Christ, a world that is characterized by its impending end in the *parousia* (see Heidegger 2004, 48). According to Heidegger, Paul believed that the *parousia* would come in his lifetime (see Heidegger 2004, 81). This realization that the world will end, linked to the insight that Christ will soon return and change the form of the world, is characteristic for Christian life according to Heidegger's reading of Paul. Heidegger is not interested in the question of whether this belief is true or not. Obviously, Paul's belief that the *parousia* would come in his own lifetime was false because the *parousia* has not happened. Heidegger's primary interest is how this belief changed the concrete lives of the early Christians.

It is Heidegger's contention that a phenomenon can only be properly understood when one considers its content, the relation to the content and the enactment of this relation. According to Heidegger, the history of philosophy has been dominated by a prejudice toward the formal. For example, take a random stone. In Heidegger's view, philosophy has never been interested in the properties of this specific stone, but only in its stone-ness, its essence. This is a purely formal determination that is uninterested in the content of the phenomenon at hand and is blind to the enactment. It is a purely theoretical—that is, only the idea of the stone is deemed important—view of the stone and of philosophy.

The question is, now, what this means for how Heidegger deals with the content of Paul's factical religious experiences recounted in his letters? The content of Paul's proclamation is not Heidegger's primary concern, but it is clear that Heidegger could not have developed his ideas on temporality without the specific content of Paul's letters. Heidegger reads what Paul says and then thematizes how this changes the lives of the Christians. Heidegger's interest in the content is guided by the questions of relation and enactment.

So, Heidegger is not interested in the content of the Pauline letters in the same way that believers or theologians are. He does not give a theological reading of Paul. It has already been noted that Heidegger finds a different account of temporality in the Pauline letters, but how does he find this? How does he read Paul's texts? He reads them as proclamation.

Now, the central question can be asked. In this phenomenology of Pauline proclamation, how does Heidegger thematize faith? About this he states: "The πίστις is not a taking-to-be true, or else the ὑπεραυξάνει would have no meaning; the πιστεύειν is a complex of enactment that is capable of increase. This increase is the proof of genuine consciousness" (Heidegger 2004, 76).

Heidegger begins by stating that faith is not a taking-to-be-true. Here, he rejects a very common interpretation of faith, in which faith is an epistemological category. With this, Heidegger shows himself to be well aware of the conflated conception of faith which is predominant in a certain philosophical tradition. He most notably opposes Nietzsche's account of Pauline faith, which he develops in *The Antichrist*. In it, Nietzsche claims Paul understood faith in terms of a taking-to-be-true and then concludes that Pauline faith is a "not-wanting-to-know what is true" (Nietzsche 2004, 157). Nietzsche interprets faith as an epistemological act and then concludes that it is a denial of truth. Heidegger, on the other hand, is more nuanced. He sees that there is an interpretation of faith that is a taking-to-be-true, but he, the Pauline conception of faith, is precisely not this (see McManus 2013, 146–47).

What, then, is Pauline faith? Heidegger continues by stating that having faith is a complex of enactment (*Vollzugszusammenhang*) (see Heidegger 2004, 76). That is to say, faith only becomes meaningful when it is enacted. What this means is that faith should be understood as a relation. It is a way of relating to a content that needs to be enacted in life. Now, the question is: What is this content? The content to which one relates faithfully is also the content of Paul's proclamation, namely, the message that the world has changed through the coming of Christ and his imminent return in the *parousia*. In Heidegger's reading of Paul, faith is the relationship one has to the *parousia*, to the fact that the world has changed and the remaining time is short. This is still relatively abstract. With the phenomenon of your wife, you relate to her as being specifically your wife. How should this be understood with faith? Why is the relation to the imminent *parousia* faith?

The shape of the world has changed. Time has grown short and the imminent return of the Messiah will change everything even more. This is the content of Paul's proclamation according to Heidegger. Faith is the way in which Paul relates to this content and the people who have heard and accepted his message. Relation is the question how a certain content is experienced. Faith, in this sense, is not in the first place a belief about a state of affairs in the world, but it is the belief that the first and imminent second coming of the Messiah affect my life concretely. Faith, then, is the realization that the world has changed and that, as a consequence, life also has to change. This change in life is the way in which faith is enacted. Faith needs to be enacted in lived life (see Fehér 2010, 47). For Heidegger, in his reading of Paul, the question of faith becomes the question of how faith is to be enacted.

About the enactment of faith, Heidegger states:

> Christians must be κλητοί, those who are called, as opposed to those who are cast away. . . . Paul sets those who have understood him up against those who, in more imminent expectation of the παρουσία, no longer work and loiter idly. . . . These people make an idling out of unconcern for the contingencies of life. They are concerned in a worldly manner, in all the bustling activity of talk and idling, and become a burden to the others (cf. I Thess. 4:11). Thus they have understood the first letter otherwise.
>
> Heidegger 2004, 76

In Heidegger's view, Paul demands that faith should be enacted in a very specific way by the Christians. Being a Christian, that is: Being faithful to the proclamation means living life as being called. Paul specifically rejects those people who enact their faith by sitting around and waiting idly. For Paul, sitting around and waiting for the *parousia* to happen is an improper enactment of the faith in the *parousia*. As Simon Critchley puts it, "faith … is not some passive state of bovine tranquility" (Critchley 2012, 170). This is the message of Paul's first letter to the Thessalonians.

In the second letter to the Thessalonians Paul only reinforces this. About this, Heidegger states:

> The second letter presents a response to the present standpoint of the congregation. There are those in the congregation who have understood Paul, who know what is crucial. If the παρουσία depends upon how I live, then I am unable to maintain the faith and love that is demanded of me; then I approach despair. Those who think this way worry themselves in a real sense, under the sign of real concern as to whether or not they can execute the work of faith and of love, and whether or not they will hold out until the decisive day. But Paul does not help them; rather he makes their anguish still greater.
>
> Heidegger 2004, 75

In the first letter, Paul announced the coming *parousia* to the Thessalonians. However, Paul does not precisely say at what time the *parousia* will happen. Rather, he only writes that it will come soon. This elicits two responses from the Thessalonians, two forms of enactment. The first way enacts faith by sitting around and waiting for the *parousia*. The second way continues life in its everydayness, but understands that something has changed radically. In the second letter, Paul addresses these two responses. Paul clearly rejects the first way of enacting faith, while accepting the second way as the proper enactment.

This raises two important questions. First, what does this so-called proper enactment entail, and second, why is it the proper way? The question of enacting faith is the question of how the proclamation changes the lives of the Christians. Heidegger notes: "Christian factical life experience is historically determined by its emergence with the proclamation that hits the people in a moment, and then is unceasingly also alive in the enactment of life" (Heidegger 2004, 83). Here, Heidegger clearly states that being a Christian means enacting the relation to the proclamation. How does life change through the proclamation? About this, Heidegger states: "For all its originality, primordial Christian facticity gains no exceptionality, absolutely no special quality at all. In all its absoluteness of reorganizing the enactment, everything remains the same in respect to the worldly facticity" (Heidegger 2004, 83). So, the enactment of life, which is lived in the world, is thoroughly changed, but the world itself is not. The world remains the same, but the relation to it is changed. Heidegger states: "The indeed existing [*daseienden*] significances of real life are lived ὡς μή, as if not" (Heidegger 2004, 84). The Christian should enact his or her faith in a very specific way. Heidegger states:

> The relational sense is not changed, and still less the content. Thus: the Christian does not step out of this world. If one is called as slave, he should not at all fall into the tendency [to suppose] that something could be won for his Being in the

> increase of his freedom. The slave should remain a slave. It is a matter of indifference in which surrounding-worldly significance he stands. . . . These directions of sense which refer to the surrounding world, to one's vocation, and to that which one is (self-world) determine in no way the facticity of the Christian.
>
> Heidegger 2004, 85

So, the Christian does not abandon the world, nor does he or she expect the world to have changed. The facticity of the worldly life of the Christian has not changed through the proclamation. The Christian still has to work and live in the world. What has changed however, is how he or she relates to the world. He or she should be indifferent toward the factical conditions of his life. The Christian should not let the world determine who he or she is. As Paul emphasizes in Romans 12:2, a Christian should not take on the shape of the world. An example might help to understand this point. Take everyday life. Everyday life is filled with small and big problems and concerns. You have to work to earn money, keep your house clean, go grocery shopping. These are the concerns of life. Everyday factical life tends to lose itself in these concerns. They are almost elevated to the central problems of life. The Christian should enact his or her faith in such a way that he or she still lives life and does work, but always with the realization that the world is not the final or most important concern in his or her life. His or her life should not be determined by the world, but by the relationship of the Christian's self to God. The proper enactment of faith means living as he or she lived before the proclamation, but with the realization that there are more important matters in life.

Now, on to the second question: Why is this the proper enactment of faith? Both Heidegger and Paul do not call this enactment proper and the other improper, but it is clear that enacting faith through not taking on the shape of the world is a better way of enacting faith. It is clear why Paul preferred this form of enactment to sitting around idly. People who sat around and stopped working while waiting for the *parousia* to happen were a practical problem for the budding Christian congregations. However, Heidegger does not share Paul's practical concerns. Nor does he reject that way of enacting faith, because "Paul says so." Why, then, does Heidegger insist on the point that there is a right and a wrong way to enact faith?

The answer to this is deceptively simple. Enacting faith is integrating one's relation to the proclamation into daily life. This presupposes that daily life is actually lived. The "rejected" as Paul calls them sit around and wait. They do not participate in the world, and as such, do not live life. Rather, they separate themselves from life and the world. This makes enactment impossible. They do not enact their faith. They cannot "execute the work of faith and of love" (Heidegger 2004, 75). If one enacts faith in such a way, it becomes a theoretical construction about life, but it is no longer lived. If one understands faith in this way, then Nietzsche would be completely right about faith.

Now, I want to return to the problem of knowledge. According to Heidegger, faith in Paul is not a taking-to-be-true, but Heidegger does discuss knowledge in relation to the Christian way of life. Heidegger states that the Christians have gained knowledge with their conversion. It is knowledge of their new situation (see Heidegger 2004, 66). It is important to note that this knowledge is not theoretical or scientific knowledge. Rather, it is a primordial understanding of what it means that the being of the Christians has been changed through accepting the proclamation. It is truly faith's knowledge as one commentator calls it (see Arrien 2013, 33). The knowledge that is gained is the understanding of what has happened to the early Christians. They have a pretheoretical understanding of how their lives have changed. This knowledge is not knowledge of a specific content—not knowledge of what—but it is knowledge of how the lives are enacted. As Heidegger notes, this knowledge cannot be separated from the actual enactment. It can be considered as a kind of practical knowledge.

So, faith is the way one relates to the content of the proclamation. The *parousia* will come, and one has to relate to this in faith. However, faith would be meaningless if it is not enacted in life. According to Heidegger's analysis of faith, it should be enacted in such a way that one does not sit around, idly waiting for the *parousia*. Rather, worldly life needs to be continued as it was before the conversion. However, this relationship to the world, while the conditions of it remain the same, should be lived in a different way. One should no longer take on the shape of the world, but one should live as a self before God.

3. Phenomenology and theology

A few years after Heidegger's lecture course on Paul, Heidegger develops a decidedly different account of faith. Twice Heidegger gave the same lecture called *Phenomenology and Theology*, once in Tübingen in 1927 and once in Marburg in 1928. The second part of the Marburg lecture, together with a letter Heidegger wrote in 1964, has been published as the text *Phenomenology and Theology*. In this text, Heidegger discusses the concept of faith.

The central issue in *Phenomenology and Theology* is the relationship between philosophy and theology. Heidegger explicitly opposes "[t]he popular understanding of the relationship between theology and philosophy," which "is fond of opposing faith and knowledge, revelation and reason" (Heidegger 1998, 40). Instead, Heidegger sees "the problem of the relationship differently from the very start. It is for us rather a question about the relationship of two sciences" (Heidegger 1998, 40). Heidegger accepts that philosophy and theology are both sciences. They differ from each other, however, in the fact that theology is a positive science and philosophy is not. He writes: "Our thesis, then, is that theology is a positive science, and as such, therefore, is absolutely different from philosophy" (Heidegger 1998, 40).

Being a positive science theology has a positum, that is, a certain domain of entities that are studied in that science. The being of those entities is not characterized in that science; rather, that is the task of ontology (see Heidegger 1998, 41). The positum of Heidegger's account of theology is Christianness, the essence of what it means to be a Christian. Heidegger continues by stating that faith is what makes Christianness Christian (see Heidegger 1998, 43). In this way, Heidegger develops faith as the central concept in theology. The analysis of the concept of faith, then, takes up a large part of *Phenomenology and Theology.*

Before turning to Heidegger's account of faith in *Phenomenology and Theology*, two preliminary remarks need to be made, one about Heidegger's language in *Phenomenology and Theology*, and one about what Heidegger means with the term Christian.

First, both in the lectures on Paul as well as in *Phenomenology and Theology*, Heidegger speaks about faith. However, his vocabulary in 1928 is similar in some respects, but different in others. Two differences are especially poignant. First, in 1928, Heidegger had already written and published *Being and Time*, while in 1920–21 he had no idea he would write this book. So, his vocabulary in 1928 is partly the vocabulary he developed in *Being and Time*. Second, in *Phenomenology and Theology*, Heidegger uses theological terms. A reason for this is that in *Phenomenology and Theology*, Heidegger tries to define theology as a science. To this end, he has to take recourse to theological terms.

Second, what does Heidegger mean with Christian? In the lectures on the letters of Paul, Heidegger engages with Paul's Christianity. This is the primordial Christianity that was not yet influenced by Greek metaphysics (see Heidegger 2004, 49). In *Phenomenology and Theology*, however, Heidegger addresses Christianity as he saw it around him. In that text, Christian denotes twentieth-century German Christianity.

About faith, Heidegger remarks in *Phenomenology and Theology*:

> We call faith Christian. The essence of faith can formally be sketched as a way of existence of human Dasein that, according to its own testimony—itself belonging to this way of existence—arises not from Dasein or spontaneously through Dasein, but rather from that which is revealed in and with this way of existence, from what is believed. For the "Christian" faith, that being which is primarily revealed to faith, and only to it, and which, as revelation, first gives rise to faith, is Christ, the crucified God.
>
> Heidegger 1998, 43–44

The difference in Heidegger's vocabulary immediately becomes clear. Instead of speaking about life or religious life, Heidegger uses the term *Dasein*. Dasein is the concept Heidegger uses in *Being and Time* to denote something along the lines of man, the subject or life without using any of these words. Heidegger uses the term *Dasein* to avoid connotations that the other terms have. For the purposes of the comparison between his concepts of faith in 1920 and 1928, the notion of Dasein is functionally equivalent to the word *life*, which Heidegger uses in his lectures on the letters of Paul. Furthermore, Heidegger developed his concept of Dasein partly based on his analysis of Christian facticity in his lectures on Paul.

There is, however, one noticeable difference. In his reading of Paul, Heidegger spoke of life or religious life by which he meant a concrete, lived life. Of course, Heidegger was not interested in the life of any specific person, but his analysis does pertain to life as it is lived. In the analysis of Dasein, the question is posed of how a religious Dasein is possible. But Dasein is not life as it is lived, but rather the structure of life as such. The analysis of religious Dasein, then, is a more formal analysis that thematizes the structure of religious life, not religious life as it is lived.

Heidegger is not interested in faith as a concrete phenomenon, but only faith as a concept. About this concept, Heidegger states that it is a way of existence. Faith is not just a part of life in Heidegger's analysis. It is not one characteristic of certain people, but it is all-defining and all-encompassing. It is a way of existence. Dasein that has faith understands everything through the lens of faith.

Faithful Dasein belongs to faith. It owes its existence to it. But the reverse is not true. Faith does not belong or owe its existence to Dasein. Rather, faith originates in revelation. One cannot decide to become faithful and to have their way of existence changed. It has to happen to someone. Faith is not of Dasein's own making.

How, then, does the revelation relate to Dasein? Heidegger notes: "The imparting of this revelation is not a conveyance of information about present, past, or imminent happenings; rather, this imparting lets one 'par-take' of the event that is revelation (= what is revealed therein) itself. But the par-taking of faith, which is realized only in existing, is given as such always only through faith" (Heidegger 1998, 44).

Revelation makes Dasein a part of itself. This already became clear from Heidegger's statement that Dasein's entire existence becomes faithful. However, this does not give special knowledge about the past, present or future. However, because it changes Dasein's entire existence, it also affects Dasein's understanding. Heidegger continues: "The crucifixion, however, and all that belongs to it is a historical event, and indeed this event gives testimony to itself as such in its specifically historical character only for faith in the scriptures. One 'knows' about this fact only in believing" (Heidegger 1998, 44). Faithful Dasein does not gain any insight nor any inherent interest in the crucifixion as an historical event. Rather, partaking in the crucifixion changes Dasein's existence. Dasein enters into a different mode of life. The crucifixion is only inherently important for the Christian by virtue of its ability to change Dasein's existence.

So, although being faithful does not grant Dasein new knowledge about the past, present or future, it does change Dasein's existence and also its way of understanding. Faithful Dasein understands everything through faith. Faith, then, although not a strict taking-to-be-true does have epistemological features because it determines how Dasein understands the world and itself. It is in this broad sense that faith is an epistemological characteristic. About this, Heidegger writes: "Thus faith understands itself only in believing" (Heidegger 1998, 44). Faith takes on a totalizing tendency. Once the revelation has happened to Dasein, there is no longer any Dasein outside of this faith. To become faithful means to leap away from an old life into a new one. Faithful life implies an annulment of a previous life. Life as it is lived has to be completely reconfigured. Thus, for Heidegger "the proper existentiell meaning of faith is: faith = rebirth" (Heidegger 1998, 44).

So, how does Heidegger understand faith in *Phenomenology and Theology?* Life is completely changed by the event of the crucifixion. Through partaking in the event Dasein is reborn as faithful Dasein. This changes Dasein's entire existence. Not only does faithful Dasein understand itself only through faith, it also understands reality through the lens of faith. Becoming faithful means being reborn into a new life. As Heidegger states: "Rather, faith is an appropriation of revelation that co-constitutes the Christian occurrence, that is, the mode of existence that specifies a factical Dasein's Christianness as a particular form of destiny. Faith is the believing-understanding mode of existing in the history revealed, i.e., occuring with the Crucified" (Heidegger 1998, 45).

In *Phenomenology and Theology*, Heidegger adopts what I like to call a totalizing perspective on faith. Faith determines the lives of the Christians completely. As such, faith can only be understood as a mode of life. It is a complete and completely different way of living. But different from what? Heidegger denies that the difference between philosophy and theology is based on the opposition between faith and reason, which by no coincidence he links to the opposition revelation and knowledge. For Heidegger, the difference between philosophy and theology is that philosophy is the science of being and theology is a positive science of a specific domain of being, namely, the domain of faith.

Both everyday Dasein—that is, Dasein as it is in its everydayness, in this case that means non-Christian Dasein—and the Dasein that has faith have a nontheoretical knowledge. Their knowledge is an understanding mode of interacting with the world. However, next to this Christian Dasein gains a special kind of knowledge. Knowledge which is not related to the world, but which one gains "in believing." Heidegger mentions the crucifixion in this regard. The crucifixion is a historical event, but this event is only "known" through faith. Faith, then, offers Dasein special knowledge (see Heidegger 1998, 44).

Heidegger does not oppose faith and reason in a traditional sense in *Phenomenology and Theology*. However, he does make a distinction between knowledge which is gained from dealing with the world and knowledge that comes from the revelation. Heidegger unwittingly maintains the faith-reason opposition in *Phenomenology and Theology* by opposing "natural" knowledge which comes from interacting with the world to "special" knowledge from the revelation as two sources for two different modes of being. Heidegger not only maintains the opposition, but also makes it absolute because these two modes of Dasein are incompatible. In the more traditional view expounded in the introduction, reason could be supplemented by faith, but with Heidegger's totalizing approach to faith, this becomes impossible.

4. Comparison

In *Phenomenology of Religious Life* and *Phenomenology and Theology*, Heidegger gives two different accounts of faith. But faith is in both cases the same phenomenon. According to Heidegger it is Christian faith that follows the conversion to Christianity. The question is what the differences between the two accounts are precisely, and more importantly, what the meaning of those differences is.

In the lectures on Paul, Heidegger states that one comes to faith through hearing and accepting the proclamation. Heidegger sees faith as the relation one takes toward the *parousia*. This relation, that is, faith, can only be meaningful when it is enacted in life. Because it needs to be enacted, faith is necessarily a part of life itself. It does not grant the faithful any special knowledge. The *parousia* is proclaimed to them, and because of the relation to the *parousia*, the believers start to enact their lives differently. This different enactment is not just limited to faith, but it is a different enactment of life and the world. The content of the world remains the same and the relation the believers have to the world too. However, the way they enact this relation is changed. They no longer take on the shape of the world.

In *Phenomenology and Theology*, faith is given to Dasein through revelation. This revelation is imparted on the believers through the crucifixion. The event of the crucifixion makes Dasein a participant in faith. This changes Dasein entirely. Its entire existence becomes a faithful one. Faith is being reborn. It is an entirely new life. The old Dasein is transformed into a faithful Dasein. This also affects its understanding. Dasein understands everything through the lens of faith. This includes the world itself.

Between these two accounts, four major differences can be defined. First, Heidegger makes a transition from speaking about primordial Christianity to speaking about Christianity in Heidegger's own day. Although the basic phenomenon is the same, namely, Christianity, the form it takes is different. These two forms of Christianity are separated by two thousand years of tradition. The Christianity Heidegger speaks about in *Phenomenology and Theology* is the Christianity as he saw it around him in the twentieth century, whereas primordial Christianity is the Christianity of the first century. However, there is a more fundamental difference. Turning to primordial Christianity is an attempt to find an original Christianity that can inform the analysis of factical life. The analysis of Christianity in *Phenomenology and Theology*, however, is an analysis of the phenomenon as it was encountered in twentieth-century Germany.

This immediately brings us to the second difference. A phenomenon cannot be understood without its content. In both the texts, faith has a clear content. The *parousia* in 1920–21 and the crucifixion in 1928. The *parousia* is dealt with extensively by Heidegger. The content of Paul's proclamation and the meaning of this content are a matter of great concern for Heidegger. He spends a great amount of time explaining how Paul's proclamation should be understood, and Heidegger also stresses the fact that this is precisely what Paul himself did. Paul also explained the content of his letters. This is how the second letter to the Thessalonians should be understood according to Heidegger, namely, as an explanation of the first letter. In *Phenomenology and Theology*, however, Heidegger is not interested in the content. He only briefly mentions the crucifixion as being the content of faith and he does not comment on it. The crucifixion remains an entirely empty concept in *Phenomenology and Theology.* It is empty in the sense that Heidegger could have exchanged it for many other theological concepts. Instead of the crucifixion Heidegger could have used the resurrection as the basis of faith and this would have changed nothing in his analysis. In this sense, crucifixion is an empty concept for Heidegger.

The third difference is the relationship between faith and life. In the early conception faith is a part of factical life. Being faithful is not a new mode of existing. Rather, it happens within factical life. Becoming faithful changes life, but it does not suspend the old worldly relations. Someone becomes faithful and then continues living. In Heidegger's later analysis faith is a rebirth. It is a leap away from an old life into a new one. Seen in this way, faith implies a rupture with the former life and with the former worldly relations.

Last, there is the difference in the concept of knowledge. In both texts, knowledge is linked to faith. Through faith, a new kind of knowledge is gained. This is not theoretical knowledge. It is not knowledge of a specific content. Heidegger continually insists that no knowledge of specific events is imparted to the Christians in their conversion. Rather, knowledge should be understood as a framework for understanding the world. In the Paul lectures, the faithful Christian understands the world "as not." Similarly, faithful Dasein understands everything through faith. The difference between the two is that, in the earlier text, religious life is factical life, but in the later text, Christian Dasein is a different mode of being next to everyday Dasein. In Heidegger's analysis of Paul, the Christian way of life is a way of living factical life in a temporal way. Although Christian life is lived toward the *parousia*, Paul gives an account of factical life as it is lived in relation to time that is ending. According to Heidegger, Paul gives an account of factical, everyday life, whereas faithful Dasein is a mode of being next to everyday Dasein.

5. Conclusion

The concept of religious faith is a difficult, but interesting concept in the work of Martin Heidegger. During the course of his career, Heidegger gives different accounts of religious faith and his evaluation of this concept for philosophy is ambiguous. In this essay, I have focused on this concept in to different texts by Heidegger, the lectures he gave on Paul in 1920–21 and *Phenomenology and Theology* of 1928.

These two concepts of faith have many similarities, but there are also four major differences. First, Heidegger bases his two analyses of religious faith in different conceptions of Christianity. Second, in the earlier text, faith is informed by the content of Christian faith, whereas in *Phenomenology and Theology*, faith is entirely formal. Third, in the lectures on Paul, faith is an integral part of life, but it does not annul living in the world. In *Phenomenology and Theology*, on the other hand, faith is a rebirth. It is a rupture with the earlier life. Fourth, in 1920–21, faith is factical life. In 1928, however, faith is a mode of life next to factical life.

There is one further difference between the two accounts of faith that has not yet been discussed. It is the difference of Heidegger's evaluation of the two accounts of faith. In his lectures on Paul, Heidegger is more positive about faith. Paul stresses the importance of enactment for life in his proclamation, which is something that everyday life had forgotten. Everyday life covers up enactment. This was the case in Paul's time, but it is also so in Heidegger's time. As such, faith provides an alternative to the dominance of everyday life, which tends to forget that there is more to life than the everyday concerns of life itself.

In *Phenomenology and Theology*, Heidegger has a different view on faith. He calls faith the mortal enemy of philosophy, and because for Heidegger philosophy always has to do with life, of life itself (see Heidegger 1998, 53). Heidegger is so critical about faith because it is all-encompassing. It changes Dasein in such a way that it sees everything through the lens of faith. This means that Dasein is no longer intellectually free. The world can no longer be truly understood because it is always seen through faith.

Heidegger's critical evaluation is understandable, and indeed, when faith is considered in the way Heidegger considers it in *Phenomenology and Theology*, one can hardly come to another conclusion than that faith and philosophy are mortal enemies. However, does Heidegger's later analysis do justice to the concept of faith? I argue that it does not. Heidegger does not look at, nor does he thematize religious faith as it is lived by the faithful. Rather, he makes a theoretical construction of what faith is based on theological presuppositions. He analyses theological concepts, such as revelation and faith, and does not wonder if this does justice to faith as it is actually lived. This is in complete opposition to his earlier account of faith. In the earlier text, Heidegger was clearly trying to understand the phenomenon of faith as it was portrayed in the letters of Paul. In *Phenomenology and Theology*, Heidegger has lost his attention for how faith is lived, and as such, has also lost his openness in questioning the concept of faith.

References

Arrien, Sophie-Jan. 2013. "Faith's Knowledge: On Heidegger's Reading of Saint Paul." *Gatherings: The Heidegger Circle Annual* 3: 30–49.

Cimino, Antonio. 2011. "Begriff und Vollzug. Performativität und Indexikalität als Grundbestimmungen der formal anzeigenden Begriffsbildung bei Heidegger." *Internationales Jahrbuch für Hermeneutik* 10: 215–39.

Critchley, Simon. 2012. *The Faith of the Faithless: Experiments in Political Theology.* London/New York: Verso.

Fehér, István M. 2010. "Religion, Theology and Philosophy on the Way to Being and Time: Heidegger, Dilthey and Early Christianity." In *A Companion to Heidegger's Phenomenology of Religious Life*, edited by Sean J. McGrath and Andrzej Wierciński, 35–66. Amsterdam: Rodopi.

Heidegger, Martin. 1998. *Pathmarks.* Edited by William McNeill, translated by James Hart and John Maraldo. Cambridge: Cambridge University Press.

Heidegger, Martin. 2004. *The Phenomenology of Religious Life.* Translated by Matthias Fritsch and Jennifer Anna Gosetti-Ferencei. Bloomington: Indiana University Press.

McManus, Denis. 2013. "Heidegger, Wittgenstein and St. Paul on the Last Judgement: On the Roots and Significance of 'The Theoretical Attitude.'" *British Journal for the History of Philosophy* 21 (1): 143–64.

Nietzsche, Friedrich. 2004. *Ecce Homo and The Antichrist.* Translated by Thomas Wayne. New York: Algora Publishing.

9

The Experience of Contingency and the Attitude to Life:

Nietzsche and Heidegger on Paul[1]

Gert-Jan van der Heiden

The basic significance of the difficult notion of experience may be captured in one sentence: "every experience worthy of the name thwarts [*durchkreuzt*] an expectation" (Gadamer 2004, 350). This description by Gadamer, which is as simple as it is elegant, tells us that in a true experience, we encounter the world in a particular way: While we may have our expectations about what happens in the world, we only truly experience the world when it turns out to be different than we thought it to be. If this is indeed an experience, and if to be experienced means to be someone who often experienced that the world is different than expected, it makes sense to say that a *radical* experience is an experience of the very *possibility* of such an experience itself. Rather than explaining the possibility that the world can show itself to be different than we expected in terms of the limited and finite capacities of human beings and their expectations, we might conceive of this possibility as pertaining to the nature of the world itself. In this latter case, a radical experience is nothing less than the experience that the world *can be different* than expected or than usually encountered. Thus, following this train of thought, a radical experience is the experience of the world's "potentiality-of-being-otherwise."[2] That is to say, a radical experience experiences that the world can also be other or can also not be. Usually, this latter modality of being—something that can also be other or can also not be—is called contingency. Thus,

1 The present essay is part of the project *Overcoming the Faith-Reason Opposition: Pauline* Pistis *in Contemporary Philosophy*, financed by the Netherlands Organisation for Scientific Research (NWO; project nr. 360-25-120), carried out at Radboud University and the University of Groningen.

2 The expression "potentiality-of-being-otherwise" refers to Heidegger's expression *Seinkönnen* from *Being and Time*, which is translated as "potentiality-of-being" (Heidegger 1996, 247), as well as to Meillassoux's expression *pouvoir-être-autre* to describe contingency (Meillassoux 2006, 54).

an experience deserves to be called radical if in it, the world is experienced in its contingency.

In this essay, I suggest that in the first letter to the Corinthians, Paul is concerned with such a radical experience. In particular, this concern announces itself in his reflections on the *schēma tou kosmou toutou*, the figure, form or shape of the present world, about which he writes: "the form of this world is passing away" (1 Cor. 7:31). Although the world has a specific present form or order—the world *is* now in a particular mode—Paul announces this figure of the world to the members of his community in Corinth as one that is passing away. Does this not mean that in this passage, Paul lets the world appear in its potentiality-of-being-otherwise or its potentiality-of-being-not?

Following this line of inquiry, I also argue that the contemporary interest of philosophers in the letters of Paul is concerned with exactly this latter question and that these present-day readings explore the possibility of retrieving philosophically—in Heidegger's sense of *Wiederholung*—the particular radical experience that speaks from this passage from the first letter to the Corinthians. Moving away from Nietzsche's insistence on the resentment and nihilism at work in Paul, as I suggest, the contemporary debate is highly influenced by some of the basic aspects of Martin Heidegger's understanding of Paul's experience of the cosmos.

Finally, for Paul, the experience of the world he communicates in 1 Corinthians 7:31 is intrinsically related to a particular comportment to the world or attitude of life, namely, the one of faith. Therefore, a philosophical retrieval of Paul must include a reflection on this comportment of faith and the related attitude of life to which Paul incites the members of his community in Corinth; moreover, it must connect this comportment to the ontological commitment of Paul that speaks from 1 Corinthians 7:31. Also, here, the present-day reading of the passages from 1 Corinthians 1 and 7 offers the outlines of such a philosophical retrieval of Paul's experience of the world and the accompanying attitude to life that *discloses* (rather than simply follows from) the possibility of such an experience—and again, the difference with Nietzsche's reading of Paul is striking.

1. The order of the cosmos and its interruption

Although it is difficult to collect the multifarious present-day philosophical readings of Paul under one heading, let us proceed from one insight they seem to share: Paul's letters offer an alternative to a certain metaphysical perspective of the world. His account of the cosmos *cannot* be understood, as one may put it in Heidegger's vocabulary, in terms of the onto-theological framework that determines the crucial features of metaphysics throughout the history of philosophy. For instance, despite the critical comments concerning Heidegger's thought one may find elsewhere, Alain Badiou affirms the German philosopher in at least one respect: "Paul prescribes an anticipatory critique of what Heidegger calls onto-theology, wherein God is thought as supreme being, and hence as the measure for what being as such is capable of" (Badiou 2003, 47). Onto-theology is the thought that proceeds from the idea that permanent presence is the determining dimension of being. This permanent presence is unified and grounded in one being, which is named God in the history of metaphysics. Similarly, to use the concept of God that Aristotle develops in Book Lambda of the *Metaphysics*, the cosmos and all its movements are ultimately grounded in and unified by God as the *archē* or principle determining the order of this cosmos.

Paul, as Badiou argues in the above quote, offers an alternative to such an approach of reality because for him, God is not simply the one who sustains and chooses what is, but rather chooses what is not. Referring to the first letter to the Corinthians in which Paul writes that God chose "things which are not, to bring to nought things that are" (1 Cor. 1:28), Badiou writes: "the Christ-event causes nonbeings rather than beings to arise as attesting to God" (Badiou 2003, 47). Hence, for Paul, God is not simply the principle that offers a unifying ground causing and accounting for all that is, but is rather the opposite principle that accounts for the interruption of the totality of beings.[3] If we loosely understand the Greek word *kosmos* as describing the order of the world in which all beings are taken up and have their proper place, one might say that for Paul, God is the principle that makes sure that the present configuration or shape of this *kosmos* will pass away since what is, will be brought to nothing, and what is not, will be granted being.

A similar interruptive dimension in Paul's understanding of the cosmos is at work in Jacob Taubes's reading. To account for the difference between Nietzsche's and Paul's conception of the world (as *kosmos*)—and I will come back to Nietzsche's reading of Paul below—Taubes argues that in contrast to Nietzsche's

[3] For a different account of how the question of onto-theology forms the point of departure for contemporary developments in ontology, see Van der Heiden 2014.

immanent conception of the world, Paul offers us an account of the cosmos in which a *miracle* is possible, that is, in which the immanent laws that fix the order of the world may be interrupted by something that cannot be explained from within this order; as Taubes writes: "And it's a different matter whether one decides, in whatever way, to understand the cosmos as immanent and governed by laws, or whether one thinks the miracle is possible, the exception" (Taubes 2003, 85). Hence, like Badiou, Taubes claims that Paul's letters offer us a principle that is the opposite of the famous metaphysical principle of sufficient reason (which, as Heidegger argues [1997, 20], is the principle par excellence of onto-theology): Rather than giving a sufficient ground for all that is, as the immanent laws that govern the cosmos do, Paul argues that there is another principle at work that may interrupt these laws and that accounts for the possibility that events may occur that transgress to these laws. Seen from the perspective from these immanent laws, this possibility is nothing less than the possibility of a miracle. Hence, both Badiou and Taubes argue that Paul's letters attest to an account of the cosmos in which the cosmos is not regulated by a fixed principle alone, but allows for exceptions and events that do not obey the laws of the cosmos. In sum, for Badiou and Taubes, Paul's cosmos is marked by the possibility that something new or unexpected may happen.

Yet, as one may simply ask: Are these accounts of Paul's ontological commitment justified? Does it not remain to be seen what, from the point of view of new testamentary research, Paul's cosmology exactly amounts to?[4] Moreover, is it true that Paul's letters indeed offer an alternative to onto-theology? While the second question lies beyond the scope of what I can do here, the third question can be addressed. An answer to this third question should not simply offer an interpretation of Paul's theory of the cosmos—this will not solve anything since opposing suggestions have been made—but should embed this theory in the particular experience of the world that speaks from Paul's letters and the attitude to life to which he incites the believers. The latter requirement immediately shows that experience and comportment are more primordial than the particular theoretical commitment. Therefore, the question of Paul's cosmology can probably only be properly settled in light of the comportment to the world he proposes and the experience of the world that goes together with it.

4 How, for instance, should one interpret the new testamentary attention to Christ's subjugation of the cosmic powers in the context of the question of the onto-theological character of Paul's cosmology? "Christ's gradual subjection of the present cosmos is thought to continue till the end of time. According to Paul this end is imminent and will actually come about within a life-span" (Van Kooten 2003, 103).

To show *both* how this ontological commitment may be embedded in a specific attitude to life *and* how this may lead to an opposed account of Paul's cosmology, let us first turn to the philosopher that deserves to be called the great antagonist of the present-day readings of Paul: Nietzsche. For Nietzsche—and this is the obvious (but perhaps not most fundamental) reason why so many present-day readers reject his interpretation—Paul's letters offer all but an alternative to metaphysics. Although the term *onto-theology* is not Nietzsche's, it is not difficult to reconstruct which of the different versions of onto-theology he would ascribe to Paul.

For Nietzsche, Paul's understanding of reality is based on an opposition between faith and truth, which he finds in the famous words of Paul, also from the first letter to the Corinthians: "Hasn't God made foolish the wisdom of this world [*sophian tou kosmou*]?" (1 Cor. 1:20). Hence, as well as many present-day readers, Nietzsche refers to this Pauline letter for obtaining a basic insight in Paul's conception of the world. Moreover, this passage seems intrinsically related to the phrase that the form of this world is passing away: Because the present fashion and form of *this* world pass away, the wisdom of *this* world is foolish. Yet, for Nietzsche, this does not mean that Paul would subscribe to a radical experience as defined above. Rather, he derives Paul's ontological commitment from his interpretation of the epistemological opposition between faith and truth that speaks from this quote. The wisdom of the world, as Nietzsche argues, is called science today and is therefore motivated by nothing but a will for truth: Science only wants to know the true nature and order of the world in which we live. If this wisdom is made foolish, Nietzsche continues, this means that the quest for truth itself is suspended and replaced by a faith that does not want to know the truth, and subsequently prefers lies and illusions; as Nietzsche writes: "'Faith' as an imperative is the veto against science—in praxi, the lie at any price ... Paul perceived that the lie—that faith was necessary" (Nietzsche 2004, 151).

It is important to note that the epistemological opposition between faith and truth is not the most basic one for Nietzsche: It is itself founded in a more prior opposition of two orientations of the will. In opposition to the wanting-to-know of science and truth, "'faith' means not *wanting*-to-know what is true," as Nietzsche writes (2004, 157). These opposed wills underlying truth and faith correspond to two different attitudes to life. Whereas the will of science—wanting-to-know—leads to "the service of truth," which "is the hardest service" in which "almost everything on which the heart otherwise clings, our love, our trust in life, has had to be surrendered," Paul's will of faith—not wanting-to-know—leads into the opposite direction that turns him away from the uneasy truth of this world toward an other world in which harmony and blessedness reign—"Belief makes blessed: consequently, it lies" (Nietzsche 2004, 155).

Thus, referring to the same passage as Badiou, namely, 1 Corinthians 1:28, Nietzsche arrives at the opposite conclusion: When Paul writes that God has chosen the foolish and weak things—the things that are not—over the things that are, he does this out of a particular *rejection* of the world as it is; this rejection marks his sentiment or attitude to life, which is nothing but an attitude of resentment in which those who are nothing, who are suffering, who are not noble or mighty, envy those who are something, who rule the world by their nobility and power.

This particular Pauline will or attitude to life does not only shape the epistemological distinction between faith and truth, but also discloses the ontological distinction that goes hand in hand with it: *this* world is rejected in the name of another, eternal and divine world. By affirming this distinction, Paul's Christianity is a form of Platonism, as Nietzsche often argues: Paul adopts the distinction between the sensible and the intelligible world, between the world we inhabit and the harmonious, eternal world the believer dreams of. When Nietzsche speaks of "the lie at any price" that characterizes Paul's faith, this refers especially to the metaphysical illusion that constitutes Paul's ontological commitments: faith imagines a harmonious, eternal world, but this other world does not exist and is only invented to *devalue* the world we inhabit; as Nietzsche writes elsewhere: "The concepts 'other world,' 'true world' invented in order to devalue the only world there is—in order to leave no goal, no reason, no task remaining for our earthly reality!" (Nietzsche 2004, 97).

Thus, we may finally reconstruct how Nietzsche might interpret Paul's words "the shape of this world is passing away": The end of this world should be understood in light of the arrival (or, rather, the faithful acknowledgment) of the other, eternal, true world, which for Nietzsche is the false, nonexisting world invented by faith. The Platonic dualism of a sensible and an intelligible, eternal world, however, is one of the major forms of onto-theology since it grounds our everyday reality in the pure presence of this eternal world.

When comparing this with what we saw before in our brief account of Badiou and Taubes we may draw two conclusions. First, according to Nietzsche, Paul's cosmology is not concerned with the contingency of this world, but rather with the affirmation of a fictional eternal world over the world in which we live.

Second, however, and more interestingly, Nietzsche's account does help us to further our specific inquiry into the importance of the attitude to life for Paul's cosmology: Nietzsche derives Paul's cosmology from a particular (illusionary) experience of the world and its related attitude to life, namely, the rejection of this world. In this sense, Nietzsche helps us to see how, in Paul, the ontological and epistemological commitments can only be understood out of Paul's *comportment* to and *experience* of the world. Since the "other world" is a lie, as Nietzsche argues, the attitude to life that speaks from Paul's letters—Paul's resentment—should ultimately be characterized as nihilistic: it affirms *nothing* in the existing world, experiences the world as *nothing* and only wants and welcomes the world's *coming to nothing* exemplified by the phrase "the form of this world is passing away."

2. Radical experiences and the imminence of the *Parousia*

Nietzsche's reading offers a clear account of how Paul's ontological commitment to the *other* world and his epistemological account of faith as belief that the other world exists, is rooted in an experience of and comportment to *this* world. This means, for Nietzsche, that both the other world and the faith of Paul are in a particular way dishonest: They hide the primordial dimension from which this ontological and epistemological commitment derives, from our view; they hide the motivating will—not wanting-to-know, resentment—and attitude—rejecting this world—from sight.

Yet, one might wonder whether one may not discern a more direct connection between Paul's ontological commitments and his experience of the world and it remains to be seen whether Nietzsche's account of faith as an epistemological category that hides the underlying attitude to life is a very fortunate one: Is it not more convincing to see in Paul's usage of faith and in his proclamations to the believers as believers not a comportment to the world itself? Differently put, is faith for Paul an epistemological category or rather a mode of being or an attitude to life itself? Pursuing these questions implies a critique of Nietzsche that adopts and radicalizes one of Nietzsche's basic lessons, namely, that Paul's cosmology should be understood in relation to a more primordial experience of the world that corresponds to a particular attitude to life.

Taubes's understanding of the difference between Nietzsche and Paul, as briefly discussed in the previous section, might offer a first orientation for such an approach. Rather than maintaining Nietzsche's opposition between the affirmation of this world versus the affirmation of the other, nonexisting world, Taubes argues that the difference between Nietzsche and Paul is the difference between, on the one hand, a thought that affirms pure immanence (and thus, affirms the order of this cosmos), and on the other hand, a thought that allows for the possibility of an exception, and thus, for a transgression of this order. This second thought identifies Paul's ontological commitment not with the (false) belief that the other world exists, but rather with the possibility that the order of the cosmos *can be violated*. In Taubes's reinterpretation, the dispute between Nietzsche and Paul is not a dispute concerning two worlds, but rather concerning the mode of being of the world itself. Whereas in Nietzsche's understanding Paul is presented as rejecting life, Taubes's reinterpretation shows that Paul's position comprises the possibility of a critique or a disruption of the given order of the world, whereas Nietzsche confines himself to affirming this order.

In one respect, Taubes's reinterpretation of Paul is exemplary for what happens in present-day thought. Rather than calling for resentment and nihilism, the present-day readings suggest that the attitude of life Paul advocates is concerned with the *interruption* of the order of the world because the world *can be different* and allows for the appearance of something utterly new, unpredictable and unexpected.[5] This line of thought is already present in Heidegger's reading of Paul. To show this, let us once more start with Paul's words that the form of this world is passing away.

If 1 Corinthians 7:31 attests to Paul's ontological commitment, Heidegger argues, it is crucial to understand that this commitment derives from a certain enactment (*Vollzug*) of life, rather than with the theoretical claim of the end of this world at a certain moment in time. To substantiate the idea that Paul is mainly interested in the attitude to life accompanying this idea of the end of the world, Heidegger refers to another passage in which Paul uses the same word *schēma* or form in the relation to the world: "And be not conformed [*suschēmatizesthe*] to this world [*aiōn*]" (Rom. 12:2). Paul advises the Corinthians not to conform to (become of the same form as) this world or era. Here, as Heidegger notes, it is clear that *schēma* refers first and foremost to a particular attitude to life, a certain mode of being: The way in which "the world" does things

[5] It will not come as a surprise that Badiou objects exactly to Nietzsche's interpretation of Paul's resentment (2003, 60–62), as does Heidegger (1995, 120).

and the way in which the worldly people live their lives is distinguished from the way in which the believers do (the same) things.

In light of our specific interest in the complex of the experience of the world and the related attitude to life, Heidegger's emphasis on enactment leads to two questions: (1) How, according to Paul, is the world experienced in the comportment of faith as enactment? (2) Does Paul give a more positive description of this nonconformist attitude to the world? Whereas the first question, which concerns a further elaboration of the ontological commitment of Paul, is treated in the rest of this section, the second question, which is more directly concerned with the attitude to life, is discussed in the third section.

Heidegger's answer to the first question leads us to the crucial theme of the *parousia*, the second coming of Christ (Heidegger 1995, 102–4). When we truly want to understand the ontological commitment of Paul, Heidegger seems to argue against Nietzsche, we should understand Paul's explicit reference to the *parousia*, which seems to characterize his singular conception of the world much more than the vague, Platonic idea of the other world. It indeed seems reasonable to suggest that we can only interpret Paul's words on the passing away of the form of this world, if we understand what the *parousia* means for him: After all, the second coming of Christ exemplifies the end of this form of the world. Heidegger follows this suggestion as can be seen most clearly from his insistence on the theme of enactment to understand both the passing away of the form of this world and the *parousia*.

One might think that the *parousia* is an event that will take place at some distant point in the future and that Paul understands it as such a future occurrence. Yet, as Heidegger insists in reference to the first letter to the Thessalonians, Paul is not so much concerned with the *parousia* as an occurrence that will take place at a specific time, but rather with the question of how this coming event affects the way in which the believers live their lives. Therefore, Paul reproaches those members of the community who try to predict the time and date of the *parousia*: the day of the *parousia* will come as a thief in the night (1 Thess. 5:2; Heidegger 1995, 102–4). Thus, for Paul, the *parousia* is the very paradigm of what cannot be foreseen and which thus makes an experience of the world possible: For us, things are concealed and obscure, and therefore, we may encounter things in the world we did not expect. Moreover, since we are dealing here with the passing away of the form of this world, the experience of the *parousia* makes possible a *radical* experience.

A further explication of the *parousia* supports the idea that Heidegger's reading aims to show that Paul's account of the believers' comportment to the world concerns a radical experience of the world. As long as the *parousia* remains a fixed moment in the future, it cannot affect the actual enactment of life, here and now. Yet, in Paul's understanding, the unexpectedness and unforeseeable nature of the *parousia* relate it immediately to the *enactment* of life. For the believers, the *parousia* is not a moment in the future, but it is rather *at every moment imminent*: for the believers, every moment of their lives is a moment in which the *parousia* can take place. Consequently, the *parousia* is not simply the last point on the timeline of this (form of the) world; rather, as imminent possibility, it is present here and now; it *may happen* at this very moment.[6] This explains why Heidegger argues that the *parousia* affects the enactment of life: The lives of the believers are not divided into a life in this world and another life, in another world that starts at some moment in the future when the *parousia* will have taken place; rather, the believers should live their lives in the faith that the *parousia* can happen here and now. Consequently, life should be lived, for Paul, in accordance with the radical experience of the world opened up by the unexpectedness of *parousia*.

Looking back on Nietzsche's claim concerning faith's illusion of the other world, we see now how Heidegger's account of the *parousia* offers another orientation to Paul's words that the figure of this world is passing away. The *parousia* is not a future moment in which the other world becomes manifest; rather, it is the Pauline name for the principle that the order and the form of the world *can* change, here and now, at this very moment. (In Taubes's words, it is the principle that the exception and the miracle are *possible*.) This principle concerns the potentiality-of-being-otherwise of the order of this world; the present figure of the world can pass away at this very moment. Such a Heideggerian reading of 1 Corinthians 7:31, in which the reference to Nietzsche's other world is avoided, is affirmed by Agamben's account of the figure (*schēma*) of the world: "In pushing each thing toward itself through the as not, the messianic does not simply cancel out this figure, but it makes it pass, it prepares its end. This is not another figure or another world: it is the passing of the figure of this world" (Agamben 2005, 24–25). Finally, in this Heideggerian reading of

6 By emphasizing that the Pauline experience of the *parousia* concerns the very experience of its imminence, here and now, Heidegger offers another account of this imminence than is done in some strands of new testamentary research, cf., for example, the following quote in which this imminence is understood in terms of a future moment: "In Paul's view, many or at least some of the member of the Christian community at Rome and Corinth will experience the imminent end of time at some moment in the next few decades while still alive" (Van Kooten 2003, 103).

Paul, the faith does not coincide with the epistemological belief that the other world exists—which is as certain as it is false—but faith is rather the comportment that *discloses* the principle of the passing away of the figure of this world; this comportment is marked by the "distress" and "constant insecurity," as Heidegger emphasizes: Only the believers who await the *parousia*, will not be overtaken by it as by a thief in the night since they do not ignore the *parousia*, but experience it in its imminence (Heidegger 1995, 98, 105; 2004, 67, 73). Thus, in Paul's letters, faith is the comportment in and by which a radical experience of the world is possible as the experience of the imminent passing away of the form of this world. Of course, one may wonder whether this form of faith does not introduce its own illusions: What if the world indeed has an immanent order that allows for no exception? Yet, if one wants to pursue this question of the illusory character of faith in a Nietzschean manner, one should be aware of how this question has changed its character by Heidegger's analysis: The difference between conforming to the world and not conforming to the world is no longer understood in terms of the metaphysical dualism between this world and the other world, but rather between immanent order and imminent change, that is to say, between two accounts of the ontological structure of *this* world: immanence versus imminence.

3. Comportment and contingency: The meaning of Paul's *hōs mē*

The analysis of the imminence of the *parousia* leads us back to the second question, which was left unanswered above: What does a more positive description of the nonconformist attitude to the world looks like? By the reference to some crucial passages in the first letter to the Corinthians (in particular, 1 Cor. 1:26–27, 1 Cor. 7:17–31), it becomes clear that Heidegger does not only object to the ontological commitment Nietzsche ascribes to Paul, but also to the underlying attitude to life. According to Heidegger, Nietzsche has misunderstood Paul when describing the latter's attitude to life as nihilistic and resentful (Heidegger 1995, 120). First, the passages concerning God choosing the weak and those that are not mighty or noble (1 Cor. 1:26–27) are not concerned with ethics or resentment, according to Heidegger, but rather with the enactment of Christian life: Everything that is considered to be *significant* in this order of the world becomes *insignificant* because the world is passing away. Yet, this does not mean that anyone (mighty or not, noble or not, slave or master) needs to change his or her position (Heidegger 1995, 119). Rather, Paul calls on everyone to remain in the position in which they were when they were called to faith: "Let every man abide in the same calling wherein he was called" (1 Cor. 7:20; Heidegger 1995, 119). Hence, Paul does not call on people to withdraw from this order of the world; yet, even though nobody should change his or her position, the way in which one enacts his or her position should change. As Heidegger summarizes: "something remains unchanged, and yet it is radically changed" (Heidegger 1995, 118; 2004, 85).

Exactly at this point, we see why Heidegger argues that Nietzsche has misunderstood Paul: What is described in these passages is not a form of resentment that expresses Paul's envy of people who were mighty or noble; nor do they offer any descriptions of an afterlife in which all wrongs are made undone. Rather, Paul calls on the members of his community in Corinth to adopt a specific comportment to the world and to the life they lead: no longer affirming the significances of the world, but rather enacting the task given to them in this world in the faith that this world is passing away. This is the attitude to life that arises exactly as soon as the world we inhabit is experienced in its contingency.

To clarify this paradoxical attitude to life in which all callings remain the same, but the way in which these callings are lived is fundamentally altered, Heidegger refers to 1 Corinthians 7:29–31, in which Paul uses the expression *hōs mē* or "as not" to describe this paradoxical mode of living: "those that weep should be as not weeping," "those that rejoice should be as not rejoicing," "those that have wives should be as not having wives" (1 Cor. 7:29–31)—and the slave should remain a slave in relation to his or her master, but should be a slave as not being a slave. *Hōs mē* thus expresses the new comportment to the old significances of life (Heidegger 1995, 116; Heidegger 2004, 83).

Before elaborating the meaning of this *hōs mē*, let me retake the question that also inspired the previous section: Does this reading of the passages from the first letter of the Corinthians offer a convincing critique of Nietzsche's account of Paul's attitude to life? Perhaps Heidegger is right in his refusal of the term *resentment* because there does not seem to be a resentful tone in Paul's letters. Yet, if we recall that for Nietzsche this resentment is also related to *nihilism*, that is, as a form of rejecting rather than affirming this world and this life, one might wonder whether Heidegger's explication of the new comportment to life to which Paul calls the members of his community does not reinstate the problem of nihilism: Should we not read the explication of the new comportment to life as *hōs mē* as a way of privileging the *mē onta*, the things that are not?

This question inspires Simon Critchley's understanding of the contemporary readings of Paul when he argues that, referring to the importance of 1 Corinthians 7:29–31 in these readings, they are marked by a certain "meontology" (2012, 177–83): "Paul is preaching a meontology, an account of things that are not. Furthermore, his is a double meontology: on the one hand, the form of this world is passing away or falling away and becoming nothing. This is the nihilism of world politics" (Critchley 2012, 178). This insight into the nihilism in the words of Paul that the form of this world is passing away, which Critchley borrows from Taubes, is immediately connected to another crucial feature of Taubes's account of how Paul influenced Western thought: According to Taubes, what dominates Western thought is Marcion's reading of Paul (which, in the nineteenth century, reappears in Von Harnack's theology). According to Critchley, this influence of Marcion is still present in the readings of Agamben, Badiou and Heidegger to such an extent that they deserve to be called crypto-Marcionists (Critchley 2012, 195–202).

Although this reading seems to follow some basic elements in Taubes's lectures on Paul, it is of crucial importance to note that Critchley connects Paul's meontology to Marcion's reading of Paul in a way that goes against the basic insight of Taubes's interpretation of Paul's influence of Western thought. For Taubes, Marcion is responsible for the idea, still present in Nietzsche's reading, that Paul is committed to an ontological dualism, that is, to a rejection of this world in light of an affirmation of the other world. By calling the contemporary readings of Paul crypto-Marcionist, Critchley forgets that Heidegger, Agamben as well as Taubes explicitly *reject* Marcion's insistence on a Pauline ontological dualism. Although it remains unclear in Critchley's text what the precise meaning of the prefix "crypto" is, it seems obvious that by referring to crypto-Marcionism, he accuses these authors of the same form of nihilism to which Nietzsche objected in Paul. Yet, it is not clear at all that the nihilism to which Nietzsche objected, is the same "nihilism" as the one Taubes mentions in reference to 1 Corinthians 7:31 and connects to the *hōs mē* (Taubes 2003, 72).

For Taubes, there is a crucial difference between the nihilism of Nietzsche's Paul that rejects life because of a lie and an illusion and the Pauline awareness that the passing away of this world order requires a specific attitude to this order. Hence, by conflating Nietzsche's nihilism with Paul's meontology, Critchley loses sight of the characteristic subtlety of Taubes's position since Taubes rejects the Marcionist reading of Paul, but embraces a more "messianic" reading of Paul.

This conflating of Nietzsche's nihilism with Paul's meontology is not only confusing Taubes's reading of Paul, but also affecting a proper understanding of Heidegger's as well as Agamben's account of the *hōs mē*. When describing the specific tension—"the messianic tension"—that the *hōs mē* introduces between weeping and itself ("as not weeping"), Agamben emphasizes that the *hōs mē* does not lead us toward another world:

> The messianic tension thus does not tend toward an elsewhere, nor does it exhaust itself in the indifference between one thing and its opposite.... According to the principle of messiance *klēsis*, one determinate factical condition is set in relation to itself—the weeping is pushed toward the weeping, the rejoicing toward the rejoicing. In this manner, it revokes the factical condition and undermines it without altering its form.
>
> Agamben 2005, 24

Hence, rather than leading to a variation of Nietzschean nihilism, the formula *hōs mē* is concerned with "revok[ing] the factical condition" and undermining the present form of life and the present form of the world. Of course, in our quest for a positive account of the new comportment to which Paul inspires, the terms *revoking* and *undermining* are not yet enough since they are negative terms; yet, this quote also makes clear that to understand the "meontology" of Agamben, one should start by clarifying the difference between these negative terms and the nihilism Nietzsche discerns in Paul's letters. I leave this clarification in Agamben's case to another occasion, but proceed here with Heidegger.

By describing Heidegger as a crypto-Marcionist, Critchley tends to conflate Nietzsche's nihilism with Heidegger's understanding of Paul's *hōs mē*. In this way, it becomes impossible to understand why Heidegger insists on their difference. Therefore, it is crucial to offer an interpretation of the difference between the nihilism arising from Marcion's ontological dualism and Paul's insistence that the present form of the world passes away. Since we have already analyzed Nietzsche's account of nothingness in Paul, namely, the illusion of the other world offered by faith, we can limit ourselves to addressing the question of which type of nothingness is at stake in Paul's *hōs mē* by departing from the insight that, for Heidegger, Paul is not so much concerned with the affirmation of a nonexisting world, but rather with thinking the imminent transformation of the world, here and now, affecting the lives of the believers.

Nietzsche's distinction between an affirmation of the world as it is (which is the world of becoming) and a rejection of any illusion of a nonexisting, eternal or permanent world, does not acknowledge the possibility of an *other* nothingness, located paradoxically between what is and what is not. This other nothingness is captured by the concept of contingency. Something is called contingent if it is, but can also not be (Agamben 1999, 261). To say that the form of the present world is passing away means to say that it is, but can also not be. For Nietzsche, Paul's nihilism consists in *wanting* this world to *become* nothing (in name of something that does not exist). Thus, Nietzsche suggests that this form of the world is all there is. To a certain extent, this is correct since there is no second, permanent world. Yet, in another respect, this suggestion is incomplete as we can see when looking at this form of the world from the perspective of its contingency: The concept of contingency does not refer to Paul's *wanting* the world to *become* nothing, but rather refers to a possibility that precedes any will.[7] It points to the *intrinsic* nothingness of the form of the present world itself, which is given only in the modality of possibility: it *can* also *not be.*

In light of this determination of the nothingness, the comportment to which Paul incites his community can no longer be understood in terms of the difference between the affirmation and the rejection of this world. The attitude to life that Paul recommends neither affirms life in a Nietzschean gesture nor rejects life in the way Paul does according to Nietzsche. Rather, as Heidegger strikingly indicates, the attitude to life as expressed by the formula *hōs mē*, leaves the form of the world and the modes of living it implies unchanged. All believers remain in their own calling. Yet, this calling, as Agamben suggests, is revoked by the *hōs mē*; this calling is enacted as not significant, as not being called (Agamben 2005, 23). Neither rejecting the present order of the world nor affirming it, this comportment corresponds to a third attitude excluded by the opposition of affirmation and rejection. This comportment thus requires a *suspension* of this opposition so that another attitude is disclosed that allows for experiencing the contingency of this form of the world: This form of the world *is*, and therefore, all remain in their calling; yet, this form of the world *can* also *not be*, and therefore, everyone is recommended to enact their calling *as not* being called. Only in this way, one participates in the configurations this world has to offer without being absorbed in them.

7 For the idea of potentiality without will, a *potentia absoluta* as distinct from a *potentia ordinata*, see Agamben's comments (1999, 253–55).

In reference to the first letter to the Thessalonians, Heidegger mentions that Paul makes a radical distinction between those that are fully absorbed in computing the "when" of the *parousia* and those who have a more sober relation to it and are more awake. Heidegger writes: "Paul's answer to the question of the When of the παρουσία is thus an urging to awaken and to be sober. Here lies a point against enthusiasm" (Heidegger 1995, 105; 2004, 74). Affirmation of this world and rejection of this world in name of a future event that will come on a particular day are ultimately of the same type for Heidegger's Paul since they are examples of the same comportment of being absorbed in and under the spell of one particular form of the cosmos—whether it is the present cosmos, or the other form of the cosmos, which will be at a certain point in the future. Against the enthusiastic affirmation of both this world and the other world, Paul calls for a more sober and awake comportment, namely, one that experiences the form of the world in light of its imminent change, in light of its contingency. For Paul, such a radical experience of the world is equiprimordial with the comportment of faith that discloses it. Rather than a passionate and willful affirmation or an equally passionate and willful rejection of this world, the comportment expressed by *hōs mē* amounts to a sober, awake attitude in which one participates in the order of life the present world offers, but does not get absorbed in or possessed by it; rather, in this comportment, one experiences the form of the world in which one acts and lives, here and now, in light of its contingency, its imminent passing away.

References

Agamben, Giorgio. 1999. *Potentialities: Collected Essays in Philosophy*. Translated by Daniel Heller-Roazen. Stanford, CA: Stanford University Press.

Agamben, Giorgio. 2005. *The Time that Remains: A Commentary on the Letter of the Romans*. Translated by Patricia Daley. Stanford, CA: Stanford University Press.

Badiou, Alain. 2003. *Saint Paul: The Foundation of Universalism*. Translated by Ray Brassier. Stanford, CA: Stanford University Press.

Critchley, Simon. 2012. *The Faith of the Faithless: Experiments in Political Theology*. London: Verso.

Gadamer, Hans-Georg. 1990. *Gesammelte Werke*, vol. 1: *Wahrheit und Methode*. Tübingen: Mohr Siebeck.

Gadamer, Hans-Georg. 2004. *Truth and Method*. Translated by Joel Weinsheimer and Donald G. Marshall. London: Continuum.

Heidegger, Martin. 1995. *Gesamtausgabe*, vol. 60: *Phänomenologie des religiösen Lebens.* Edited by Claudius Strube. Frankfurt am Main: Klostermann.

Heidegger, Martin. 1996. *Being and Time.* Translated by Joan Stambaugh. Albany, NY: SUNY Press.

Heidegger, Martin. 1997. *Gesamtausgabe*, vol. 10: *Der Satz vom Grund.* Edited by Petra Jaeger. Frankfurt am Main: Klostermann.

Heidegger, Martin. 2004. *The Phenomenology of Religious Life.* Translated by Matthias Fritsch and Jennifer Anna Gosetti-Ferencei. Bloomington: Indiana University Press.

Meillassoux, Quentin. 2006. *Après la finitude: Essai sur la nécessité de la contingence.* Paris: Seuil.

Nietzsche, Friedrich. 2004. *Ecce Homo and The Antichrist.* Translated by Thomas Wayne. New York: Algora.

Taubes, Jacob. 2003. *The Political Theology of Paul.* Translated by Dana Hollander. Stanford, CA: Stanford University Press.

Van der Heiden, Gert-Jan. 2014. *Ontology after Ontotheology: Plurality, Event, and Contingency in Contemporary Philosophy.* Pittsburgh: Duquesne University Press.

Van Kooten, George H. 2003. *Cosmic Christology in Paul and the Pauline School: Colossians and Ephesians in the Context of Graeco-Roman Cosmology.* Tübingen: Mohr Siebeck.

10

Paul as a Challenge for Contemporary Philosophers:

Nietzsche, Heidegger and Agamben[1]

Antonio Cimino

An appropriate assessment of the pivotal role Paul plays in the context of contemporary philosophy should also take into consideration the deep ambiguity that characterizes the philosophical reception of Pauline themes.[2] As a matter of fact, Paul represents a challenge to the very self-understanding of a number of contemporary thinkers. In the following essay, which focuses on Nietzsche, Agamben, and above all, Heidegger, I intend to show the extent to which Paul is an important interlocutor for these philosophers, especially with regard to basic questions about the nature of philosophical thought. In doing so, I develop an interpretive hypothesis that, in my opinion, does justice to the complex and ambiguous reception of Paul in contemporary continental philosophy. According to this hypothesis, both Heidegger's and Agamben's readings of the Pauline letters comprise a substantial and complete refutation of Nietzsche's anti-Pauline commitment. According to Nietzsche's polemical considerations in *The Anti-Christ*, Paul should be considered as the real founder of Christianity as an institutionalized religion, and is therefore one of the most radical opponents of the authentic philosophical spirit that Nietzsche wants to initiate. On the other hand, according to Heidegger and Agamben, one can defend the very opposite reading and argue that Paul is a revolutionary figure who can provide relevant

[1] The present essay results from my postdoctoral research project *The Truth of Conviction: Attestation, Testimony, and Declaration*, financed by the Netherlands Organisation for Scientific Research (NWO). It is part of a larger project, *Overcoming the Faith–Reason Opposition: Pauline* Pistis *in Contemporary Philosophy* (project no. 360-25-120), carried out at Radboud University and at the University of Groningen. See Cimino 2013b, 2014, 2015.

[2] Over the last few years, much research has been devoted to the reception of Paul in contemporary philosophy. See, for example, Scilironi 2004; Caputo and Alcoff 2009; Blanton and de Vries 2013.

starting points for a radically new conception of philosophy. This ambiguity, as it unfolds in the work of Nietzsche, Heidegger and Agamben, can ultimately be said to constitute the entire reception of Paul in contemporary thought, which could also be understood as the attempt to answer the questions of whether and to what extent Paul can be regarded as a philosopher or as an antiphilosopher.

In the following comparative analysis, I explain how Nietzsche, Heidegger and Agamben formulate and answer these questions, paying particular attention to the position these thinkers assign to Paul within the framework of the Western philosophical and religious tradition.[3] The philosophical potential of Paul emerges in Heidegger's thought in a very clear way. Heidegger's interest in Paul's letters might be explained with reference to various factors (the historical context, biographical motives, his interaction with other philosophers or theologians, etc.), but if one wants to elucidate the authentic philosophical commitment underlying his reading and to do so against the background of Nietzsche's anti-Pauline attitude, then it makes sense to consider the radical anti-Platonism of his early Freiburg lectures. According to Heidegger's interpretive framework there, the predominant tendency in the Western philosophical tradition is the theoretical attitude, that is, a distanced and objectifying comportment toward the prescientific life-world. The project of a phenomenological hermeneutics of factical life is meant to provide a nontheoretical interpretation of human existence, and in the final analysis, a "destruction" (see Heidegger 2010, 19–25) of Platonism, which accords primacy to such a theoretical attitude. Within this framework, Heidegger's interpretation of Paul should be considered not merely as an application of his own revised phenomenological method, but above all, as an attempt to find inspiring starting points for a new form of phenomenological thinking. Thus, in Heidegger's approach to Paul, we see a radical reversal of Nietzsche's perspective. For Nietzsche, Paul belongs to the Platonic-Christian theological-philosophical

[3] In order to appreciate the real importance of the Pauline challenge that comes into consideration here, however, one should also stress the fact that such an ambiguity does not only belong to the readings of Paul in contemporary philosophy, but also defines an essential part of the philosophical reception of the Pauline letters in general. In this connection, it makes sense to mention Spinoza's position in his *Theological-Political Treatise*, in which an entire chapter (11) is devoted to the question concerning the nature of apostolic announcement. According to Spinoza, the apostolic function can be considered from two different perspectives. In some respects, it can in fact be traced back to prophecy, inasmuch as apostleship presupposes imagination (*imaginatio*) as its own cognitive faculty. Nevertheless, apostles also make use of argumentation, most notably in their letters, in order to convince, to debate, to formulate opinions and also to explain the foundations of religion. If we follow Spinoza's approach here, we can see in Paul a strong philosophical attitude (Spinoza 2007, 162).

tradition he wants to overcome, whereas for Heidegger, a phenomenological interpretation of Paul stands in contrast to the traditional Platonic tendency. The opposition between Paul and Platonism emerges, in particular, with reference to the problem of temporality and historicity. According to Heidegger, the Platonic tendency is not able to do justice to the factical character of human existence, that is, either to its primordial temporality or to its self-experience independent from theoretical commitments because Platonic philosophers consider facticity as a secondary dimension in comparison to atemporal being. In contrast to this, Paul can be said to provide a genuine account of facticity as such, even if it is not explicitly philosophical, once viewed from a phenomenological perspective.

In Agamben's reading of the letter to the Romans, the ambiguity that determines the reception of Paul becomes apparent in an emphatic way insofar as Agamben stresses both Paul's philosophical potential and his radical opposition to some traditional philosophical frameworks. I focus on two aspects of his approach. On the one hand, Agamben formulates an extremely interesting hypothesis, according to which there are essential starting points for Hegel's conception of the dialectic to be found in Paul, most notably, for the notion of sublation (*Aufhebung*). On the other hand, due to his messianism, Paul enacts a new experience of language, which does not accord with traditional logic and represents a substantial alternative to both the denotative character of language and allegedly obvious distinctions (e.g., essence vs. existence, subject vs. predicates). In the end, Nietzsche's ideological and tyrannical Paul disappears completely in Agamben's reading, which, in line with Heidegger's, presents Paul as a deeply antidogmatic personality, who, on the basis of his profound messianism, acts against institutionalizations of religion, the abstract codification of norms and the reification of language.

1. Nietzsche's anti-Pauline paradigm

Nietzsche's anti-Pauline manifesto, *The Anti-Christ*, outlines a very negative and one-sided account of Paul (Nietzsche 1990, 166).[4] Indeed, the real target of Nietzsche's violent attack is not Christianity as such, but the institutionalized Christian ideology allegedly founded by Paul, who is considered to be one of the

4 For discussions of the relationship between Nietzsche and Christianity, see especially the following studies: Jaspers 1963; Welte 1964; Valadier 1974; Biser 1982, 2002; Kee 1999; Hübner 2000. As regards Nietzsche's interpretation of Paul, see Havemann 2002.

most radical opponents of the authentic philosophical spirit Nietzsche wants to establish against the Platonic-Christian tradition (Nietzsche 1990, 131). Actually, the genuine intention of Nietzsche's anti-Christian commitment is clearly revealed in his very different evaluations of Jesus and Paul. In his explanation of the history of Christianity, Nietzsche lays special emphasis on the sharp opposition between Jesus and Paul, that is, between the authentic essence of the primordial Christian religion, on the one hand, which allegedly already disappeared after Jesus' death (Nietzsche 1990, 163–64), and Christianity as a purely ideological construction, on the other hand. According to Nietzsche, Jesus is the only real Christian and represents the concrete embodiment of authentic Christianity (Nietzsche 1990, 163–64), which does not refer to any faith or dogmatic system, but only to a concrete way of life (Nietzsche 1990, 157–58). As a matter of fact, Nietzsche entirely disregards and degrades faith and dogma, considering them as mere cognitive or ideological epiphenomena that do not allow one to see the real nature of the Christian religion (Nietzsche 1990, 178–87).

Against this background, Nietzsche attributes to Paul the falsification of the history of Christianity, and above all, the pure invention of the theological-metaphysical paradigm of Christianity, especially with regard to the immortality of soul, which is, according to Nietzsche, an ideological conception Paul shares with Platonism.[5] In doing so, Nietzsche claims to discover the real intentions of Paul, which, according to him, are political because the genuine goal of Paul was to get power by establishing a clerical elite and controlling the masses. In the end, Paul made use of the Christian religion as an *instrumentum regni* (Nietzsche 1990, 166–67). According to Nietzsche's virulent criticisms, this Pauline-Christian ideological construction had a fatal impact on the conception of life developed and experienced in the European tradition because it prevented the experience of life in its genuine nature and deprived it of its intrinsic, instinctual power, passing off afterlife as the real meaning of life (Nietzsche 1990, 167–69). In the final analysis, Nietzsche thinks Paul to be a typical proponent of the Platonic-Christian ideology he wants to fight in order to establish not only an alternative philosophical paradigm, but also a new humankind.

[5] See especially Nietzsche's definition of Christianity as "Platonism for the 'people'" (2014, 2).

2. Heidegger and his reversal of Nietzsche's position: Paul as an anti-Platonist and as a starting point for a new conception of philosophy

Heidegger's phenomenological interpretation of Paul can be addressed from very different perspectives.[6] In this essay, I deliberately avoid any historical or biographical approaches because I intend to focus on the purely philosophical commitment underlying Heidegger's analysis of the Pauline letters in his early Freiburg lecture courses. Accordingly, I make use of the opposition between Platonism and anti-Platonism, considering this as a privileged framework for explaining the real impact of Paul on Heidegger's thought. First of all, however, it makes sense to clarify Heidegger's conception of Platonism in his lecture on the phenomenology of religious life. This is especially pertinent because his notion of Platonism does not refer to Plato as such,[7] but only to modern and contemporary thinkers, who can be classified as Platonists for many reasons.[8]

As a matter of fact, Heidegger's notion of Platonism in his early Freiburg lecture courses is extremely vague. Nevertheless, it is possible to identify four basic elements that, according to Heidegger, define the Platonic framework. First, Platonism should be understood as a theoretical attitude, that is, as a distanced and objectifying comportment toward the prescientific life-world (Heidegger 2004a, 27). In fact, in modern Platonism, which includes Husserl, the neo-Kantians (Heidegger 2004a, 33) and the various philosophers of values, the reception of the original theoretical commitment of Greek thought entails an essential tendency to view philosophy as science (Heidegger 2004a, 12). Second, Platonism is a metaphysical paradigm that establishes a basic dualism between the ideal, that is, atemporal or extra-temporal, and the empirical, that is, temporal and historical (Heidegger 2004a, 27). Third, Platonism neglects not only the specific ontological status of human existence, but also temporality and historicity as basic features of human facticity.[9] Fourth, Platonism is not able to

[6] With regard to Heidegger's reading of Paul in his early Freiburg lectures, I recommend the following analyses: Pöggeler 1996; Brejdak 1996; Savarino 2001; Molinaro 2008; Vedder 2007, 2009; Camilleri 2011. See also the comprehensive collection of essays McGrath and Wierciński 2010.

[7] Since scholarly research on Heidegger and Plato is very extensive, I mention only the following contributions: Seron 2001; Petkovšek 2004; Cimino 2005; Partenie and Rockmore 2005; Peluso 2008; Ralkowski 2009.

[8] Regarding Heidegger and modern Platonism, see Brach 1996 and Kim 2010.

[9] In this case, Heidegger refers paradigmatically to Rickert's neo-Kantian Platonism and emphasizes the fact that he is not able to take seriously the philosophical question concerning human life as such. See Heidegger 2004a, 34.

give a proper philosophical account of facticity, since facticity is neglected or considered as a secondary dimension in contrast to the ideal (Heidegger 2004a, 27). Manifestly, in modern Platonists the four characteristics mentioned above become apparent in very different ways and combinations. In the final analysis, however, these various Platonic approaches lead to the same result. Platonistic philosophies do not have adequate access to factical life as such, which represents the principal issue and theme of philosophical inquiry for Heidegger. Such a Platonism can be considered the most important opponent for Heidegger's hermeneutics of facticity so that his philosophy is characterized by a fundamental anti-Platonic tendency. In this regard, one notices clear resemblances between Heidegger's early philosophical program and Nietzsche's basic intentions. In fact, they both commit themselves to a strong anti-Platonic attitude, criticizing in particular the metaphysical positing of ideal values, norms or entities, and also stressing the need for a philosophical perspective that would understand life starting from life as such—without the allegedly Socratic-Platonic idea of a scientific philosophy.[10]

Even if Heidegger and Nietzsche share a basic anti-Platonism and antimetaphysical attitude, the consequences of this for their respective readings of Paul could not be more different. As has been said, Nietzsche considers Paul a paradigmatic proponent of the metaphysical-theological tradition he wants to overcome. For him, as explained, Paul is a significant manifestation of the Christian-Platonic ideology that prevents a genuine experience and philosophical account of life as such. For Heidegger, in stark contrast, Paul paves the way for a real overcoming of the afore-mentioned Platonic features of philosophical thought.

In Heidegger's anti-Platonism, one can also see the deep ambiguity that defines his project of a hermeneutics of facticity. On the one hand, this project is antiphilosophical insofar as Heidegger intends to dismiss the philosophical tradition, which is considered to be the interplay among the four Platonic elements mentioned above, especially in the case of contemporary philosophy. On the other hand, his hermeneutics of facticity does not intend to dismiss philosophy as such, because Heidegger's aim is to emancipate philosophical thought from the Platonic commitment that becomes evident in the idea of a scientific philosophy. In doing so, he claims to do justice to the real nature of

10 As concerns Heidegger and Nietzsche, see Giugliano 1999; Müller-Lauter 2000; Denker et al. 2005; Casale 2010; Babich, Denker and Zaborowski 2012.

philosophy. In the end, Heidegger's project of a hermeneutical phenomenology of factical life is indeed both antiphilosophical and philosophical, in a very radical way.

Within this framework of an essential ambiguity between philosophy and antiphilosophy, one should also understand the reasons why Paul becomes a relevant starting point for Heidegger's hermeneutics of factical life. In fact, Heidegger's philosophical and antiphilosophical perspective is also a specific feature of his approach to Paul. This means one cannot understand Heidegger's approach to Paul without considering this basic ambiguity of his early phenomenological hermeneutics. On the one hand, Heidegger sees in Paul an essentially antiphilosophical attitude because Paul's religious experience is articulated differently from Greek philosophy. Given these premises, Heidegger is not interested in possible or documented connections between Paul and ancient philosophy because he basically focuses on the antiphilosophical potential of Paul. On the other hand, however, Heidegger's use of Paul does not have any theological or religious intentions (Heidegger 2004a, 47) because his concern is and always remains philosophical, even if not in the traditional (Platonic) sense of philosophy.

3. Heidegger's Pauline commitment

The Pauline character of Heidegger's early philosophy can be revealed if one considers how suitable Paul's famous remark (1 Cor. 3:19) about "the wisdom of this world" (*sophia tou kosmou toutou*) would be as a motto for Heidegger's program of a hermeneutics of factical life. While it is, of course, evident that the substance of Heidegger's argumentation against Greek philosophy cannot be reduced to Paul's remark, one should nevertheless place a special emphasis on the convergence between Heidegger's Pauline motives and his phenomenological destruction of the Greek *sophia*. In the following analysis, I explain why Heidegger's early philosophy can be read as an alternative to the Greek *sophia* and how his Pauline inspiration—*not Paul as such*—is consistent with his own opposition to the Greek *sophia*.[11]

Heidegger's philosophical program implies a "destruction" of the Greek primacy of *sophia* because he considers *sophia* as the theoretical attitude rooted

[11] Sommer (2005) offers a detailed presentation of the interplay between Christian anthropology and Greek sources in Heidegger.

in a mundane, that is, inauthentic, self-understanding of human life. In connection with this, one should mention the paradigmatic interpretation of *sophia* in the Marburg lecture course on Plato's *Sophist* (Heidegger 1997, 122). According to Heidegger's account, *sophia* expresses the typical Greek self-understanding of human existence and also of philosophical inquiry as such. Heidegger is convinced that the Platonic-Aristotelian idea of philosophy as a theoretical attitude is essentially different from the modern idea of theoretical experience because the former is not shaped by the modern (i.e., Galilean-Newtonian) paradigm of science. Nevertheless, for him, *sophia* does not imply any proper or authentic self-understanding of human being or of philosophy because it basically remains world-oriented. In fact, *sophia* is essentially connected with the tendency to assimilate itself to eternal beings.

From this viewpoint, Heidegger's philosophy—both his hermeneutics of facticity and his existential ontology—has an essentially Pauline character since it contests the primacy of *sophia* as a mundane self-understanding, but also because his alternative to *sophia* is shaped in Pauline terms. In order to avoid misunderstanding, it is important to stress that Heidegger's commitment to the Pauline rejection of the mundane Greek *sophia* does not entail the elimination of philosophy as such since, on the contrary, Heidegger intends to make use of the antiphilosopher or anti-Platonist Paul against what he considers an inauthentic enactment of philosophical existence. Otherwise put, the antiphilosopher Paul should pave the way for a truly philosophical enactment of philosophy inasmuch as Paul's articulation of factical life enables one to understand facticity starting from facticity as such and apart from theoretical or *sophia*-related preconceptions.

In this sense, Paul plays a very seminal role for Heidegger's phenomenological enactment of philosophy because his religious articulation of facticity has a strong philosophical impact, being an essential alternative to traditional Platonic-Aristotelian theoretical comportments. At the end of the day, Heidegger makes use of the antiphilosophical potential of Paul's articulation of facticity in order to establish *philosophically* deeper foundations for his hermeneutics of human life. The framework sketched above can be clarified in a more concrete way by emphasizing Heidegger's opposition of his Pauline account of authentic life to the inauthentic, world-oriented Greek existence (see Brejdak 1996).

According to Heidegger, *sophia* is an unconcerned contemplative attitude characterized by inauthentic tendencies. Generally speaking, Heidegger maintains that human existence does not take seriously the primordial characteristics of its own facticity, which refer to the essential finitude and insecurity of human life as such. This tendency toward self-assurance articulates itself philosophically in the positing of ideal dimensions or levels of reality. The paradigmatic example is Plato's world of ideas, which later reemerges in Husserl's idealism. In order to avoid this tendency, Heidegger is convinced that the hermeneutics of facticity should pay attention to Paul's and Augustine's emphasis on the fundamental insecurity of factical life.[12]

Paul's experience of facticity represents an important alternative to traditional metaphysical frameworks precisely because it attests to the primacy of temporality, historicity and insecurity that defines human existence. In this regard, the radically anti-Platonic character of Paul is extremely clear since Heidegger starts from the Pauline experience of temporality in order to reverse the Platonic metaphysical paradigm. In fact, according to Heidegger, Paul neither attempts to escape life as such, nor establishes the ideological primacy of the afterlife, but, on the contrary, paves the way for a genuine understanding of human existence in its radical facticity and finitude. For Heidegger, temporality and historicity in Paul are not understood in opposition to eternal entities, as is the case with Greek philosophy, but are instead understood and experienced as such, that is, in their primordial character.

It is possible to summarize by saying that, within the framework of Heidegger's reading of Paul, the Pauline account of temporality, historicity and insecurity is radically opposed to the Greek ideal of *sophia*. It makes sense to refer again to Heidegger's lecture course on Plato's *Sophist*, where he formulates the following point:

> Herein resides the peculiar tendency of the accommodation of the temporality of human Dasein to the eternity of the world. The abiding with what is eternal, θεωρεῖν, is not supposed to be arbitrary and occasional but is to be maintained uninterruptedly throughout the duration of life. Therein resides for man a certain possibility of ἀθανατίζειν (1177b33), a mode of Being of man in which he has the highest possibility of not coming to an end. This is the extreme position to which the Greeks carried human Dasein.
>
> Heidegger 1997, 122

The Greek ideal of *sophia* as *theōrein* and *athanatizein* is the exact opposite of Heidegger's experience of being-toward-death (Heidegger 2010, 227–55), which, in turn, draws its primordial inspiration from the Pauline *hōs mē* and also from

[12] On Heidegger and Augustine, see de Paulo 2006.

the experience of *parousia*.[13] One could also say that Heidegger makes use of the Pauline experience of *parousia*, which is future-oriented and essentially linked to the experience of human finitude, in order to overcome Plato's and Aristotle's accounts of *parousia*, which, by contrast, are rooted in a mundane self-understanding and do not take human mortality seriously. Heidegger ultimately formulates his own philosophical program in opposition to the Greek "wisdom of this world," where this is understood not only in the sense of the *genitivus obiectivus*—that is, "wisdom of this world" as wisdom that gives priority to worldly entities and does not consider the proper ontological status of human existence—but also in the sense of the *genitivus subiectivus*, so that the two senses cannot be separated at all. In this regard, the following quotation from Heidegger's *On the Essence of Ground* clearly shows that, for Heidegger, the opposition between Greek philosophy and the Pauline religious experience does not refer simply to different conceptions of the world, but to two different attitudes, or ways, of experiencing the world, which is to say, to two different ways of life:

> It is no accident, however, that in connection with the new ontic understanding of existence that irrupted in Christianity the relation between κόσμος and human Dasein, and thereby the concept of world in general, became sharper and clearer. The relation is experienced in such an originary manner . . . that κόσμος now comes to be used directly as a term for a particular fundamental kind of human existence. Κόσμος οὗτος in Saint Paul (cf. I Corinthians and Galatians) means not only and not primarily the state of the "cosmic," but the state and situation of the *human being*, the kind of stance he takes *toward* the cosmos, his esteem for things. Κόσμος means being human in the manner of a way of thinking that has turned away from God (ἡ σοφία τοῦ κόσμου). Κόσμος οὗτος refers to human Dasein in a particular "historical" existence, distinguished from another one that has already dawned (αἰὼν ὁ μέλλων).
>
> Heidegger 1998, 112

The Pauline anti-Platonism of Heidegger's early philosophy does not only concern the general framework of his "destruction" of Greek ontology. It also affects some specific elements of his hermeneutics of facticity, as I will show in what follows.

13 See the explicit reference in Heidegger 2004b, 48.

4. Pauline anthropology and the Aristotelian self-understanding of philosophy as starting points for Heidegger's conception of authentic life

With regard to the relationship between authentic and inauthentic life, Heidegger's attitude toward ancient philosophy is deeply ambiguous insofar as his approach to Plato and Aristotle cannot be reduced to a mere rejection of the philosophical life enacted in classical antiquity. In fact, although Paul represents a central interlocutor for the Heideggerian conception of authenticity, one should nevertheless stress that Plato and Aristotle also serve as models for discovering the possibility of a proper self-understanding of human life. It makes sense to clarify this point because it is of importance for understanding the multifaceted connection between primordial Christianity and ancient philosophy in Heidegger's thought.

Even if Heidegger rejects the self-understanding of philosophy as *sophia*, he nevertheless explicitly considers the Aristotelian *phronēsis* to be an enactment of authentic life. This crucial tension between *sophia* and *phronēsis* clearly emerges again in his lecture course on Plato's *Sophist*, where Heidegger focuses on Aristotle's account of *sophia* and *phronēsis*, trying to show that, according to the conception developed in his *Nicomachean Ethics*, Aristotle grants primacy to *sophia* (Heidegger 1997, 116). In the final analysis, the ontological primacy of presence and eternal beings cannot be separated from the priority of *sophia* over *phronēsis* (Heidegger 1997, 117–18). Heidegger's interpretation of *sophia* in terms of an inauthentic mode of existence can be understood against the background of the tension between early Christianity and ancient wisdom, especially because Heidegger sees a basic feature of inauthenticity in the Greek *sophia*, that is, curiosity. In fact, the primacy of sight, which becomes apparent in the contemplative, or theoretical, nature of traditional philosophy (see McNeill 1999), should be traced back to the ontological structure of human existence (Heidegger 2010, 164–67). In contrast, the Christian religious tradition provides a new critical insight into the primacy attributed to *theōrein*. In this regard, Augustine's analysis of curiosity is of central importance for Heidegger and is embedded in *Being and Time* (Heidegger 2010, 164–67; see 2004a, 165–69). In spite of the priority attributed to *sophia*, Heidegger argues that Aristotle is nevertheless able to discover an authentic possibility of human being, that is, *phronēsis*, which is interpreted as a form of conscience (Heidegger 1997, 39).

It might be possible to achieve a clearer articulation of the ambiguity characterizing Heidegger's attitude toward Aristotle's anthropology if one takes into consideration the temporal dimension of the basic division between *sophia* and *phronēsis*. Heidegger criticizes Aristotle's emphasis on *sophia* and refers to the alleged primacy of the Greek ontology of presence, but on the other hand, he discovers in Aristotle not only the possibility of authentic life as *phronēsis*, but also the specific temporal structure of the related experience. Such a temporality of *phronēsis* could be considered as Pauline, inasmuch as it is kairological.

This crucial intersection of Pauline temporal experience with Aristotelian anthropology is well documented in those passages in which Heidegger refers to the two fundamental starting points for the kairological conception of temporality (Heidegger 2004a, 71–72; 1988, 288). For Heidegger, Paul's fundamental contribution to a philosophical understanding of temporality consists in the emphasis on a primordial experience of temporality, that is, "primordial" in the sense of an experience free from Platonic and scientific misconceptions. Platonic conceptions regard temporality as a secondary dimension, and scientific approaches consider temporality first and foremost on the basis of linear time. In contrast to these, Paul enables Heidegger to see a temporality rooted in factical life as such and related to the concrete situation of the "I am," wherein the positing of ideal dimensions or objectifying experiences of temporality plays no role whatsoever.

Although Heidegger's reiterated remarks on the primacy of presence in ancient philosophy do not seem to leave open other interpretive approaches, closer consideration reveals that one should also emphasize Aristotle's contribution to a phenomenology of authentic temporality, or more precisely, Heidegger's Pauline reading of Aristotle's kairological conception of the authentic temporality specific to *phronēsis*:

> The instant is a primal phenomenon of original temporality, whereas the now is merely a phenomenon of derivative time. Aristotle already saw the phenomenon of the instant, the kairos, and he defined it in the sixth book of his *Nichomachean Ethics*; but, again, he did it in such a way that he failed to bring the specific time character of the kairos into connection with what he otherwise knows as time (nun).
>
> Heidegger 1988, 288

This passage makes clear the extent to which Heidegger identifies an essential inconsistency in Aristotle's philosophy of temporality since a clear distinction is made between the kairological account and the chronological one such that the former refers to the primordial temporality of human existence and the latter to the derivative experience of the now. According to Heidegger, in the end, Aristotle is not able to clarify the final connection between these two experiences of temporality.

5. Pauline features of Heidegger's hermeneutics of facticity

Heidegger's Pauline reversal of Platonism in his early Freiburg period also offers more concrete starting points for outlining a hermeneutics of facticity. I want to place special emphasis on three basic themes of Heidegger's interpretation of Paul, that is, the Pauline model of pretheoretical self-knowledge, the hermeneutical feature of the Pauline announcement and the Pauline inspiration for formally indicative conceptuality.

The first Pauline element is the possibility of a pretheoretical self-knowledge rooted in the primordial facticity of human existence. In Paul, Heidegger sees a clear example of a self-articulation of human existence that does not make use of traditional philosophical categories and does not rely on the theoretical commitment common to Greek philosophical thought. Facticity as such already has a primordial self-understanding, which is situation-related and addresses the individual as such. In explaining the connection between "knowledge" and "having-become," Heidegger discovers in Paul this fundamental phenomenon of a pretheoretical self-experience defining human facticity:

> This knowledge is entirely different from any other knowledge and memory. It arises only out of the situational context of Christian life experience.
>
> Knowledge about one's own having-become poses a very special task for the explication. From out of this the meaning of a facticity is determined, one which is accompanied by a particular knowledge. We tear the facticity apart from the knowledge, but the facticity is entirely originally co-experienced. Especially in this problem, the failure of the "scientific psychology of experience" can be shown. Having-become is not, in life, [just] any incident you like. Rather, it is incessantly co-experienced, and indeed such that their Being [*Sein*] now is their having-become [*Gewordensein*]. Their having-become is their Being now.
>
> Heidegger 2004a, 65–66

This point is of absolute importance within the framework of Heidegger's hermeneutical philosophy because the entire project of his hermeneutics of facticity, and that of his existential ontology too, cannot be understood without the basic assumption that human existence is characterized by a primordial self-understanding that belongs to its being as such and is independent of purely scientific or philosophical epistemic commitments. Otherwise put, Heidegger finds in Paul a relevant confirmation of the essential hermeneutical feature of human life.

This peculiar approach of Heidegger is readily apparent if one pays attention to the fact that he interprets Christian facticity in terms of an enactment-based self-experience. In this connection, even though Heidegger focuses on the specific features of Christian facticity, he nevertheless clarifies the structures of facticity as such because enactment-sense constitutes the basic phenomenal character that he always emphasizes in his phenomenological analyses of factical life:

> The conversion to Christian life experience concerns the *enactment*. In order to raise the relational sense of factical life experience, one must be careful that it becomes more "difficult," that it is enacted ἐν θλίψεσιν. The phenomena of enactment must be entwined with the sense of facticity. Paul makes of enactment a theme. It reads: ὡς μή, not οὐ. This μή indicates the tendency toward that which has the character of enactment. μή refers back to the enactment itself.
>
> Heidegger 2004a, 86

Heidegger's analyses cannot be understood in terms of a psychological account of Paul's self-experience, since his phenomenological approach consistently implies a suspension of such explicative schemas. Furthermore, he avoids fictitious oppositions such as practical versus theoretical, which are deeply inadequate if one wants to grasp the actual meaning of the enactment-based self-knowledge belonging to Christian facticity (Heidegger 2004a, 87–88). Starting from the enactment-based meaning of the primordial self-understanding rooted in the Christian facticity, Heidegger is in a position to give a phenomenological account of two basic terms of the Pauline anthropology, that is, "flesh" and "spirit." In this regard, the phenomenological character of Heidegger's interpretation is concretely shown by the fact that he avoids any Platonizing reading of these two concepts (i.e., flesh and spirit as substantial parts of human being), and instead, interprets them as notions referring to the phenomenal dynamics of facticity. To put it differently, for Heidegger, flesh and spirit represent basic tendencies of factical life that are, more or less directly, related to inauthentic life and authentic existence respectively (Heidegger 2004a, 88).

We can go one step farther and underline the phenomenon of announcement, which is central in Heidegger's reading of Paul, as another fundamental starting point for Heidegger's analysis of the hermeneutical character of human life. In this case, it makes sense to render explicit some conceptual connections that are not initially self-evident. As a matter of fact, the hermeneutical feature of Paul's apostolic announcement becomes apparent if we take into consideration both Heidegger's emphasis on the original meaning of hermeneutics and the phenomenon of attestation analyzed in the existential ontology (see Cimino 2013b).

6. The hermeneutical feature of the Pauline announcement

Even if Heidegger shaped the hermeneutical character of his thought in very different ways according to his various conceptions of philosophy, he always describes hermeneutics in terms of announcement or making known (*Kundgabe*).[14] This characteristic relation of hermeneutics to announcement concerns not only the specific task of philosophy, but also a central phenomenon of Heidegger's existential analytic, that is, "attestation" (*Bezeugung*). In fact, Heidegger characterizes attestation not as a mere epistemic phenomenon, but rather as a kind of making known or giving-to-understand which human existence bears in itself and which can be traced back to conscience (*Gewissen*) (see Cimino 2013b). It might be worthwhile to draw together some paradigmatic passages (Heidegger 2010, 257, 259–61) in which the hermeneutical features of attestation as call of conscience are well-documented. The key idea here is that the specific enactment of attestation can be characterized as a "giving-to-understand" (Heidegger 2010, 261). The basic hermeneutical feature of both philosophical discourse and attestation concerns the fact that hermeneutical givenness is essentially different from theoretical or scientific givenness. Both in the case of the hermeneutical enactment of philosophical thinking and in the case of the hermeneutically shaped giving-to-understand that defines attestation as the call of conscience, the related givenness is neither the result nor the starting point of a scientific reasoning or proof. Both cases are forms of enactment pertaining to the primordial (self-)understanding of human existence. In both

[14] See, for example, Heidegger 2010, 35.

cases, in fact, Dasein gives itself something to understand. One could also say: Dasein announces something to itself.

The announcement-related hermeneutical feature of the Pauline discourse becomes apparent if one focuses not only on etymological or conceptual connections—in this regard, one could mention some clear resemblances in German: *Kundgabe, Verkündigung, Bekundung* and so on—but above all on the concrete phenomenon analyzed in Heidegger's hermeneutical phenomenology of the Pauline announcement. In fact, Heidegger develops a phenomenological account of Paul's announcement and takes into consideration its content-sense, relational sense and enactment-sense (Heidegger 2004a, 97–111). He thus shows the extent to which Paul's announcement is irreducible to any traditional philosophical or scientific discourse, and should be considered in reference to its concrete factical situation (Heidegger 2004a, 63–74), as is the case with Heidegger's hermeneutics of facticity.

7. The Pauline inspiration for the formally indicative conceptuality

The philosophical potential of the Pauline factical experience also becomes apparent in Heidegger's elaboration of the methodical strategy he calls "formal indication."[15] In this case, one can say that Paul serves as a model both thematically and methodologically. Thematically, the philosophical relevance of Paul for the elaboration of formally indicative concepts consists in the fact that the Pauline experience shows the primacy of the enactment-sense (see Crowe 2006). It is precisely the enactment-sense that constitutes the basic phenomenal theme formally indicative concepts have to articulate and to express. Under these premises, the Pauline experience insofar as it is strongly enactment-based turns out to be a concrete and privileged research field for Heidegger such that philosophy should face a basic question: How should Christian factical life be approached in order to articulate philosophical concepts that do justice to the primordial ontological character of religious life? This issue should be contextualized in the general methodological problem Heidegger elaborates in his early hermeneutics of factical life with regard to the adequate categories that enable the articulation of human existence in philosophical terms.

[15] Concerning this fundamental topic of Heidegger's methodology, see Cimino 2011.

Assuming, as Heidegger does, that the Pauline factical life experience markedly expresses some primordial features of human life, especially as concerns enactment-related characters, then a phenomenological analysis of the Pauline experience could be an appropriate starting point for elaborating the general question concerning philosophical categories of human existence. In other words, the Pauline experience represents a thematic challenge for phenomenological inquiry since it finds itself confronted with a self-articulation of human existence that cannot be approached on the basis of traditional categories.

The unfolding of Heidegger's phenomenological explications of the Pauline letters concretely shows to what extent his analysis anticipates, in many respects, his general ontology of human life, especially as regards the intentional features that define the experience of temporality and authentic life. If we consider Heidegger's ontological analysis of human existence in *Being and Time* to be a formal explication focused on general structures, then his phenomenological interpretation of the Pauline letters is a decisive step toward such a formalization. In fact, on the one hand, in the course of his interpretation, Heidegger is interested in the concrete dynamics of the Pauline experience of factical life. On the other hand, however, his interpretation is not carried out as a mere report referring to texts, but is rather the attempt to highlight the Pauline experience phenomenologically—on the basis of the essential conceptual framework he introduces in his early hermeneutics, that is, content-sense, relational sense and enactment-sense (see Cimino 2013a, 119). This basically means that the results of his phenomenological reading reach an essential level of formality.

From a methodological viewpoint, the central role of the Pauline enactment concerns the possibility of formal experience. The formality of the Pauline experience does not mean a separation from factical contents (as would be the case, for example, with a pure ontology in the Husserlian sense) or a formality in the sense of the Heideggerian formal indication, since the Pauline experience is not a philosophical one. Rather, the peculiar formality of the Pauline experience refers to the fact that, on the basis of the *hōs mē*, it is an experience that is not absorbed in worldly contents. In this regard, the Pauline experience is not only thematically fruitful, but can be considered a model for philosophy itself, at least according to Heidegger's conception of philosophy in his early Freiburg period.

It is, in fact, quite clear that Heidegger conceives of philosophy in terms of authentic life, that is, a life that is not absorbed in the contents of the world, with the central phenomenal feature being the enactment-sense. Accordingly, the

Pauline experience of factical life can serve as a model that clarifies the possibility of philosophy as an authentic form of life. If, in this connection, ancient philosophy should be considered an inauthentic enactment of human life, then, conversely, Christian factical life can provide essential impulses for a new enactment of philosophy, which enables one to articulate formally indicative concepts. Formally indicative conceptuality is only possible on the basis of an experience that emancipates us from an ontology of substance and also from a worldly self-understanding of human life. Thus, in the final analysis, Paul's experience of factical life provides one with a paradigm of performativity that is of importance for the self-understanding of philosophy as such (see Cimino 2011).

8. Pauline emancipation in Agamben: A radical refutation of Nietzsche's reading

A radical reversal of Nietzsche's position can also be found in the work of Giorgio Agamben, who, in his commentary on the letter to the Romans (2005), presents a revolutionary Paul. In Agamben's work, the ambiguity that determines the philosophical reception of Paul becomes apparent in an emphatic way because he stresses both Paul's philosophical potential and his radical opposition to some traditional philosophical frameworks. In this connection, it makes sense to focus on two main points, that is, Paul's overcoming of traditional logic and the allegedly Pauline origin of Hegel's dialectic. I do not intend to provide a general account of these two points.[16] My intention is rather to explain to what extent Nietzsche's conservative, tyrannical and dogmatic Paul radically contrasts with Agamben's Paul (see Cimino 2015, 210–11), who emerges as a hero of both philosophical and political emancipation.

The messianic enactment of language emerging in Paul's religious life represents a substantial alternative to Plato's and Aristotle's ontology because Paul enacts a new experience of language that cannot be reduced to the denotative character of linguistic articulation or to allegedly obvious distinctions (e.g., essence vs. existence, subject vs. predicates). On the basis of Agamben's reading, one cannot consider Paul as a founder of institutionalized religions precisely because his conception and enactment of language does not allow any formation

16 For a general presentation, see Cimino 2014.

of dogmas. The denotative function of language acts as the basic presupposition for the codification of laws and norms, and in particular, for the separation between statements of general normative principles—and also dogmas—and the comportment of individuals.[17] According to Agamben, Paul's messianism is essentially antidogmatic and anti-institutional because it deactivates that denotative function and does not fit with the traditional distinction between general and individual. On the contrary, in dogmatized and institutionalized religions, there is a basic asymmetry between norms and individual experience, whereby statements of general principles become preponderant and self-sufficient, that is, separate from individual enactment. Paul's deactivation of law as such runs in the exact opposite direction because it is committed to a strong unity between individual religious experience and the statement of principles, between utterance and concrete comportment.

9. Agamben and the Hegelian reception of Paul's performative and antidogmatic deactivation

In his commentary on Paul's letter to the Romans, Giorgio Agamben (2005, 99–104) formulates a suggestive hypothesis about the relationship between the Pauline deactivation (*katargein*), which denotes the new experience of law performed by Paul, and Hegel's conception of the dialectic, especially regarding the notion of sublation (*Aufhebung*). According to Agamben, the much-debated theme of the link between faith and law in Paul cannot reduce these terms to mutually exclusive alternatives. Instead, one should focus on the specific meaning intended by Paul's use of the word *katargein*. The messianic deactivation does not, in fact, mean a pure destruction or abolition, but a deactivation that, in turn, implies a preservation and also a completion or perfection (Agamben 2005, 99). Here, Agamben identifies a strong connection with Hegel's notion of sublation, which he bases on a philological hypothesis. Hegel's reception of the Pauline deactivation can be traced back to Luther's frequent translation of *katargein* as *aufheben*, with Luther being aware, according to Agamben, of the particular double meaning that characterizes the German verb, that is, an overcoming (abolishment, de-activation), and at the same time, a preservation that culminates

[17] As for the relationship between politics and language in Agamben, see especially Agamben 2011.

in a more complete, or perfect, condition (Agamben 2005, 100). In formulating this proposal, Agamben argues that the idea of messianic deactivation is the inspiration for Hegel's account of the dialectic since, on the basis of the messianic deactivation, the law is simultaneously deactivated and fulfilled:

> This is how a genuinely messianic term expressing the transformation of the law impacted by faith and announcement becomes a key term for the dialectic. That Hegel's dialectic is nothing more than a secularization of Christian theology comes as no surprise; however, more significant is the fact that (with a certain degree of irony) Hegel used a weapon against theology furnished by theology itself and that this weapon is genuinely messianic.
>
> Agamben 2005, 99

In order to understand the reason why Agamben is connecting law (*nomos*) and faith (*pistis*) within the messianic dynamics of the Pauline deactivation, one should also consider an important presupposition underlying his interpretive approach, a presupposition that, on closer consideration, enables him to connect the Pauline deactivation with the Hegelian dialectic. Law and faith belong to a primordial sphere that encompasses both of them and can be characterized as law in the broad sense. Law is opposed to faith insofar as *nomos* is understood in the narrow sense of the normative, or prescriptive, *nomos*, that is, as *nomos tōn entolōn* or *nomos tōn ergōn*. As Agamben stresses, however, there is also a different form of *nomos*, which is not normative, but promissive: "The messianic law is the law of faith and not just the negation of the law. This, however, does not mean substituting the old *miswoth* with new precepts; rather, it means setting a non-normative figure of the law against the normative figure of the law" (Agamben 2005, 95). In the final analysis, Agamben can only argue for the dialectical character of the deactivation because he assumes that the Pauline deactivation unfolds within the sphere of the *nomos* in the broad sense. Apart from the philological and historical plausibility of Agamben's hypothesis, it also makes sense to focus on a further conceptual implication he draws in reference to the Hegelian reception of the Pauline deactivation, especially considering the problem of time. Here, Agamben emphasizes not only a connection between Hegel and Paul, but also a substantial difference:

> When the Torah is rendered inoperative in messianic *katargēsis*, it is not caught up in a deferment or in an infinite displacement; rather, the Torah finds its *plērōma* therein. We find a genuinely messianic exigency reemerge in Hegel in the problem of the *plērōma* of times and the end of history. Hegel, however,

> thinks the *plērōma* not as each instant's relation to the Messiah, but as the final result of a global process.
>
> Agamben 2005, 100–101

Agamben sees a substantial ambiguity in Hegel's reception of Paul's messianic conceptual framework. On the one hand, he underlines the messianic feature of the problem concerning the end of history with reference to the Pauline notion of fulfillment (*plērōma*). On the other hand, however, Agamben notices that Hegel does not make a clear distinction between messianism and eschatology, since fulfillment is not seen within the framework of a qualitative transformation of time—that is, as the messianic transformation, which primarily affects the present—but essentially from the perspective of the end of history and time, that is, as concerns the final stage of the Hegelian dialectical process. In the end, despite the allegedly Pauline resonances, Hegel is not in a position to assimilate Paul to the dogmatic aspects of his dialectical conception.

References

Agamben, Giorgio. 2005. *The Time That Remains: A Commentary on the Letter to the Romans*. Translated by Patricia Dailey. Stanford, CA: Stanford University Press.

Agamben, Giorgio. 2011. *The Sacrament of Language: An Archaeology of the Oath*. Translated by Adam Kotsko. Stanford, CA: Stanford University Press.

Babich, Babette, Alfred Denker and Holger Zaborowksi, eds. 2012. *Heidegger and Nietzsche*, Amsterdam: Rodopi.

Biser, Eugen. 1982. *Gottsucher oder Antichrist? Nietzsches provokative Kritik des Christentums*. Salzburg: Mueller.

Biser, Eugen. 2002. *Nietzsche—Zerstörer oder Erneuerer des Christentums?* Darmstadt: Wissenschaftliche Buchgesellschaft.

Blanton, Ward, and Hent de Vries, eds. 2013. *Paul and the Philosophers*. New York: Fordham University Press.

Brach, Markus J. 1996. *Heidegger—Platon: Vom Neukantianismus zur existentiellen Interpretation des* Sophistes. Würzburg: Königshausen & Neumann.

Brejdak, Jaromir. 1996. *Philosophia crucis: Heideggers Beschäftigung mit dem Apostel Paulus*. Frankfurt am Main: Lang.

Camilleri, Sylvain. 2011. "Heidegger, lecteur et intèrprete de Saint Paul." *Freiburger Zeitschrift für Philosophie und Theologie* 58 (1): 145–62.

Caputo, John D., and Linda M. Alcoff, eds. 2009. *St. Paul among the Philosophers*. Bloomington: Indiana University Press.

Casale, Rita. 2010. *Heideggers Nietzsche: Geschichte einer Obsession*. Bielefeld: transcript.
Cimino, Antonio. 2005. *Ontologia, storia, temporalità: Heidegger, Platone e l'essenza della filosofia*. Pisa: ETS.
Cimino, Antonio. 2011. "Begriff und Vollzug: Performativität und Indexikalität als Grundbestimmungen der formal anzeigenden Begriffsbildung bei Heidegger." *Internationales Jahrbuch für Hermeneutik* 10: 215–39.
Cimino, Antonio. 2013a. *Phänomenologie und Vollzug: Heideggers performative Philosophie des faktischen Lebens*, Frankfurt am Main: Klostermann.
Cimino, Antonio. 2013b. "Attestation and Facticity: On Heidegger's Conception of Attestation in *Being and Time*." *Journal of the British Society for Phenomenology* 44 (2): 181–97.
Cimino, Antonio. 2014. "Messianic Experience of Language and Performativity of Faith: Agamben's Interpretation of Pauline Faith." *Freiburger Zeitschrift für Philosophie und Theologie* 61 (1): 127–40.
Cimino, Antonio. 2015. "Seeing the Truth and Living in the Truth: Optical Paradigms of Truth and Pauline Countermodels." In *Phenomenology and the Metaphysics of Sight*, edited by Antonio Cimino and Pavlos Kontos, 208–23. Leiden: Brill.
Crowe, Benjamin D. 2006. *Heidegger's Religious Origins: Destruction and Authenticity*. Bloomington: Indiana University Press.
Denker, Alfred, Marion Heinz, John Sallis, Ben Vedder and Holger Zaborowski, eds. 2005. *Heidegger und Nietzsche*. Freiburg im Breisgau: Alber.
Giugliano, Antonello. 1999. *Nietzsche, Rickert, Heidegger (ed altre allegorie filosofiche)*. Napoli: Liguori.
Havemann, Daniel. 2002. *Der "Apostel der Rache": Nietzsches Paulusdeutung*. Berlin: De Gruyter.
Heidegger, Martin. 1988. *The Basic Problems of Phenomenology*. Translated by Albert Hofstadter. Bloomington: Indiana University Press.
Heidegger, Martin. 1997. *Plato's Sophist*. Translated by Richard Rojcewicz and André Schuwer. Bloomington: Indiana University Press.
Heidegger, Martin. 1998. *Pathmarks*. Edited by William McNeill. Cambridge: Cambridge University Press.
Heidegger, Martin. 2004a. *The Phenomenology of Religious Life*. Translated by Matthias Fritsch and Jennifer Anna Gosetti-Ferencei. Bloomington: Indiana University Press.
Heidegger, Martin. 2004b. *Der Begriff der Zeit*. Edited by Friedrich-Wilhelm von Herrmann. Frankfurt am Main: Klostermann.
Heidegger, Martin. 2010. *Being and Time*. Translated by Joan Stambaugh, revised by Dennis J. Schmidt. Albany, NY: SUNY Press.
Hübner, Hans. 2000. *Nietzsche und das Neue Testament*. Tübingen: Mohr Siebeck.
Jaspers, Karl. 1963. *Nietzsche und das Christentum*. München: Piper.
Kee, Alistair. 1999. *Nietzsche against the Crucified*. London: SMC Press.

Kim, Alan. 2010. *Plato in Germany: Kant—Natorp—Heidegger*. Sankt Augustin: Academia Verlag.
McGrath, S. J., and Andrzej Wierciński, eds. 2010. *A Companion to Heidegger's "Phenomenology of Religious Life."* Amsterdam: Rodopi.
McNeill, William. 1999. *The Glance of the Eye: Heidegger, Aristotle, and the Ends of Theory*. Albany, NY: SUNY Press.
Molinaro, Aniceto, ed. 2008. *Heidegger e San Paolo: Interpretazione fenomenologica dell'Epistolario paolino*. Roma: Urbaniana University Press.
Müller-Lauter, Wolfgang. 2000. *Heidegger und Nietzsche*. Berlin: De Gruyter.
Nietzsche, Friedrich. 1990. *Twilight of the Idols* and *The Anti-Christ*. Translated by Reginald John Hollingdale. New York: Penguin Books.
Nietzsche, Friedrich. 2014. *Beyond Good and Evil / On the Genealogy of Morality*. Translated by Adrian Del Caro. Stanford, CA: Stanford University Press.
Partenie, Catalin, and Tom Rockmore, eds. 2005. *Heidegger and Plato: Toward Dialogue*. Evanston, IL: Northwestern University Press.
Paulo, Craig J. N. de, ed. 2006. *The Influence of Augustine on Heidegger: The Emergence of an Augustinian Phenomenology*. Lewiston, NY: Mellen.
Peluso, Rosalia. 2008. *Logica dell'altro: Heidegger e Platone*. Napoli: Giannini.
Petkovšek, Robert. 2004. *Le statut existential du platonisme: Platon dans l'analytique existentiale de Heidegger*. Bern: Lang.
Pöggeler, Otto. 1996. "Martin Heidegger und die Religionsphänomenologie." *Edith-Stein-Jahrbuch* 2: 15–30.
Ralkowski, Marc. 2009. *Heidegger's Platonism*. London: Continuum.
Savarino, Luca. 2001. *Heidegger e il cristianesimo (1916–1927)*. Napoli: Liguori.
Scilironi, Carlo, ed. 2004. *San Paolo e la filosofia del Novecento*. Padova: Cleup.
Seron, Denis. 2001. *Le problème de la métaphysique: Recherches sur l'interprétation heideggerienne de Platon et d'Aristote*. Bruxelles: Ousia.
Sommer, Christian. 2005. *Heidegger, Aristote, Luther: Les sources aristotéliciennes et néo-testamentaires d'*Etre et temps. Paris: PUF.
Spinoza, Benedict de. 2007. *Theological-Political Treatise*. Edited by Jonathan Israel, translated by Michael Silverthorne and Jonathan Israel. Cambridge: Cambridge University Press.
Valadier, Paul. 1974. *Nietzsche et la critique du christianisme*. Paris: Ed. du Cerf.
Vedder, Ben. 2007. *Heidegger's Philosophy of Religion: From God to the Gods*. Pittsburgh: Duquesne University Press.
Vedder, Ben. 2009. "Heidegger's Explication of Religious Phenomena in the Letters of Saint Paul." *Bijdragen. International Journal in Philosophy and Theology* 70 (2): 152–67.
Welte, Bernhard. 1964. *Nietzsches Atheismus und das Christentum*. Darmstadt: Wissenschaftliche Buchgesellschaft.

Index